# Data Management for eRobotics Applications

Von der Fakultät für Elektrotechnik und Informationstechnik
der Rheinisch-Westfälischen Technischen Hochschule Aachen
zur Erlangung des akademischen Grades eines
Doktors der Ingenieurwissenschaften
genehmigte Dissertation

vorgelegt von



Diplom-Informatiker
Martin Hoppen
aus Bad Honnef

Berichter: Universitätsprofessor Dr.-Ing. Jürgen Roßmann
Universitätsprofessor Dr. rer. pol. Matthias Jarke

Tag der mündlichen Prüfung: 7. Juni 2017

**Bibliografische Information der Deutschen Nationalbibliothek**
Die Deutsche Nationalbibliothek verzeichnet diese Publikation in der Deutschen Nationalbibliografie; detaillierte bibliografische Daten sind im Internet über http://dnb.ddb.de abrufbar.

Martin Hoppen:

Data Management for eRobotics Applications

1. Auflage, 2017

Gedruckt auf holz- und säurefreiem Papier, 100% chlorfrei gebleicht.

Apprimus Verlag, Aachen, 2017
Wissenschaftsverlag des Instituts für Industriekommunikation und Fachmedien an der RWTH Aachen
Steinbachstr. 25, 52074 Aachen
Internet: www.apprimus-verlag.de, E-Mail: info@apprimus-verlag.de

Druck: KN Digital Printforce GmbH, Stuttgart

ISBN 978-3-86359-542-5

D 82 (Diss. RWTH Aachen University, 2017)

# Acknowledgment

First of all, I want to thank my supervisor Professor Juergen Rossmann for giving me the opportunity and support for writing this thesis at the Institute for Man-Machine Interaction. I also want to thank my co-supervisor Professor Matthias Jarke for accepting this work. Furthermore, I want to thank my senior engineer Michael Schluse for his continuous support and the numerous discussions, which often gave direction to my work. Likewise, I am very grateful for the many discussions with my colleagues Ralf Waspe and Malte Rast and for their expert opinions. Special thanks go to Michael Schluse and Malte Rast for proofreading this work. Also, I want to thank all my other (current and former) colleagues for their support, especially Petra Krahwinkler for encouraging me to keep to writing. Last but definitely not least, I want to thank my wife Anne for her support and for enduring the countless hours I spent with this thesis rather than with her.

# Abstract

The development and the whole lifecycle of robotic and general mechatronic systems features a high degree of complexity. The eRobotics approach aims at making this complexity manageable by combining the usage of electronic media, modern 3D simulation techniques and robotics concepts. The basis for any eRobotics application is a Semantic World Model – a comprehensive 3D model of the developed system and its operational environment featuring closeness to reality and a self-describing meaning. These highly complex models require an efficient data management that goes beyond the traditional flat file.

The work at hand offers a solution to this problem by presenting a new universal data management approach for eRobotics applications that efficiently manages Semantic World Models in a distributed database. The basic idea is to combine multiple instances of a simulation database (SimDB) with a common external database (ExtDB). SimDB is an active, in-memory simulation database that serves as the core data management component of a 3D simulation system. It caches the Semantic World Model and realizes its execution. ExtDB's duty is the central management and provisioning of the shared Semantic World Model, providing a persistence back-end and a versioning mechanism, and serving as a communication hub for the distributed system.

A novel database synchronization approach flexibly synchronizes each pair of SimDB and ExtDB on schema, data, semantics as well as on version level. It is based on a sound theoretical basis using methods adopted from Model-Driven Engineering. The approach is universally specified in terms of the Unified Modeling Language's (UML) metamodel making it applicable to various database paradigms while ensuring an object-oriented modeling optimally suited for Semantic World Models.

The approach's feasibility and practicability is proven by various eRobotics applications from as different fields as environment (forest, cities), industry (automation, industrial robots) and space (satellites, space robotics).

Keywords: eRobotics, Data Management, 3D Simulation, Semantic World Model, Database

# Zusammenfassung

**Datenhaltung für Anwendungen der eRobotik**

Die Entwicklung und der Lebenszyklus robotischer und mechatronischer Systeme zeichnet sich durch eine hohe Komplexität aus. Ziel der eRobotik ist es, diese Komplexität durch Einsatz von elektronischen Medien, moderner 3D-Simulationstechnik und Konzepten der Robotik handhabbar zu machen. Grundlage jeder eRobotik-Anwendung ist ein Semantisches Weltmodell – ein umfassendes 3D-Modell des entwickelten Systems und seiner Einsatzumgebung – das sich insbesondere durch Realitätsnähe und eine selbstbeschreibende Bedeutung auszeichnet. Diese hochkomplexen Modelle bedürfen einer effizienten Datenhaltungsmethode jenseits der oft üblichen einfachen Dateien.

Die vorgelegte Arbeit gibt eine Lösung für dieses Problem in Form eines neuen, universalen Ansatzes zur Datenhaltung für eRobotik-Anwendungen, der Semantische Weltmodelle in verteilten Datenbanken verwaltet. Grundidee ist die Kombination aus Simulationsdatenbanken (SimDB) mit einer gemeinsamen externen Datenbank (ExtDB). Als aktive In-Memory-Datenbank zur Zwischenspeicherung und Ausführung Semantischer Weltmodelle bildet SimDB die Kernkomponente eines 3D-Simulationssystems. Aufgabe von ExtDB ist die zentrale Verwaltung und Bereitstellung des gemeinsam genutzten Semantischen Weltmodells. Sie stellt eine Persistenzschicht dar, ermöglicht Versionierung und dient als zentrale Kommunikationsstelle des verteilten Systems.

Ein neuartiger Ansatz zur Datenbanksynchronisation synchronisiert jedes Paar von SimDB und ExtDB auf Schema-, Daten-, Semantik- und Versions-Ebene. Er basiert auf einer fundierten theoretischen Grundlage, die Methoden des modellgetriebenen Engineerings verwendet. Das Verfahren ist universal auf der Grundlage des Metamodells der Unified Modeling Language (UML) spezifiziert. Dies erlaubt seine Verwendung mit verschiedensten Datenbankparadigmen und stellt zugleich eine objekt-orientierte Modellierung sicher, die für Semantische Weltmodelle optimal ist.

Die Umsetzbarkeit sowie die Praxistauglichkeit des Verfahrens wird durch zahlreiche Anwendungen der eRobotik aus den unterschiedlichsten Gebieten wie Umwelt (Wald, Städte), Industrie (Automatisierungstechnik, industrielle Roboter) und Weltraum (Satelliten, Weltraumrobotik) nachgewiesen.

Schlagwörter: eRobotik, Datenhaltung, 3D Simulation, Semantisches Weltmodell, Datenbank

# Contents

# List of Figures

# List of Tables

# Chapter 1

# Introduction

Complex system structures and expensive hardware prototypes characterize modern robotic applications and their development. To cope with this complexity and to bring down costs, the eRobotics [1] research field was established. It aims at providing a comprehensive software environment that integrates the usage of electronic media, simulation technology as well as robotic concepts and that addresses the entire lifecycle of complex robotic systems.

The initial focus of eRobotics was on robotic applications. However, due to its flexible technologies, its usage spread to other fields of application, in particular, general mechatronic systems (like satellites), modeling and simulation of the environment (forest, cities, buildings) or industrial automation. Some examples from this thesis are shown in Figures 1.1–1.3.

**Figure 1.1:** *Exemplary environmental eRobotics applications.*

Core technologies of eRobotics are simulation ("the preparation, execution and evaluation of targeted experiments with a simulation" [2]) and the so-called Virtual Testbed. A simulation usually examines only specific aspects of a system in detail, e.g., a single laser scanner (Figure 1.4, left). In contrast, a VTB (Virtual Testbed) is a more holistic approach that considers the entire system in its operational environment, e.g., a wood harvester with a laser scanner based navigation within a forest (Figure 1.4, middle). A VTB can also be seen

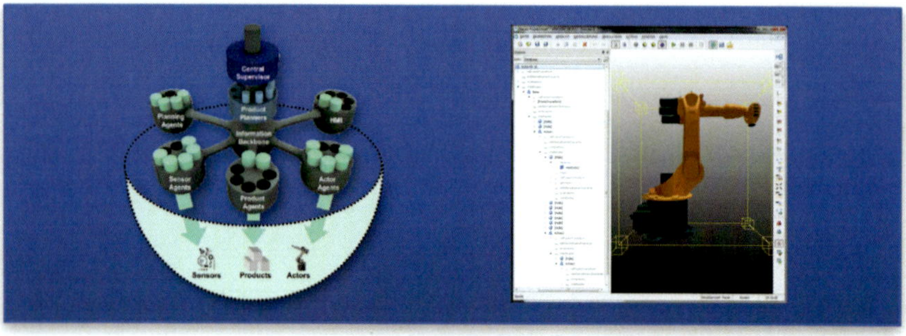


**Figure 1.2:** *Exemplary industrial eRobotics applications.*

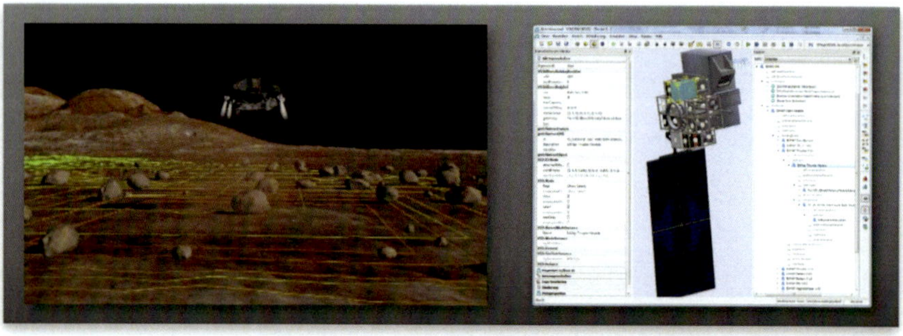

**Figure 1.3:** *Exemplary space eRobotics applications.*

as a sophisticated digital twin [3] of the considered system, together yielding a cyber-physical system. As such, it can be used for so-called

- *Simulation-based Optimization* to optimize the properties of a system under development itself,
- *Simulation-based Reasoning* as a mental model of the system in operation to optimize decision-making, or
- *Simulation-based Control* to develop a control in simulation and identically use it on the target hardware, i.e., reusing the developments from the VTB in live operation (Figure 1.4, right).

These three concepts can be summarized by the term *Simulation-based X*.

Figure 1.5 summarizes the overall structure of eRobotics. Its *Concepts* particularly comprise the VTB and Simulation-based X. Its *Processes* apply these concepts to realize simulation-based agile development processes. Both are realized in terms of computerized *Methods*.

Basis for any simulation is a model ("a simplified reproduction of a planned or existing system" [2]). In 3D simulation, the focus is on a system's *spatial* properties and behavior

**Figure 1.4:** *Example for the basic idea of the Virtual Testbed and Simulation-based X (adopted from [1]).*

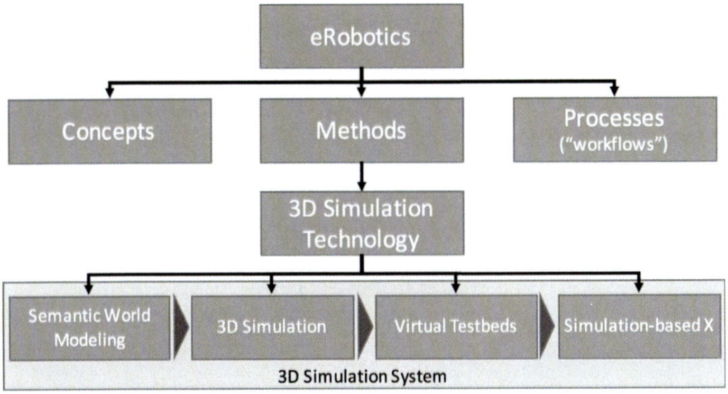


**Figure 1.5:** *Structure of eRobotics (adopted from [1]).*

that corresponding 3D models must reproduce. The basis for eRobotics applications are so-called Semantic World Models (Figure 1.6). These are comprehensive 3D models of a system in its environment that aim at closeness to reality and a self-describing meaning. Thus, in contrast to a purely geometric description (e.g., optimized on rendering), a Semantic World Model represents a more intuitive modeling approach of a system with a focus on the problem domain, which allows for the interpretation of its components' meaning and models the environment in which the system operates. Altogether, eRobotics integrates methods for Semantic World Modeling, 3D simulation, VTBs, and Simulation-based X into a 3D simulation system (or "simulator" [2]).

Thus, the basis for any eRobotics application is a Semantic World Model. Similar to CAD (Computer-Aided Design) data, typically, they consist of a huge number of parts of many different types, often with only few instances. Moreover, these parts are hierarchically structured and have interdependencies. In contrast, traditional business data (like banking data) is less complex and comprises only few types each with a huge number of instances. According to [4], such data is best modeled in an object-oriented approach. In contrast, a relational modeling approach only provides a limited representation of real-world objects

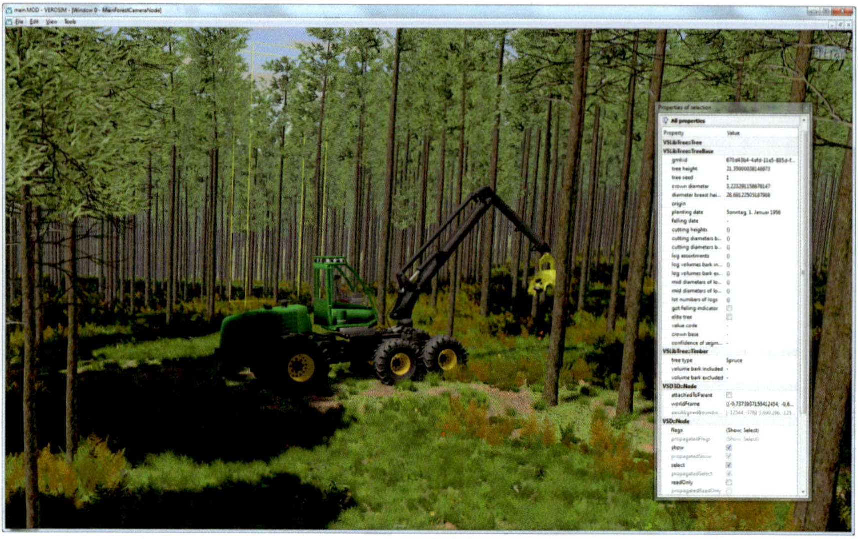

**Figure 1.6:** *Exemplary Semantic World Model of a wood harvester and its working environment.*

(e.g., due to normalization) and the necessary navigation along object structures is often inefficient.

To cope with the consequential complexity of Semantic World Models, an appropriate data management approach is necessary. In contrast to flat files, database technology provides several advantages for that purpose.

First of all, as the systems developed by and the problems solved by eRobotics applications get more complex, more and more users and different subsystems of the application need to be involved in often distributed processes. Besides simulation itself, these are processes for data processing as part of model building, e.g., when processing huge amounts of raw geodata. Likewise, general collaborative modeling (e.g., with CAD tools), on-site and often offline data acquisition for natural environment models, or complex control architectures for flexible automation systems need a distributed data management approach. Again, only using database technology, a Semantic World Model can efficiently be built up, managed and provisioned to all distributed participants. In contrast to simple model files, this is enabled by databases' multiuser support, access rights management, support for concurrent access, safe transactions, and DDB (Distributed Database) techniques. Moreover, active databases can build the basis for communication as well as collaboration via the Semantic World Model and to make the data management component an active part of the simulation. This avoids the need for additional communication or synchronization protocols where the state of the model may deviate from communicated changes or events.

Semantic World Models also tend to get huger, in particular, in case of environmental models of forests or cities, but also in case of complex space scenarios like the International Space Station. In the long term, only database technology makes such amounts of data manageable, e.g., by providing query interfaces or (spatial) indexing.

Furthermore, well-defined access points using a query language or an API (Application Programming Interface) of the DBMS (Database Management System) and a client-server architecture simplify an eRobotics application's subsystems access to the shared Semantic World Model. Adding additional services on top of a DBMS allows to provide standardized interfaces to even more subsystems. For example, applications with an environmental model in a geo database take advantage of an additional WFS (Web Feature Service) supported by many software tools in the field of GIS (Geo Information System).

In current eRobotics applications, Semantic World Models are described by a (domain specific) application schema, e.g., CityGML for city models, ForestGML for forest and forestry models, IFC (Industrial Foundation Classes [5]) for building information modeling, AutomationML (Automation Modeling Language [6]) in industrial automation, or SysML (Systems Modeling Language [7]) for system specifications. Only by using databases, such schemata are made explicitly available and enforced throughout all subsystems of an eRobotics application making it their common language.

Semantic World Models are time-dependent. They change in modeling processes as well as during simulation runs. With a file-based data management approach, additional mechanisms for version control and simulation logging (and replay) are necessary to capture these processes over time. Using a temporal database allows for an integrated versioning or logging to archive and access different versions or temporal snapshots of the model. Most importantly, this makes simulation results easily analyzable using (temporal) database queries.

Finally, eRobotics applications in general and live 3D simulations in particular make high demands on data management performance. Highly optimized (simulation) file formats may seem favorable for this scenario by itself. However, they lack the aforementioned advantages provided by database technology. Using in-memory databases, an adequate performance (not only) for simulation is achieved.

All in all, based on these considerations, eRobotics applications make the following five main demands on a data management based on database technology:

1. *Support object-oriented data modeling!* – The complex structure of Semantic World Models is best modeled in an object-oriented approach.
2. *Distributed Architecture!* – Support distributed simulation, data processing, modeling (i.e., collaboration), data acquisition, or control architectures. For that purpose, data must be replicated to different clients, sites as well as projection screens and must be kept in sync.
3. *In-Memory Database!* – Provide the necessary performance for (live) 3D simulation.

4. *Be schema-adaptive!* – Enable a universal applicability of the data management concepts by supporting the various schemata or modeling languages (e.g., CityGML, ForestGML, AutomationML, X3D, VSDML, ...) of eRobotics applications.
5. *Support Simulation-based X!* – Support the specific requirements of Simulation-based X. While Simulation-based Optimization and Reasoning particularly need to store and compare different simulation runs (i.e., need temporal data management), Simulation-based Reasoning and Control require the reuse of the identical model and data management in live operation as used within simulation.

Today, in the general field of applications with a 3D context, some scenarios exist that employ database technology. Their motivations for doing so are diverse and similar to those identified for eRobotics applications. Each data management approach covers some aspects also required for managing Semantic World Models. For example, while some store only metadata within the database others store the entire 3D model. Some provide an object-oriented modeling, a distributed approach, the usage of different schemata, or a temporal data management. The work at hand presents a new universal data management approach for eRobotics applications that fulfills all of the identified demands at once based on a consequent usage of database technology. An overview of its architecture is given in Figure 1.7.

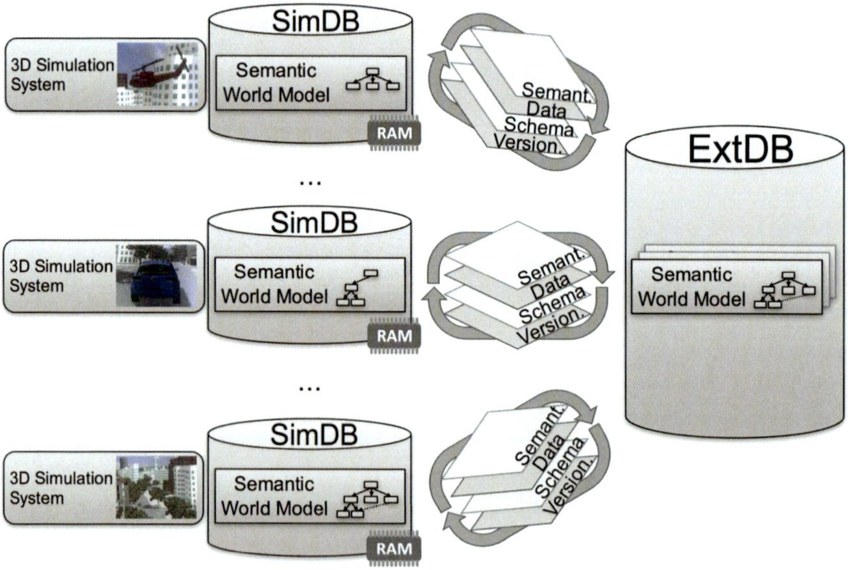


**Figure 1.7:** *Architecture of the new data management approach for eRobotics applications presented in this thesis.*

The basic idea is to combine two types of generic databases: A simulation database (SimDB) and an external database (ExtDB). SimDB is an active, in-memory simulation database, which serves as the core data management component of a 3D simulation system. It caches the Semantic World Model and realizes its execution. Multiple instances of the 3D simulation system and SimDB are connected to a single ExtDB. Its duty is the central management and provisioning of the shared Semantic World Model, providing a persistence back-end as well as a versioning mechanism, and serving as a communication hub for the distributed system of SimDBs and ExtDB.

A novel database synchronization approach synchronizes each pair of SimDB and ExtDB. A basic prerequisite of this approach is the compatibility of the two databases' modeling concepts. To support its flexible application, the approach does not depend on specific database paradigms (relational, object-oriented, XML, ...). In this thesis, compatibility is formally specified using a new approach based on MDE (Model-Driven Engineering) methods: Modeling concepts are represented in terms of database metamodels and their compatibility in terms of model transformations. In this context, the UML (Unified Modeling Language [8]) metamodel is added as a pivot to guarantee the object-oriented modeling concepts optimally suited for Semantic World Models and to provide a language with well-known semantics for a universal and neutral specification of the synchronization approach suited for various database systems. Figure 1.8 illustrates the scenario.

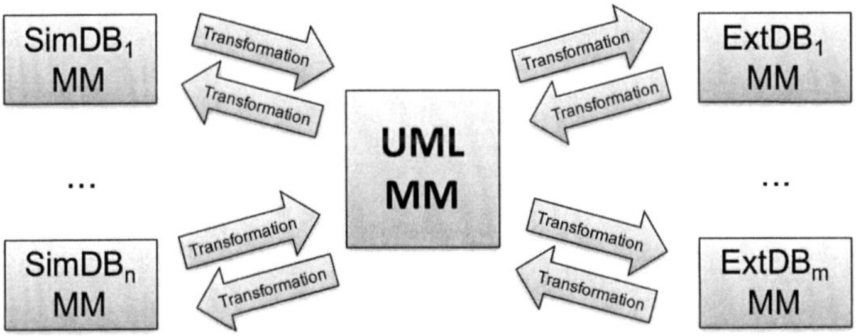


**Figure 1.8:** *Database compatibility and support for object-oriented modeling concepts is stipulated in terms of model transformations to and from the UML metamodel (MM) for each SimDB and ExtDB metamodel.*

Based on these conceptual compatibility requirements, the synchronization approach is specified on four levels:

- Initially, on **schema level**, the common schema of the Semantic World Model in ExtDB is synchronized to (each) SimDB, distributing it within the overall system.
- On **data level**, based on the synchronized schema, (parts of) the model's instance data is replicated from ExtDB to SimDB making it available to the simulation system. Changes to the replicated data are resynchronized to ExtDB yielding persistence. From there, changes are propagated to other instances of SimDB making ExtDB a communication hub for the distributed system.

- On a **semantic level**, functional data synchronization is used to selectively translate parts of the Semantic World Model from third party schemata (e.g., CityGML, AutomationML, ...) to proprietary structures of the simulation system to enable their interpretation.
- Underneath, on a **version level**, from the multiple versions of the Semantic World Model managed within ExtDB (in this context, a temporal database) a snapshot is synchronized to SimDB. Likewise, changes to the replicated data are resynchronized with corresponding timestamps or timestamp tuples for multiple time dimensions.

This thesis is structured as follows. In Chapter 2, related approaches for the usage of databases in the context of 3D applications are examined and discussed. Chapter 3 summarizes the fundamentals of database technology, MDE and UML as needed in this work. In Chapter 4, the particularly MDE-based system requirements for the presented approach are postulated, before, in Chapter 5, the novel synchronization concept itself is described in full detail. Reference implementations fulfilling the system requirements and realizing these specifications are presented in Chapter 6. They build the basis for the various eRobotics applications shown in Chapter 7. Finally, the results of this work are summarized in Chapter 8.

# Chapter 2

# Related Work

In this chapter, fields of application with a 3D context that are similar to eRobotics are examined for data management approaches incorporating databases. Different fields are identified: VR (Virtual Reality), AR (Augmented Reality) and training, collaborative 3D environments, city modeling and planning, the usage of VRML (Virtual Reality Modeling Language [9]), and PDM (Product Data Management) systems. Their common feature is their usage of a 3D model and its (partial) management by a database.

## 2.1 Augmented Reality and Training

Following [10], AR is a variation of VR, where a user is not completely immersed in a VE (Virtual Environment) but he rather sees the real world with superimposed virtual objects. Thus, one important aspect in AR applications is portability leading to a focus on portable data management.

### 2.1.1 BARS: Battlefield Augmented Reality System

A mobile AR system using databases is described in [11]. The "Battlefield Augmented Reality System" uses an information management system that combines distributed object management with object instantiation from databases. Its purpose is to save bandwidth by distributing only relevant data to mobile users. An object-oriented data model describes the hierarchically structured city data.

Objects are distributed shallowly by creating "ghost" copies retaining a master copy only at one site of the distributed system. Such a ghost is a non-fully replicated copy of its master allowing simplified object versions to be transmitted (e.g., with sufficient parameters for rendering). Changes to the master copy are pushed to all its ghosts. Remote systems can change a master copy by sending it a change request.

A so-called "Connection and Database Manager" (ConMan) is responsible for object distribution. It keeps track on all objects (master and ghost), on which machine they reside and where they are located spatially. Connections for communication between objects are build up or terminated based on proximity and other rules. Objects may also be archived in relational databases. When they are required in an interaction with another object they are instantiated into an object by the ConMan. This requirement may also be determined by the object's proximity. Changes to such an instantiated object are made persistent by writing them back to the corresponding database entity.

### 2.1.2 BrahmsVE

"BrahmsVE" [12] combines a multi-agent DES (Discrete Event Simulation) system (Brahms [13]) with a 3D framework (OWorld) and a 3D browser plugin (Adobe Atmosphere). Brahms - specialized in the simulation of work practice - can thereby be used in VE training scenarios.

The client-server architecture of BrahmsVE consists of the client-side browser plugins (OWorld and Atmosphere), a Brahms server for the DES and a BrahmsVE server. The latter is based on MySQL [14] and PHP (PHP: Hypertext Preprocessor [15]) and provides central services like scene graph and animation script building, web page delivery and synchronization of activities. It also provides events from the client-side Virtual Environment (e.g., collisions) to the Brahms server using a dedicated table in the MySQL database.

In the case study "SimStation Online," BrahmsVE was extended to allow collaboration by querying and updating multimedia information on scene graph nodes managed in a common SQL (Structured Query Language) database. Furthermore, the construction of a Virtual Environment from predefined file-based components using queries to a MySQL database was added.

### 2.1.3 Studierstube

In the context of the research project "Studierstube" [16], a DBMS (Database Management System) was used as a back-end for mobile AR applications. The authors' motivation was to provide efficient data management for the highly structured AR data while supporting large-scale models with detailed information. Therefore, a proprietary object-oriented modeling language called BAUML (Building Augmentation Modeling Language) was developed. Based on XML (Extensible Markup Language), it supports hierarchical data modeling. Its high degree of flexibility in adding application specific semantic details using standard XML techniques also suited the authors' demand for rapid prototyping of AR applications.

For the actual data management, an XML DBMS called "Muddleware" [17] was developed. During runtime, it stores its data as a DOM (Document Object Model) and provides XPath (XML Path Language) for data access. It has a client-server architecture and supports persistence, a locking mechanism and several APIs (Application Programming Interfaces) like C++, Java and the XML-based Muddleware Script. By providing a notification system, it also represents an active database where clients can subscribe to changes. Thus, Muddleware itself supports collaboration though the proposed mobile AR application does not use this feature. Furthermore, Muddleware facilitates rapid prototyping as it does not impose a schema on the managed XML data.

For data delivery, an AR client queries a subset of BAUML encoded data, which is subsequently converted into a ready-made scene graph by an on-the-fly XSLT (Extensible Stylesheet Language Transformation [18]), a transformation language for XML data (itself based on XML). This view generation process creates a scene graph that not only contains the scene information but also the complete application logic, effectively creating an AR application on user request, which can be interpreted by a generic AR scene graph browser. The system does not allow to write back changes from this scene graph to the database.

## 2.2 3D City Modeling and Planning

As 3D city models tend to be huge, both data management as well as visualization and simulation are challenging tasks. The focus on the following selection of systems from the context of 3D city modeling and planning is on approaches incorporating database technology.

### 2.2.1 Karma VI

The "Karma VI" system described in [19] provides a multi-view approach to the representation and manipulation of geodata from within a VR environment. The authors' work was motivated by the different needs in the different phases of infrastructure planning. In the orientation or planning phase, the classic 2D view on buildings and the like was preferred, in the modeling phase a 2.5D bird's eye view and in the presentation phase a detailed 3D view.

The approach combines a geo database (SDE (Spatial Database Engine [20])) with a scene graph (WTK (WorldToolKit)) and CAD (Computer-Aided Design) components in a client-server architecture. On server-side, SDE - based on an Oracle [21] RDBMS (Relational Database Management System) - provides tables containing features with 2D geometric as well as attribute data. On client-side, a feature's 2D geometry is loaded into the scene graph. The plan view is represented by a node holding the 2D geometry itself. The node for the model view contains a 2.5D version of the 2D geometry, extruded by an arbitrary scalar attribute of the feature. For the world view's node, an associated 3D CAD model is imported, aligned with the 2D geometry and scaled. The three nodes are subsumed by a LOD (Level of Detail) node representing the feature in the scene graph. It contains the database key to identify the feature (e.g., for query results) and the feature's center coordinates on which all its views are positioned. Manipulations, modeling and analysis of the geo data is set up on client-side (operators, parameters, etc.) and executed on server-side.

### 2.2.2 Databases and Virtual Environments for cultural sites

In [22], a relational multimedia database is used. Such a database provides special multimedia data types, e.g., for video or audio data [4]. Here, it is used to provide additional multimedia information on artifacts modeled in a VE of a culture site. By selecting a scene object, the user can retrieve the related information. For that purpose, a scene graph node's name can contain an identifier, which is subsequently used as a key for database queries. Vice versa, scene objects corresponding to a database entry can be retrieved and highlighted by searching the appropriately named node in the scene graph.

### 2.2.3 CityServer3D

In [23], an integrated system for the storage, management and Internet-based distribution of 3D geodata called "CityServer3D" is presented. One of the authors' main motivation was the unification of different import and export formats used in the context of 3D geodata (e.g., CityGML [24, 25], VRML, GML (Geography Markup Language [26]), SVG (Scalable Vector Graphics), SHP (Esri Shapefile)). Therefore, a three-tiered architecture was designed, consisting of a client, a server and a data tier.

The data tier can contain different data sources with different schemata. Primarily, an Oracle spatial database with a dedicated schema called GeoBase21 is used, which corresponds to the server tier's so-called metamodel (not to confuse with the concept of metamodels as described in Chapter 3) for runtime data. Other schemata are supported using converters in the server tier's layer for database access. The metamodel builds the system's core, decoupling the various data formats and allowing unified data processing methods. Finally, a variety of interfaces (HTTP (Hypertext Transfer Protocol), WMS (Web Map Service), W3DS (Web 3D Service)) provide data access to proprietary and 3rd party clients with read or read-write support.

GeoBase21 is a generic relational schema based on a central "feature3d" table following the OGC (Open Geospatial Consortium) Simple Feature specification. A feature3d entity can reference into its own table to build hierarchies, can reference geometric data with different LODs and can reference a table for attribute registration to flexibly define application specific data. Furthermore, multiple feature3d can be grouped together (thematically or spatially).

In [27], motivated by the increasing complexity of CityServer3D, the authors extended their approach of decoupling the data sources from the metamodel. Direct SQL database calls were replaced by the Java persistence framework Hibernate [28], separating business logic from database access.

On the server tier, data access is handled using a so-called data provider object (DPO) for every database schema, e.g., a GB21DPO for the GeoBase21 schema. A DPO provides access to the data from its corresponding data source using classes of the server's runtime metamodel. Thus, it loads data from the database into the runtime model while providing a static mapping between both schemata. A DPO combines DAOs (Data Access Objects) with converters. While the DAOs provide the actual access to the database in the form of objects corresponding to the native database schema, converters provide their necessary conversion to the metamodel. Within the DAOs, Hibernate, enhanced by support for spatial database extensions, is used for database access.

## 2.3 Collaborative Environments

For 3D systems with multiple users, collaboration is an interesting and important aspect. Different authors focus on this problem of interchange between the clients using database technology.

### 2.3.1 Virtual Space Teleconferencing

In [29] a "Virtual Space Teleconferencing" system is described that uses a distributed "Virtual World DataBase" (VWDB; not to be confused with [30, 31, 32]). It implements a NVE (Networked Virtual Environment) for communication among remote sites. Within such a virtual conferencing room, participants have a virtual representation (avatar). They use its virtual eyes to look into the room and see each other's avatars, move their own avatar in the room, communicate with each other, and see as well as (cooperatively) manipulate virtual objects within the room.

The authors classified NVE into categories of increasing degree of networking, where level 0 represents VEs without networking. On level 1, a VWDB is shared with read-only access so participants can neither change the environment nor see each other. Level 2 adds distribution of each site's status so participants can see a virtual representation of other sites allowing simple communication (e.g., pointing at objects) but no further cooperation, as the VE cannot be manipulated. Not until level 3, users can cooperate by changing virtual objects, but only independently. Therefore concurrency control is needed so one object can only be manipulated by one user at the same time. Level 4 removes this limitation and allows mutual interaction with multiple users changing objects (e.g., grasping the same object) at the same time, which needs a more sophisticated concurrency control.

Because of the need for cooperation and ease of implementation, the Virtual Space Teleconferencing was realized as a level 3 NVE. The approach is based on the assumption that manipulating one object of the virtual world does not interfere with other objects. This improves interactivity by allowing parallel manipulation of different objects. For such a system, the authors identified consistency, mutual exclusion and interactivity as key problems they addressed in the design of their distributed architecture. It consists of a master site holding a master copy of the VWDB being distributed as a whole to all client sites on system startup. To keep the copies consistent, manipulations are reported to the master, which updates its

VWDB accordingly and distributes the change to all client sites. Simultaneous changes to the same object are prevented by mutually exclusive access to virtual objects. To manipulate an object, clients have to ask the master, which only grants access to currently free objects. Simultaneous requests are ruled based on client priorities. The data redundancy supports interactivity as the copies of the VWDB can be rendered locally at each site. Furthermore, local manipulations are not only reported to the master, but also directly update the local copy of the VWDB.

### 2.3.2 Virtual World Database

In [30] and [31] the "Virtual World Database System" (VWDB) combines a Virtual Reality system with an OODBS (Object-Oriented Database System) to provide Virtual Reality as a multi-modal database interface for queries and updates.

In VWDB, a database schema is described using a proprietary language ("VWDB Schema Definition Language") to define classes ("categories") with their base classes, simple attributes, references and behavior (methods). Subsequently, it is appropriately translated for the target database management system. On system startup, the Virtual Reality model data is loaded from the OODB (Object-Oriented Database) into a WTK-based scene graph.

Using commands of a multi-modal (gestures and speech) language, the user can perform queries and updates, which are subsequently executed on the original data by the database management system. The multi-modal language is defined using automata for multi-modal interactions like "move object." By analyzing voice and gestures, sequences of input symbols are first identified and then verified using these automata. Finally, such sequences are translated into query messages for the OODB back-end.

In VWDB2 [32], collaborative work support was added to the system with multiple VR clients (now Java3D[1]-based) connecting to the OODB back-end. Main issues were update propagation, a transaction concept and solutions to consistency problems.

For update propagation to all connected clients, changes to the now shared VE are first issued as transactions to the central database. After an interference check at the back-end, they are commited and then distributed to all clients by an additional messaging service using a multicast[2] approach.

The authors' transaction concept first differentiates between local and global transactions where local transactions need no propagation to the the back-end (e.g., a client's own movements). Global transactions are further divided into three categories: primitive, group and continuous transactions. Primitive operations cannot be decomposed (e.g., "Create box") and group operations combine them to give meaning (e.g., "Where is box A?", "Create box B", "Put A on B"). Both transaction types are commited as a whole and follow traditional

[1]Java3D is a scene graph framework for Java [33].

[2]In multicasting, one host sends data to a group of hosts (one-to-many) [34].

ACID (atomicity, consistency, isolation and durability) properties. In contrast, continuous operations combine primitive and group operations to an initially open-ended sequence (e.g., "Move box"). As such operations' progress needs to be reflected in the shared VE, each sub-transaction is immediately commited and distributed via multicast. Unlike the conservative approach for primitve or group transactions, (partially) failed continuous transactions are not discarded as a whole. Instead, the sequence to the last valid sub-transaction is regarded as being in an "aborted acceptable termination state." As this delimits atomicity of continuous transactions, only relaxed ACID properties apply.

The delay of update propagations (commit, multicast) for sub-transactions of continouos operations leads to jerky movements (observed at other clients) and wrongly detected or missed collisions due to interim inconsistencies between the back-end database and its local copies. Thus, for objects being moved a local "ghost" representation is created at each nearby client. It directly reflects the original movement using an additional P2P (Peer-to-Peer) connection to the initiating client. These "neighboring ghost objects" reduce the jerky impression of the original object's movement as they allow to anticipate its movement. Furthermore, they are used to refine collision detection.

### 2.3.3 Collaborative Urban Planner

The "Collaborative Urban Planner" described in [35] is based on the multi-user VE system DeepMatrix [36], extended by an RDBMS back-end providing persistence for the VE. The system's client is a browser-based Java3D application allowing navigation, analysis and modification of the environment. Actions may be local operations like "show details" or shared operations like "rotate object," where the latter are also sent to the server for distribution and persistence. A client's VE contains local Java3D objects (e.g., constructed for measuring) as well as shared (or local) VRML and CAD data imported from file. The server application provides concurrency control, message distribution and data management. It represents the single point of access to the database, ensuring its consistency. Data request messages of clients are processed, passed to the DBMS and sent back to the client. The database contains meta information on shared objects (position, texture), user roles with permissions and various planning data.

### 2.3.4 Virtual Office Environment

To intuitively collaborate in a "Virtual Office Environment" (VOE), the authors of [37] describe an approach that not only allows to model 3D data, but also the semantics of objects and the users' intention to perform actions using ontologies[3]. A DBMS manages the 3D as well as the associated semantic data allowing semantic-based queries and collaboration.

Each client locally constructs a scene graph including the attached semantic information by querying the common database. This scene graph can be seen as a view onto the database with nodes having the same ID (Identifier) as the database entity they are built for. It contains nodes for objects of the virtual world, associated leaf nodes for their 3D data and edges describing translations, rotations as well as the state between two objects (e.g., a node "note" associated with an edge "put away on" to another node "book shelf"). Clients' actions are issued as queries to the common database. To support collaboration, these changes are distributed to all other clients of the common VOE, which adopt the changes in their local scene graph.

## 2.4 VRML-based Approaches

VRML is an ISO (International Organization for Standardization) standardized language for modeling 3D data and was particularly developed for the world wide web. Although it has been superseded by its XML-based successor X3D (Extensible 3D [39]), it still has a widespread usage. Thus, different approaches for an efficient management of VRML data have been developed to abandon the purely file-based approach and adopt database technology instead.

### 2.4.1 VRML-object database system

An approach to manage VRML fragments structured by semantic information in object-oriented databases is presented in [40]. The authors were motivated by reuse and sharing of large amounts of VRML data, something they considered to be rather impractical when using standard VRML files. As a main problem for reuse of VRML data imported from CAD files they identified different 3D objects often being not logically separated and the lack of semantic attributes preventing the use of queries. For the sharing of data, e.g., among different enterprises in a city planning project, they added access control and dynamic hyperlink generation as important features.

Attribute information and logical structure is realized in a database containing a flexibly definable object-oriented data model based on a common "entity" class to describe real-world objects. An entity has a part-of relation to other entities for structure and attributes can be added using inheritance. Furthermore, each entity has a represented-by relation to

[3]"To support the sharing and reuse of formally represented knowledge among AI (Artificial Intelligence) systems, it is useful to define the common vocabulary in which shared knowledge is represented. A specification of a representational vocabulary for a shared domain of discourse – definitions of classes, relations, functions, and other objects – is called an ontology."[38].

a number of presentation objects. A "pobject" contains a VRML sub-tree (as a string) for one entity in one LOD and has a detail-of relation to pobjects for the other LODs of the same entity. pobjects are stored in a separate database to support reuse in different projects and to allow incremental discovery of entity structures. In another database, access control is defined per entity by the maximum LOD a user can get pobjects for. VRML-hyperlinks are dynamically created using query pairs defining the set of source and target entities.

The system is implemented as a web front-end with a commercial OODBMS (Object-Oriented Database Management System) back-end called O2. In a "spatial view generation" process, a user queries entities with certain attribute properties. Based on the user's access rights, pobjects corresponding to the query result are assembled into a VRML scene graph and hyperlinks are added by evaluating the query pairs.

### 2.4.2 VRML and SQL3D

In [41], the author states the need to "redeploy" VRML to integrate it into the mainstream of IT (Information Technology). As its main drawbacks he identifies its purely file-based approach, the missing concurrency support, a monolithic architecture and centralized data management. He introduces an architectural proposal called SQL3D that combines scene-graph-based 3D clients with a federation of databases for the distributed management of scene data, connected by a so-called "fabric" based on real-time CORBA (Common Object Request Broker Architecture)[4]. Thus, the approach brings together the competencies of the 3D group, the database management group and the object management group.

For the redeployment of VRML, a corresponding VRML schema must be derived for each type of employed database architecture (OODBMS, RDBMS, ORDBMS (Object-Relational Database Management System)) of the heterogeneous federation. Query languages like SQL might have to be extended to express VRML structures and behavior. In the federation, data is distributed on several databases providing scene objects and other "knowledge." For example, a client can fetch a triangle from one database and determine its color by querying another. Dedicated servers provide central services for geometry simplification or for additionally caching scene data.

On the client-side of SQL3D, a local OODBMS provides an in-memory scene object cache, which is connected to the federation by the same fabric using an ORB. The cached objects are replicated to the scene graph of the adopted 3D framework and bidirectionally kept in sync. This can either be done statically using a precompiler that inserts the necessary redirection code into the client application or by using a mechanism for dynamic extension

[4]CORBA is a middleware specification for interoperability in distributed heterogeneous, object-oriented applications [42]. It is an attempt of the OMG (Object Management Group) to standardize the ORB (Object Request Broker) approach [43]. Each application uses an ORB that manages communication and data exchange with other applications' ORBs using remote method calls on objects. Applications may be written in different programming languages like C++ or Java.

of the scene management with SQL3D during runtime. The scene management can also be dynamically replaced by SQL3D's client components. In the static approach, the application itself is aware of SQL3D, thus more of its features can be used (e.g., locking). The local object cache is kept filled by intelligent prefetching to allow the exploration of huge virtual worlds. Finally, concurrency control among the federated databases and the local object caches allows multiuser interaction between the clients.

### 2.4.3 Spatiotemporal Database Connection to VRML

The work described in [44] defines a three-tiered architecture called 3D-Spatiotemporal Internet Database that combines spatiotemporal data modeling and querying with VRML for Internet-based data access. On the presentation tier, a VRML browser is extended by additional controls for temporal navigation as well as widgets for queries and non-spatial attribute values. The underlying Internet browser communicates with a web server using a so-called Spatiotemporal DBMS Internet Client. On the middleware tier, this web server executes spatiotemporal queries on a database, translates results into VRML and adds rule-based visualizations of non-spatial data. The database tier uses an RDBMS with a spatiotemporal data model and a query language.

The proposed "3D-Spatiotemporal Data Model" isolates spatial from non-spatial data. An index table combines both parts and defines an object hierarchy using parent ids. The spatial properties of an object are modeled using implicit primitives (box, cylinder, ...) combined with appearance and positioning. Each (non-)spatial data tuple can be timestamped by a point in time to add temporal information. Two consecutively timestamped tuples can be associated by a Trend with an additional interpolation rule (linear, circular, ...), e.g., to model moving objects. Finally, a "Lifestamp" in the index table allows the definition of a predecessor-successor-relationship for a whole object (e.g., a car is scrapped).

The data can be accessed using a "3D-Spatiotemporal Query Language," an extension of SQL. It adds spatial operators for comparison (Equal, Disjoint, ...), viewpoint-dependent operators (Infront, Behind, ...), orientation-dependent operators (Upon, Beneath), temporal operators for values (At, incorporating the Trend) as well as for existence (Exists), and spatiotemporal operators for changes over time (Grow, Approach, ...).

### 2.4.4 X-VR

In his book publication [45], the author proposes the X-VR approach for dynamic database-driven VR applications. It combines two techniques: The so-called X-VRML for dynamic content modeling and the so-called X-VRDB for database modeling of virtual worlds.

The XML-based language X-VRML for modeling database-driven VR applications was motivated by the limited flexibility of static scene modeling approaches with file-based formats. Instead, X-VRML provides a template-based modeling approach where template parameters can among others be queried from databases to instantiate a concrete virtual scene, e.g., in VRML format. It supports imperative programming concepts (loops, conditional statements, ...) and object-oriented modeling techniques (objects, classes and inheritance).

Besides scene template instantiation, databases can also be accessed during runtime of the VR application. When using a server-side X-VRML interpreter, script nodes within the client-side VRML scene instance can be used to make changes persistent. With a client-side interpreter instead, X-VRML's own mechanisms can be used to read from databases to update the virtual scene or to write back changes for persistence. A client-side interpreter also allows to fully exploit X-VRML's features like user interaction and continuous manipulation of the virtual scene.

In [46], a "shared mode" for database-driven collaboration is presented. In a chess application example with two players, a shared database with the game's setting is alternately updated by the one client while being polled for changes by the other, which subsequently reflects the changes in his own virtual scene instance.

The X-VRDB approach is used for describing models of virtual worlds that can be stored in databases. These models can be instantiated as virtual scenes in scene description languages like VRML, X3D or again X-VRML.

An X-VRDB model consists of VR-Data, VR-Schema, VR-Templates and VR-Scenes. In VR-Data, VR-Objects describe single objects of the virtual world that are stored as DB (Database) records with attribute values. The VR-Schema consists of a hierarchy of VR-Classes generalizing such VR-Objects. VR-Classes are also stored as DB records describing the VR-Objects structure and general rules for their representation in different scene description languages. VR-Templates describe parametrizable virtual scenes as well as rules for their representation in different scene description languages. Particular instantiations are described in VR-Scenes, containing template parameters for selection and projection of VR-Objects. Stored VR models can either be manipulated by authoring tools or by changes from within an instantiation of the virtual world using a persistence mechanism.

The combination of X-VRDB and X-VRML allows different modeling levels. Either only VR-Objects, VR-Objects and -Classes or also VR-Templates and -Scenes can be modeled within a database using X-VRDB while the rest is modeled in an X-VRML file. In all cases, the X-VRML interpreter provides the necessary dynamics for the VR application.

## 2.5 Product Data Management (PDM)

Another field related to this work is PDM (Product Data Management) [47, 48].

### 2.5.1 PDM Basics

PDM systems are used in the industrial sector to manage all interdisciplinary product-related data, documents, and processes for all parts of an enterprise (or even multiple enterprises). For that purpose, they provide an integration platform for the often heterogeneous ecosystem of applications used in the different departments. In particular, these tools are CA$x$ (Computer-Aided $x$) software like CAD (Computer-Aided Design), CAM (Computer-Aided Manufacturing), or CAE (Computer-Aided Engineering) software – often from various vendors. The integration of a product's data and the relevant development processes is an important prerequisite for a virtual product development.

PDM systems are often used in the context of the management strategy called PLM (Product Lifecycle Management). Following [47], a PLM definition can be built bottom-up. A product is defined as any industrial product, but also products in a broader sense that may even be non-physical, e.g., insurance contracts. A product's life (Figure 2.1) then comprises phases like idea, development, manufacturing, marketing, sale, and disposal. Recycling and feedback, which can be used in the development of follow-up products, allow to speak of a product lifecycle. Finally, PLM is the management of this steady flow. It is a task of the management level that particularly relates to all departments. In the context of this strategy, a closer collaboration between these departments as well as concurrent engineering is needed to facilitate and accelerate their work. A PDM represents the engineering backbone to enable a PLM strategy.

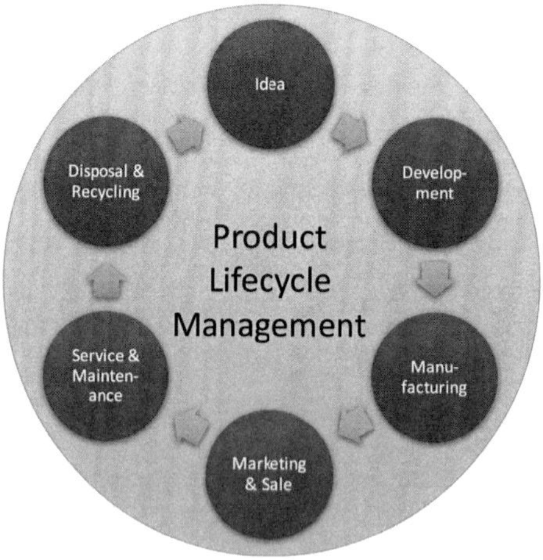


**Figure 2.1:** *Product Lifecycle Management (adapted from www.plm-info.de).*

Originating from simple shared file directories providing digital drawing cabinets for 2D CAD data, PDM systems evolved to database-driven management systems for all product data. Besides complex 3D CAD models, this includes data from all technical domains (like electrics, electronics, hydraulics etc.) and documentation. A PDM system also includes definition and control of product development processes to make the managed data appropriately available (right place, time, form) to the users. In these so-called workflows, state changes mark the phases in a product's lifecycle. Finally, a PDM system also provides a central communication infrastructure for all its users.

According to [48], a PDM system has to support the creation, update, versioning, and archival of a product structure whose elements come from (different) CA$x$ (Computer-Aided $x$) systems. It has to manage this often incompatible data, corresponding documentation, and the various relationships and dependencies in between. Figure 2.2 shows a PDM's basic setup. An alternative name for PDM is EDM (Engineering Data Management), which is more oriented towards the engineering process than to the product. A database stores metadata to describe, classify and add attributes to the file-based data (CA$x$ files, documents, etc.). The files, in turn, are stored in so-called vaults, i.e., secured file archives. Proprietary file formats of the particular applications as well as standard file formats (e.g., TIFF (Tagged Image File Format), VDAFS (Federation of the Automobile Industry, Surface Interface), or IGES (Initial Graphics Exchange Specification)) are used. The metadata represents a product's structure, i.e., a product hierarchically divided in its components or assemblies. The corresponding data model allows to link documents and other objects as well as resources and processes to the product structure itself using relationships. Finally, a PDM's data is accessed only via the database, which in turn accesses the vaults.

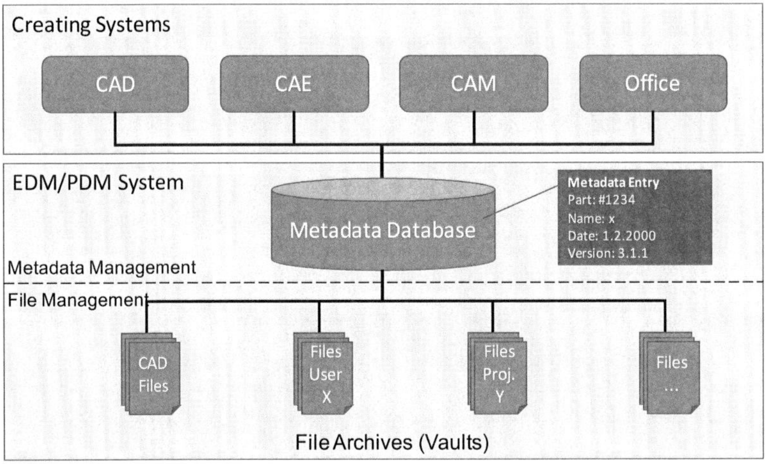


**Figure 2.2:** *Basic setup of a PDM system: A metadata database for product-related files (adopted from [48]).*

In [49], this combination of a metadata and files is called a "black box integration." The approach is said to be pragmatic for integration scenarios in heterogeneous environments (data and processes) avoiding the need for a single data model for all information.

PDM systems usually have a client-server architecture using an RDBMS (or sometimes OODBMS) as a back-end. They provide application-specific functionality like

- product data (e.g., CAD models) and document (e.g., working plans) management including version information,
- creation and management of product structures including their changing over time in terms of configurations and versions,
- extraction of parts lists,
- management of product variants,
- classifying objects or creating categories for parts,
- management of workflows, i.e., a PDM's internal representation of a controlled process,
- user and project management
- ...

PDM systems may also have a distributed architecture that is based on the utilized back-end database (see Subsection 3.4.2). For homogeneous scenarios, a distributed database is used with a main metadata server and several dependent sub-servers. In heterogeneous scenarios (possibly integrating different PDM systems), a federation of independent databases, which cooperate using special services, can be used.

Following [50], PDM data can be exchanged using the widespread neutral STEP (Standard for the Exchange of Product model data) format, standardized in ISO 10303 [51]. This format supports a wide range of CA$x$ data including geometry (i.e., 2D/3D CAD data), product structure, metadata, or organizational data. The standard also comprises a data modeling language for describing schemata called EXPRESS. Another, newer format is JT (Jupiter Tesselation) (ISO 14306 [52]) – a widespread, neutral format for 3D CAD data. Besides data exchange, it is also used to vendor-independently embed CAD data in PDM systems. JT is more focused on visualization data, supporting tesselated data of different LODs, exact geometry representations (NURBS (Non-Uniform Rational B-Splines)), product structure, attributes, and product and production information. For data exchange, the latest iterations of STEP and JT are intended to be combined using STEP for the hierarchical product structure and JT to represent (part) geometries at the hierarchy tree's leaves.

Commercially relevant PDM systems are Teamcenter (Siemens PLM Software [53]), Windchill (PTC [54]), or ENOVIA V6 (Dassault Systèmes [55, 56]).

### 2.5.2 Teamcenter (Siemens PLM Software)

According to [57], Teamcenter is especially prevalent (market leader) and thus shall be presented as a representative system in more detail. Following the same source, Teamcenter's scope goes beyond a standard PDM system, also including functionalities like Maintenance, Repair, and Overhaul or Compliance Management. It provides integration with various CA$x$ tools and other widespread software (e.g., Microsoft Office). In its latest incarnation dubbed "Unified Architecture," the different modules of Teamcenter share a common data model and use a common set of services to yield a high degree of integration.

Following [58, 50], the basic data objects to model product data in Teamcenter include

- *folders* – folders organize product data.
- *items* – basic object to represent any product information, e.g., a part or an assembly.
- *item revisions* – an item consists of one or more item revisions representing different versions or variants of the same item.
- *datasets* – item revisions have attached datasets, i.e., container objects describing and referencing vaulted files (CAD data, documents etc.). Different types of datasets exist for different file types.
- *forms* – forms are data objects representing properties (i.e., attributes) of items (revisions) for display in a predefined template.
- *relations* – relations connect objects and may also have properties describing the relationship's nature. Relations can give different, context-dependent meanings to objects.

Note that item revisions establish an explicit versioning mechanism (see Subsection 3.4.4) embedded into the product data hierarchy itself.

For asynchronous collaborative editing, Teamcenter (like other PDM solutions) provides a check-out and check-in mechanism [58]. An object can be checked-out by a user, effectively locking it and providing exclusive write access. When checking out datasets, optionally, the referenced vaulted files can be cached locally. The lock is released by a check-in of the object. A check-out (and corresponding check-in) can be performed explicitly by the user or implicitly by opening a file.

According to [59, 58], Teamcenter distinguishes between classes and business objects. Classes, more precisely called storage classes, are used to store objects in relational database tables. A storage class corresponds to a table where each row represents a stored object and columns represent the class's attributes, which obviously are persistent. Business objects are the actually used types (not instances) for data modeling comprising data and behavior. They can either be persistent (thus having an associated storage class) or exist only during runtime to represent derived data. The former may either have an individual storage class (Primary Business Object) or share the storage class of a parent business object (Secondary Business Object). Business objects have properties:

- each storage class attribute corresponds to a *persistent property* of an associated business object,
- a *compound property* represents a remote value from another business object connected by a path of relationships,
- derived, i.e., calculated values, a represented by *runtime properties*,

- relationships are modeled using *relation properties.*

Business objects and storage classes can be modeled using the "Business Modeler IDE."

Teamcenter builds on a SOA (Service-Oriented Architecture) approach, which provides business logic as services [60]. This is based on a four-tiered architecture consisting of:

- *Client application tier* providing user interfaces,
- *Web application server tier* as a web interface to the business logic,
- *Enterprise tier* providing the business logic,
- *Resource tier* for data management following the standard PDM approach (metadata database combined with file vault)

The client tier has a so-called Client Data Model (CDM), derived from the customized data model in Teamcenter. It can either be generic providing simple objects with properties. Here, reflective utility functions can be used to determine the actual object type, to access the type hierarchy, or to access property details. In contrast, a type-safe CDM – derived from a generic CDM – provides the same type hierarchy as Teamcenter's data model implemented in terms of the respective language binding used for the client application (.NET, C++, and Java). A "Data Model Manager" is responsible for un/marshaling (de/serializing) CDM objects for/from service calls, for maintaining object identity (e.g., to avoid data duplication), for providing reflective access to the data schema (see Subsection 4.2.1), and for a notification infrastructure that allows to register for changes to objects. A typical service call goes as follows:

1. on the client tier
   (a) the client establishes an authenticated connection to the web tier and
   (b) calls the client-side service stubs with the appropriate input CDM objects;
   (c) the stubs embed the marshaled objects into an XML service call document and send it to the web tier
2. on the web tier, the service request is accepted via HTTP and passed to an available business logic server on the enterprise tier
3. on the enterprise tier
   (a) the business logic server unmarshals the XML document,
   (b) calls the appropriate service implementation,
   (c) marshals the result to an XML document,
   (d) and passes it to the web tier
4. on the web tier, the result document is accepted and passed to the client via HTTP
5. on the client tier
   (a) the service stubs unmarshal the result XML document,
   (b) and creates appropriate CDM objects
   (c) that are returned to the client application

Teamcenter integrates the aforementioned JT format as a neutral visualization format [61, 58]. For that purpose, it integrates translator components for different proprietary CAD formats (e.g., CATIA from Dassault Systèmes). Translated JT files accompany the original file and can be viewed from within the PDM client without the need for the original product to be installed. Translators can be invoked manually, in batch mode, or on saving (i.e., creating or changing) the original file. Such translators also exist for other neutral formats, e.g., PDF (Portable Document Format) for different proprietary document formats.

### 2.5.3 Simulation Data Management (SDM)

Alongside the PLM strategy, there is also a concept specializing in the field of simulation and analysis called SLM (Simulation Lifecycle Management) [62]. SLM comprises SDM (Simulation Data Management), Simulation and Test Process Management, and Decision Support.

SDM can be compared to PDM, however, it focuses on the needs of simulation and analysis. Important aspects are the management of simulation specific data (geometry, model data, parameters, results etc.), optimization for large simulation data or result files, and simulation-specific query capabilities. Besides simulation, test data is equally managed, integrating virtual and physical testing into a common data model. Another important aspect is the coupling of simulation with product data, integrating it into the engineering backbone of the business. Thus, simulation models, processes or results can directly be linked, for example, to the corresponding assemblies or requirements in a PDM system.

In Simulation and Test Process Management, the execution of simulations is managed. This includes the scheduling of executions, the assignment to the hardware, the execution mode (interactive or batch mode), or the specification of the target for the results. All this shall be realized independently from discipline (e.g., finite element analysis, computational fluid dynamics, kinematics etc.) or tool vendor.

Decision Support is the third part of SLM. Here, the potentially huge amount of result data is presented and analyzed. An important aspect is the ability to compare the results of large numbers of simulation executions with different parameters.

The field is younger than PDM and has similarly evolved from simple file managing – in this case for simulation result files. SLM simplifies the usage of simulations for non-experts by providing simpler access methods in an integrated system. It enables simulation-driven design where simulation is already incorporated in the early stages of product development instead of being used only for validation in the later stages.

Two examples of SLM implementations are SIMULIA SLM (Dassault Systèmes, [62]) with an SDM component based on the same vendor's PDM ENOVIA V6, and the Teamcenter simulation process management component (Siemens PLM Software [63]) – although not explicitly using the terms SLM or SDM.

## 2.6 Discussion

To sum up, the scenarios and corresponding publications in Sections 2.1–2.5 can be classed by field of application:

- 2.1 Augmented Reality and Training
  - 2.1.1 BARS: Battlefield Augmented Reality System: [11]
  - 2.1.2 BrahmsVE: [12]
  - 2.1.3 Studierstube: [16]
- 2.2 3D City Modeling and Planning
  - 2.2.1 Karma VI: [19]
  - 2.2.2 Databases and Virtual Environments for cultural sites: [22]
  - 2.2.3 CityServer3D: [23, 27]
- 2.3 Collaborative Environments
  - 2.3.1 Virtual Space Teleconferencing: [29]
  - 2.3.2 Virtual World Database: [30, 31, 32]
  - 2.3.3 Collaborative Urban Planner: [35]
  - 2.3.4 Virtual Office Environment: [37]
- 2.4 VRML-based Approaches
  - 2.4.1 VRML-object database system: [40]
  - 2.4.2 VRML and SQL3D: [41]
  - 2.4.3 Spatiotemporal Database Connection to VRML: [44]
  - 2.4.4 X-VR: [45, 46]
- 2.5 Product Data Management (PDM): [47, 48]

First of all, many of these scenarios use an object-oriented data modeling, in particular, [11, 16, 23, 27, 30, 31, 32, 37, 40, 41, 44, 45, 46, 47, 48]. Furthermore, their motivations for incorporating database technology in their data management are diverse:

- Persistence [11, 30, 31, 32, 35, 41, 44, 45, 46, 47, 48].
- Query capabilities [30, 31, 32, 37, 40, 44, 45, 46, 47, 48].
- Multiuser support
  - with [29, 30, 31, 32, 37, 41, 45, 46, 47, 48] or
  - without [16] collaboration.
- Client-server model [16, 19, 47, 48],
  - e.g., for server side analysis or centralized data provisioning.
- Extensive model data [12, 16, 23, 27, 40, 41, 47, 48].
- Access control and rights management [35, 40, 47, 48].
- Data provisioning via Internet [12, 23, 27, 41, 44, 45, 46, 47, 48].
- Temporal data management or versioning [44, 47, 48].
- Integration of existing databases [22].
- Integration of different data formats [23, 27, 47, 48].

Thus, in existing scenarios, database technology is already used for very similar reasons as those identified for eRobotics applications in the previous chapter. However, each scenario's motivation covers only some of them, resulting in a deviated focus in corresponding data management concepts. Thus, the approach presented in this work, in its entirety, has many advantages for eRobotics applications.

In some scenarios, databases are used to store additional information (meta information, documents, films, positions, hierarchical structure ...) on scene objects or parts [22, 12, 35, 47, 48, 64, 65, 66, 67, 68, 69, 70, 71, 72]. However, for eRobotics applications, the whole Semantic World Model should be managed using database technology to obtain the referred benefits for all its objects and their properties. This ensures that every aspect is queryable, distributable, and versionable and that the complete application schema is reproduced in the database to enforce it as a common language for all subsystems.

Other systems use a database to store scene data itself, but not all of them with an object-oriented data modeling, which is ideally suited for Semantic World Models. Another important aspect for eRobotics applications is the support for arbitrary application schemata. Many systems use a generic (scene-graph-like) geometric model, in most cases with attributes [12, 19, 23, 40, 41, 44, 45]. In such scenarios, schema flexibility can be achieved to a certain extent by providing import (and export) to different file formats [23, 73, 74, 75]. Some approaches support different or flexible schemata. For example in [19], schema alteration is realized by adding attributes to generic base objects. Other systems support a selection of different static [23] or dynamic [40, 16] schemata. However, most approaches focus on a specific field of application, thus, requiring and supporting only a corresponding fixed schema. This is very common and described in many similar publications presenting applications with a 3D context, for example many from the field of BIM (Building Information Modeling) [76, 77, 78, 79, 80, 81, 82]. While PDM systems [47, 48] in principle support arbitrary schemata they are not explicitly reflected within the database schema due to their "black box integration" approach. Similar vaulting-based approaches with a 3D context can be found in other publications [83, 84, 85, 86, 87]. However, to flexibly support various eRobotics applications, arbitrary application schemata of Semantic World Models need to be explicitly supported. Most scenarios provide a distributed architecture in terms of multiuser support, a client-server model, or access control and rights management. However, only some build it on a DDB (Distributed Database)-like approach [16, 29, 41] with client-side databases. The latter is favorable for eRobotics applications, e.g., to provide schema flexibility or a query interface on client-side, as well. Finally, some approaches support temporal data management or versioning [44, 47, 48, 73, 87, 76, 88, 78, 74, 89, 75, 79, 90, 83]. In most cases, these approaches require special schema structures and many are based on file vaulting. To be flexibly used in eRobotics applications, however, it needs to be available for arbitrary application schemata.

Altogether, there are different approaches to integrate database technology in applications with a 3D context. However, none of them fulfills all the demands made on a data management approach for eRobotics applications as described in the introduction. This conclusion motivates the presented concepts and their implementation.

# Chapter 3

# Basic Principles of Databases and Data Modeling

CAD (Computer-Aided Design) applications benefit from the usage of OODBs (Object-Oriented Databases) (see Subsection 3.1.3). The same is true for 3D simulation systems in general and eRobotics applications in particular as they also extensively use 3D data. However, DBMSs (Database Management Systems) with other modeling paradigms – in particular RDBMSs (Relational Database Management Systems) – are considerably more widespread. Restricting the intended approach to OODBMSs (Object-Oriented Database Management Systems) would limit its flexibility and universality. Thus, a more general approach for synchronizing virtually arbitrary databases should be preferred. Therefore, in Section 3.1, the fundamentals of databases in general and for the different modeling approaches (relational, object-oriented, ...) are examined.

When such different database types shall be synchronized, a universal approach for describing and comparing their corresponding modeling concepts is required. Such concepts can be formalized in terms of database metamodels and can be compared using so-called model transformations, both of which are examined in the field of MDE (Model-Driven Engineering) summarized in Section 3.2.

On the one hand, modeling 3D data benefits from object-orientation (see Chapter 1 and Subsection 3.1.3), while on the other hand, other metamodel concepts for databases – mostly relational – prevail. These two opposing constraints (object-oriented data modeling and relational or other data storage) may be reconciled based on the presented MDE (Model-Driven Engineering) methods. They allow the usage of an object-oriented metamodel to describe concepts adapted to the approach's intended area of application, while other metamodels can be used as representational metamodels like the relational (see Figure 3.4). A widespread metamodel for object-oriented data modeling is the UML (Unified Modeling Language [8]). In contrast to the ODMG (Object Data Management Group) standard mentioned in Subsection 3.1.3, it is still actively in development and independent of concrete database metamodels. Thus, it serves as an ideal reference metamodel for 3D data. Section 3.3 gives an introduction to the UML subset relevant to the presented work. Details on its particular usage are given in the subsequent chapters.

Finally, this chapter closes in Section 3.4 with some more database concepts relevant to this work.

## 3.1 Databases

The following section is mostly based on [42] and [4] and gives an overview of essential database fundamentals as well as the different prevailing database metamodels.

### 3.1.1 Database Fundamentals

There are several definitions of the term database itself. In [4], a general definition is given: "A database is a collection of related data." Here, data is defined as "known facts that can be recorded and that have implicit meaning." In [42], a database is defined as "a shared collection of logically related data and its description, designed to meet the information needs of an organization." In general, a database does not even have to be software-based, e.g., it can also be a physical address book.

A database is managed by a DBMS (Figure 3.1). In [42], it is defined as "a software system that enables users to define, create, maintain, and control access to the database." A DBMS is a universal tool and serves as the entry point to databases. As mentioned above, a database not only comprises data, but also a description of the data, called its metadata (i.e., data about the data). Usually, a database is defined using a DDL (Database Definition Language). This metadata (data types, structures, and constraints) is then stored by the DBMS in the so-called system catalog or data dictionary. Data manipulation, e.g., by a DML (Data Manipulation Language), comprises the insertion, updating, deletion and retrieval of data from a database. The prevalent SQL (Structured Query Language) comprises a DDL and a DML. Furthermore, a DBMS controls access to a database by authorizing users, ensuring data consistency, controlling concurrent access for shared usage, and by providing a recovery component for the rollback to a previous consistent state in case of failures. Finally, the overall system, i.e., the combination of DBMS and database, is called the DBS (Database System). An application using a database via a DBMS is called a database application (program).

Compared to the file-based approach, using a database has several advantages. Its metadata provides a self-description. This can be used to build general purpose DBMSs to dynamically retrieve a database's structure. Furthermore, metadata can also be used by database applications. In contrast, following a file-based approach, information on file structures is usually hard-coded into applications. This also enables databases to provide so-called *program-data independence*. Changing a file format will need most applications to

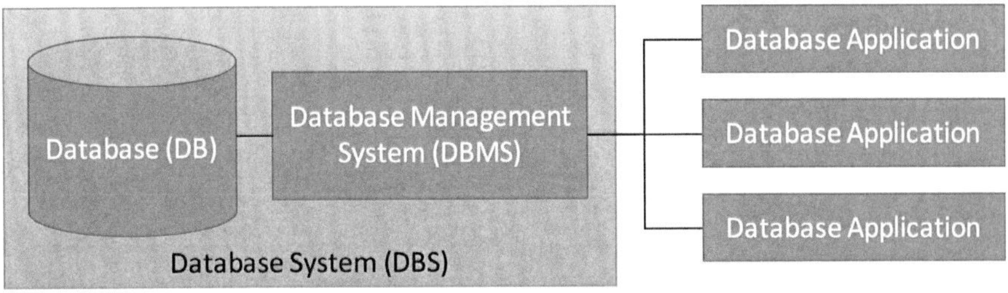


**Figure 3.1:** *Database (DB), Database Management System (DBMS) and Database System (DBS).*

be adapted. Many changes to the structure of a database, however, will not even be recognized by database applications. For example, adding another attribute to a relational database table will in most cases not affect queries on that table. However, adding information somewhere in a file record usually will need a parser to be adapted. Object-oriented or object-relational database systems additionally support operations on their data. Here, interfaces can be separated from implementations allowing the latter to be exchanged. This provides *program-operation independence*. Overall, databases offer a more conceptual view on data and behavior, abstracting from its physical storage and implementation. Another advantage of using databases is their support for different views on the same base data, providing different users with subsets or derived data ("virtual data"). Finally, it is a shared medium for data management, which can typically be used by multiple users. However, when data is updated, it must be protected by concurrency control to maintain consistency.

Moreover, databases have other advantageous properties. Instead of several data pools spread over an institution, redundancy is avoided by providing a central data management. It can also offer detailed access control as well as persistence for otherwise transient application data. Furthermore, data modeling including diverse relationships and constraint definitions is an asset of the database approach. Thus, a shared database also facilitates the provision and implementation of common modeling standards.

The structure [42] or description [4] of the data within a database is called the *database schema*, consisting of so-called schema constructs. For example, these may be table and column definitions in a relational database or class and attribute definitions in an object-oriented database. In contrast, the database's data itself, i.e., its content at a certain point in time, is called a (database) snapshot consisting of instances of schema constructs. While a database's schema rarely changes (schema evolution) its content is more frequently updated. Another term in the context of schemata is data model. However, its meaning is not yet defined consistently in literature. In this work as well as in publications like [42], a data model is a model of the database's data, i.e., its schema. In contrast, publications like [4] use it to denote the set of basic building blocks to define a database schema itself. In this work however, this is called a metamodel of a data model. Section 3.2 will provide more details on this topic. Metamodels in the database context can be categorized by level of abstraction. Conceptual metamodels provide high-level concepts without implementation constraints. Common examples are the ER (Entity-Relationship) Model (Figure 3.2) or the UML class diagrams (Figure 3.3), which are somewhat similar. The latter will be discussed in detail further down. ER diagrams (or ER models) consist of entities, relationships, and attributes. An entity is "a thing in the real world with an independent existence" [4], similar to objects in object-orientation. It has attributes with values. Entities have an entity type describing the attributes (similar to a class in object-orientation). Another integral part are relationships between entities, which belong to a relationship type (similar to links and associations in UML).

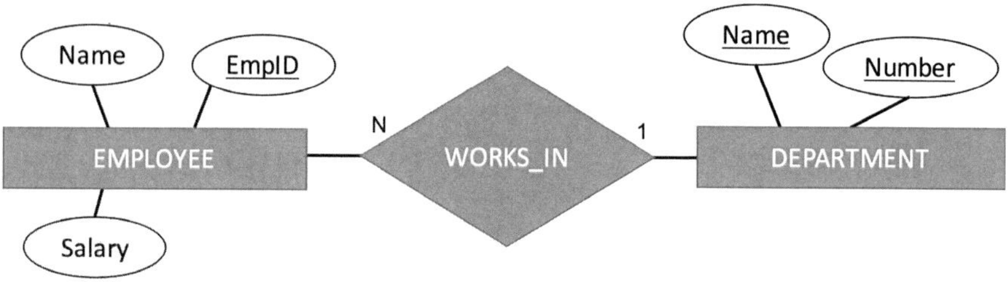


**Figure 3.2:** *Exemplary ER diagram: An EMPLOYEE entity with attributes Name, Salary and EmpID (identifying the entity), a DEPARTMENT entity (attributes Name and Number, together identifying the entity), and a relationship WORKS_IN in between (adapted from [4]).*

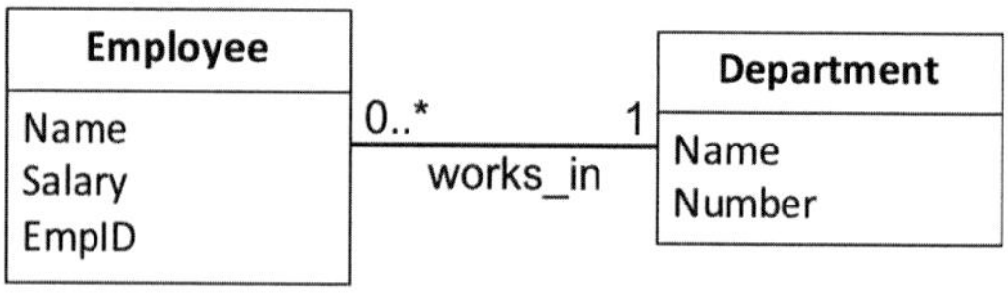


**Figure 3.3:** *Exemplary UML class diagram corresponding to ER diagram in Figure 3.2.*

Low-level physical metamodels are used for modeling data on disk. Metamodels in between are called representational [4] or logical [42]. They are abstract enough for most users to understand but also near to implementation. Here, the most widespread are the relational metamodel, object-relational metamodels, and object-oriented metamodels.

The so-called three-schema ANSI/SPARC architecture (Figure 3.4) integrates three levels of schemata for DBSs. On the internal level, an internal schema uses a physical metamodel to describe storage. On the conceptual level, a conceptual schema describes the overall structure of the database while hiding its physical implementation. Here, a representational (or logical) metamodel is used, which is often derived from a conceptual metamodel during database design. The external or view level comprises a set of external schemata or user views, likewise based on a representational metamodel. In between these tiers, mappings are defined. The architecture builds the basis for physical and logical data independence, allowing to change the storage strategy without changing the database, and to change the database without changing views and dependent applications. However, the separation between the levels is not always strict.

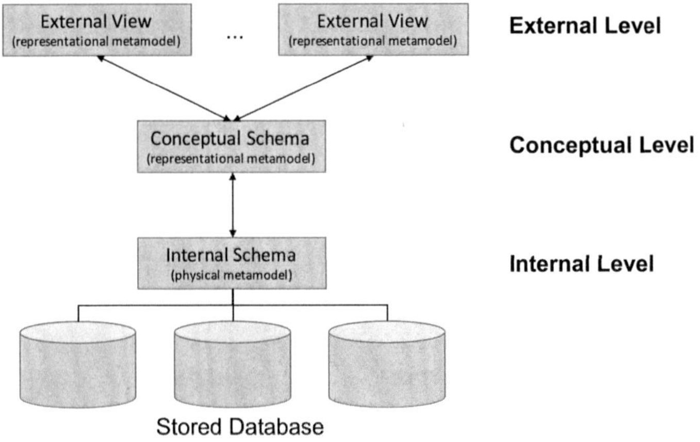


**Figure 3.4:** *The three-schema ANSI/SPARC architecture (adapted from [4]).*

Below, the main types of databases are introduced.

### 3.1.2 Relational Databases

Probably the most widespread database type is the relational. Two main advantages leading to its success are a well-defined theoretical foundation using mathematical relations and a universal query language (SQL).

The formal relational metamodel describes a database as a collection of relations. Informally, a relation is similar to a table with values (Table 3.1). Just as a table consists of rows with values for each column (header), a relation consists of tuples with values from the domain of each attribute of the relation. A domain $D$ is defined as a set of atomic values. A relation schema $R(A_1, \ldots, A_n)$ describes a relation. It consists of a name $R$ for the relation and a list of attributes $A_1, \ldots, A_n$, which are so-called roles for the domains $dom(A_i)$. A relation (or relation state) $r$ of $R$ consists of a set of $n$-tuples $t$, i.e., $r(R) = \{t_1, \ldots, t_m\}$. In turn, a tuple $t$ is an ordered list of values from the domains of $R$'s attributes or a special $NULL$ value, i.e., $t =< v_1, \ldots, v_n >$ with $t \in dom(A_i) \cup \{NULL\}$. A tuple $t$'s values for attributes $A_i, A_j$ can be denoted as $t[A_i, A_j]$. A tuple can be interpreted as a fact for the assertion represented by a relation schema. Regarding the previously mentioned ER Model, such a fact can represent an entity or a relationship while the relation schema represents an entity type or a relationship type.

**Table 3.1:** *Informal interpretation of a relation as a table. The table's name and its headers correspond to the relation schema $R$, its contents to the relation (state) $r(R)$.*

**R**

| $\mathbf{A_1}$ | $\mathbf{A_2}$ | $\mathbf{A_3}$ |
|---|---|---|
| $v_1 = t[A_1] \in dom(A_1) \cup \{NULL\}$ | $v_2 = t[A_2] \in dom(A_2) \cup \{NULL\}$ | $v_3 = t[A_3] \in dom(A_3) \cup \{NULL\}$ |
| ... | ... | ... |

Constraints restrict the set of allowed tuples in a relation. They can be implicit (enforced by the metamodel), explicit (enforced by the schema), or semantic (enforced by application programs). Implicit constraints include domain constraints restricting $t[A_i]$ to $dom(A_i)$, constraints allowing or disallowing $t[A_i] = NULL$, key constraints, and entity as well as referential integrity constraints. The last three constraints use the concept of keys. $SK \subseteq \{A_1, \ldots, A_n\}$ is called a superkey of $R$ if $t_1[SK] \neq t_2[SK]$ for any two distinct tuples $t_1, t_2 \in r(R)$. As a relation is a set of tuples, all its tuples must be distinct. Thus $\{A_1, \ldots, A_n\}$ is always a superkey of $R$. A key $K$ is defined as a minimal superkey, i.e., removing any attribute from $K$ will also remove its superkey property. This removes redundancy. Because of the uniqueness, a key (as well as a superkey) can be used to identify tuples in a relation. This property, derived from the semantics of a relation schema, is enforced by a key constraint. For relation schemata with multiple so-called candidate keys, a primary key $PK$ is chosen. Entity integrity constraints forbid $t[PK] = NULL$ so all tuples can be identified. Another concept are referential integrity constraints where foreign keys are used to refer from one tuple in relation $R_1$ to another in $R_2$. For that purpose, it must apply to all $t_1 \in r_1(R_1)$ that either $t_1[FK] = t_2[PK]$ for some $t_2 \in r_2(R_2)$ or $t_1[FK] = NULL$. Furthermore, the attributes of a foreign key $FK$ of $R_1$ must have the same domains as the attributes of the $PK$ of $R_2$.

A relational database schema $S$ is now defined as a set of relation schemata $R_i$ and a set of integrity constraints $IC$. A relational database state $DB$ is defined as a set of relations $r_i(R_i)$. $DB$ is valid when all constraints in $IC$ are satisfied.

The relational algebra is a basic set of operations for the relational metamodel. Applying them on relations yields new relations and can be used for retrieval. As relations are sets of tuples, standard set operations including UNION, INTERSECTION, SET DIFFERENCE, and CARTESIAN PRODUCT can be applied. Furthermore, specific operations of the relational algebra include SELECT, PROJECT, and JOIN (Figure 3.5). The unary SELECT (unlike SQL's SELECT) filters a relation's tuples according to some selection condition on its attribute values. PROJECT, which is also unary, performs a selection on a relation's attributes. The binary JOIN operation combines a CARTESIAN PRODUCT with a SELECT. Thus, it yields all combinations of tuples where value pairs from both participating relations fulfill some condition. A NATURAL JOIN on $r_1(R_1)$ and $r_2(R_2)$ is a special JOIN where all attributes named equally in $R_1$ and $R_2$ are implicitly accounted for with an "equal" condition in the SELECT part. In practice, query languages have additional operations like aggregation (summation) of values, which are beyond standard relational algebra. Relational algebra is used in the implementations of many RDBMS.

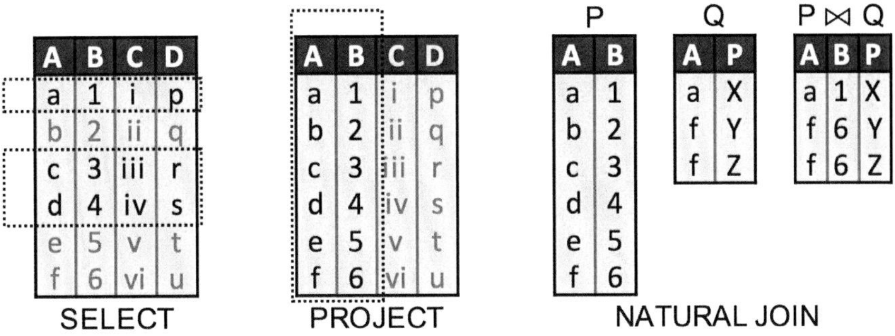


**Figure 3.5:** *Examples for the specific operations of relational algebra (adapted from [42]).*

In contrast to the algebra, the relational calculus is a declarative query language. Here, operations have no order; only the demanded information is specified, not the way how to retrieve it. It is based on predicate calculus[1] and has two variations: "In tuple relational calculus, variables range over tuples, whereas in domain relational calculus, variables range over the domains (values)" [4]. The expressive power of relational algebra and calculus are identical. A relational query language is said to be relational complete when all possible queries can also be represented in relational calculus. Thus, this definition can be used to evaluate languages. A simple query in relational tuple calculus is of the form $\{t|COND(t)\}$, where $t$ is a tuple variable and $COND(t)$ specifies a condition that must be satisfied by all tuples in the resulting relation. A condition or formula of the tuple relational calculus is composed of predicate calculus atoms. These include a specification $R(t)$ of the range relation $R$ of $t$, attribute value comparisons like $t[A] < t[B]$, logical operators, and quantifiers.

Relational calculus is not only important for its basis in mathematical logic. Furthermore, SQL is partially based on relational tuple calculus. Like the calculus, it is declarative so the RDBMS can decide on query execution order and its optimization. It has statements for

[1]While propositional logic represents knowledge using explicitly expressed facts in terms of propositions and conclusions, predicate calculus (or first-order logic) extends this concept by quantifiers, functions and predicates [91].

data definition, queries, updates, view definition, security and authorization specifications, integrity constraint definitions, and transaction control. It is divided into a core specification with an extension mechanism for special purpose components, e.g., spatial data management. SQL uses the notions of table, column and row, which correspond to relation, attribute and tuple. However, SQL tables are not always relations as query results may contain duplicates. For integration into programming languages, SQL uses so-called cursors to iterate over query results.

An important concept of relational database design is normalization. Here, formal concepts to group attributes into relation schemata are defined to assess design quality. Normalization primarily refers to stored relations and not views. The rationale for normalization includes the reduction of redundancies to optimize storage space and to reduce the risk of consistency loss during updates. Normalization is usually performed top-down from intuitively build relation schemata where attributes are grouped according to real-world entities and relationships. It leads to a vertical decomposition of relations into new part relations. A drawback is that computationally expensive JOIN operations are needed to restore the original relations in views or when querying data.

Normalization is based on so-called functional dependencies. A functional dependency $FD$ is notated as $FD = X \rightarrow Y$. $X$ and $Y$ are subsets of relation schema $R$. $FD = X \rightarrow Y$ means if $t_1[X] = t_2[X]$ then $t_1[Y] = t_2[Y]$ for every tuple $t_1$ and $t_2$ in $r(R)$. Thus, (the values for) $Y$ are functionally dependent on (the values for) $X$. Functional dependencies derive from the semantics of a relation, i.e., which legal value combinations can be found in its tuples. An $FD$ can also be seen as a constraint on a relation. Note that every subset $Y$ of $R$'s attributes is functionally dependent on $R$'s primary key $PK$ (as well as on any other key candidate or superkey of $R$).

Higher normal forms always include the requirements from lower normal forms. Corresponding examples are shown in Tables 3.2–3.5.

- The first normal form 1NF for relation schema $R$ states that $dom(A_i)$ is atomic for each $A_i \in R$ and that multi-valued attributes are prohibited. This property is basically already part of the definition of the flat relational metamodel. If 1NF does not apply the composite information in violating attributes cannot be queried with standard relational operations.

- 2NF states that *nonprime* attributes shall only be functionally dependent on the full primary key $PK$. A nonprime attribute is an attribute not part of $PK$. 2NF needs only be tested for a multi-attribute $PK$. 2NF reduces redundancy. In a violating relation where $PK' \rightarrow Y$ for $PK' \subset PK$ and a set of nonprime attributes $Y$, all tuples with the same value for $PK'$ would have the same value for $Y$.

- A relation schema is in 3NF when no nonprime attribute is functionally dependent on other nonprime attributes. Otherwise, values for a nonprime attribute are functionally determined by another nonprime attribute (or set of nonprime attributes) leading to redundancy.

**Table 3.2:** *Exemplary relation (buildings, tenanting companies and company owners) not in 1NF due to complex attribute "Companies".*

| Building | BuildName | Companies |
|---|---|---|
| 1 | Corner House | 4711: DB Makers (J. John, born 1961)<br>4712: L. C. Coding (L. Code, born 1980) |
| 2 | Main House | 4713: The Corp. (J. John, born 1961) |

**Table 3.3:** *Relation from Table 3.2 normalized to 1NF but not in 2NF: "BuildName" is only functionally dependent on "Building" and "CoName", "CoOwner" and "OBirth" only on "Company".*

| Building | BuildName | Company | CoName | CoOwner | OBirth |
|---|---|---|---|---|---|
| 1 | Corner House | 4711 | DB Makers | J. John | 1961 |
| 1 | Corner House | 4712 | L. C. Coding | L. Code | 1980 |
| 2 | Main House | 4713 | The Corp. | J. John | 1961 |

**Table 3.4:** *Relation from Table 3.3 normalized to 2NF but not 3NF: "OBirth" is functionally dependent on nonprime "CoOwner".*

| Building | BuildName |
|---|---|
| 1 | Corner House |
| 2 | Main House |

| Company | CoName | Building | CoOwner | OBirth |
|---|---|---|---|---|
| 4711 | DB Makers | 1 | J. John | 1961 |
| 4712 | L. C. Coding | 1 | L. Code | 1980 |
| 4713 | The Corp. | 2 | J. John | 1961 |

2NF and 3NF are usually generalized from $PK$ to any candidate key. Moreover, further normal forms exist, which, e.g., enforce desired properties when applying the JOIN operation on two relations.

### 3.1.3 Object-Oriented Databases

In contrast to the tuples in relational databases, OODBs (or ODBs (Object Databases) according to [4]) use an object-based metamodel to represent and store data. They are motivated by standard RDBMSs' unsuitability for certain types of novel, more complex database applications. For example in CAD, typically a huge number of types each with only a few instances is used whereas in traditional business database applications like banking there are few types each with a huge number of instances. Moreover, CAD data consists

**Table 3.5:** *Relations from Table 3.4 normalized to 3NF.*

| Building | BuildName |
|---|---|
| 1 | Corner House |
| 2 | Main House |

| Company | CoName | Building | Owner |
|---|---|---|---|
| 4711 | DB Makers | 1 | 1 |
| 4712 | L. C. Coding | 1 | 2 |
| 4713 | The Corp. | 2 | 1 |

| Owner | Name | Birth |
|---|---|---|
| 1 | J. John | 1961 |
| 2 | L. Code | 1980 |

of a huge number of hierarchically structured parts with interdependencies. Other database applications like GIS (Geo Information System) or multimedia applications need novel data types for spatial data, raster data and images, audio and video data, or large amounts of text. Moreover, application-specific operations are required, e.g., intersections on spatial data for GIS. OODBs cover most of these features, especially by combining complex object structure with inbuilt operations. Another advantage is their seamless integration in the prevalent object-oriented programming languages as both use the same modeling paradigm.

Another disadvantage of standard RDBMSs for these novel DB (Database) applications is their limited representation of real-world objects. Due to normalization, they are typically spread over several relations. Thus, rather expensive JOIN operations are needed for their reconstruction. Furthermore, there is only limited support for operations on data. The integration into procedural or object-oriented programming languages suffers from a so-called impedance mismatch: For example, relational databases do not reflect object identity or inheritance of classes. Finally, hierarchically structured data is usually accessed in a navigational manner, e.g., following a reference from a composite object to its part objects. Relational databases and SQL however use more of an associative approach for retrieval.

There are also disadvantages of object-oriented databases. In contrast to relational databases, they lack a mathematical foundation and a common standard query language. There is no universal metamodel and the standardization has been discontinued. In contrast to the well-established field of relational databases, fewer people have experience with this technology. Furthermore, competition pressure from relational and object-relational (see Subsection 3.1.4) is high. Thus, OODBMSs tend to be a niche product.

In the context of object-oriented databases, different definitions exist. One rather general is given in [42] and will be used in the following: An OODM (Object-Oriented Data Model) is defined as "a (logical) data model that captures the semantics of objects supported in object-oriented programming." Note that in this source the term "data model" is used for what is called a metamodel in this work. An OODB is then defined as "a persistent and sharable collection of objects defined by an object-oriented data model." Finally, an OO-DBMS is defined as "the manager of an OODB." This definition emphasizes the lack of a universal metamodel for OODBs. Altogether, most concepts for OODBs come from traditional database systems and from object-oriented programming. This is also reflected in the Object-Oriented Database System Manifesto of 1989 [92]. It postulates eight object-oriented characteristics:

1. complex objects; constructed using lists, sets or tuples,
2. object identity; an important concept of object-orientation where each object has a unique identity independent of its attribute values,
3. encapsulation,
4. types or classes,
5. inheritance,
6. dynamic binding,
7. a computationally complete DML and
8. an extensible set of data types.

Besides, basic DBMS characteristics are also postulated:

1. data persistence,
2. handling of very large DBs,
3. user concurrency,
4. recovery (see Subsection 3.4.1) and
5. an ad-hoc query facility.

In traditional database applications, usually, much effort has to be taken by the database application programmer for data conversion from the storage metamodel of the database (usually relational) to the runtime metamodel in the application (usually object-oriented). Using OODBs, the same (or virtually the same) metamodel is used for both. However, appropriate techniques are needed for mapping object representations on disk and in memory. For example, for object references, OIDs (Object Identifiers) are used. A technique called "pointer swizzling" is applied to resolve such references into runtime memory pointers and vice versa. Loading data from storage is also straightforward as the memory pages containing the objects are usually directly paged into main memory where they can be accessed (after some adaptions like swizzling). Another aspect in OODBMS is the handling of transient and persistent objects. In the approach of orthogonal persistence [42], three basic principles shall be fulfilled. Persistence independence demands persistence to be transparent[2] to normal program code. Following data type orthogonality, persistence should be applicable to all data types. Finally, transitive persistence uses a reachability-based approach to determine whether an object is persistent. Objects become persistent by setting a reference from another persistent object, forming a so-called reachability tree. While orthogonal persistence facilitates the use of OODB functionality for application programmers, there are also drawbacks like how queries or transaction semantics apply to transient objects. For example,

[2]Note that in the context of this work the term *transparency* is always used in its information hiding meaning.

should transient objects be included in queries and if so should they be included from every concurrent user of the system?

In the context of OODBs, normalization is also an issue. 2NF and 3NF can be reinterpreted: "Every attribute in an object is dependent on the object identity" [42]. Relationships are usually modeled using reference attributes to refer from one object to another based on its OID. For bidirectionality, back references are added to target objects. Multiplicity is realized using a list of reference attributes (or a set for uniqueness or a tuple for order). In between relationships, referential integrity must be maintained. That is, when a target object is deleted, the value of the source object's reference attribute must be reset.

An alternative to OODBs is the ORM (Object-Relational Mapping) approach. Here, the object-oriented data of a programming language is mapped from and to a relational database. However, due to the object-relational impedance mismatch mentioned above, this mapping has some problems. As stated in [93], this includes standard RDBMS lack of support for inheritance and object identity, or the different approaches to data access (navigational vs. associative) also mentioned above. To overcome these issues, the object-oriented data needs to somehow be encoded within the relational structures. Inheritance hierarchies can be mapped to tables. However, this mapping is ambiguous. Objects can either all be stored in one table for the complete hierarchy, in a table per class (each including all inherited attributes), or distributed over tables for each superclass requiring JOINs to restore original objects. Object identity can be realized by adding an OID column. Due to this encoding, tables themselves tend to lose their inherent semantics and the mapping needs to be integrated in each database application. However, these time-consuming and error-prone mapping tasks can mostly be automated using an ORM (Object-Relational Mapping) middleware like Hibernate [28].

A standardization for object data was introduced by the ODMG [94]. The specifications not only cover OODBMSs, but also systems like ORM tools that map object data to relational or other databases. Thus, the collective notion of an ODMS (Object Data Management System) is introduced that provides transparent persistence and standard database capabilities. However, after publishing their 3.0 standard in 1999, the ODMG disbanded. The standard's major components are an OM (Object Model), an ODL (Object Definition Language) as a DDL for OODBMSs, and an OQL (Object Query Language).

The Object Model is a superset of the OMG (Object Management Group) OM. It describes objects and literals. An object has a unique identity. Its structure can be atomic (a single object) or a collection of other objects. Besides a unique ID (Identifier), an object can be named making it a root of a reachability tree. Literals do not have identity. That is, they can only be distinguished by their value. A literal's type can also be atomic, a collection or structured (e.g., an interval). Atomic objects are abstracted by classes. A class defines behavior using operations and state using properties (attribute or relationship). The OM supports binary relationships. Two types of inheritance are supported. Behavior inheritance is used with so-called interfaces that only specify operation signatures and cannot be instantiated. Proper classes can also have a state, are instantiable and support an "extend" inheritance. Multiple inheritance is only supported for behavior inheritance. Types can have a so-called "extent," which contains all its instances and can be indexed. Independent of their type, objects can be transient or persistent. The OM furthermore defines metadata, e.g., for metaobjects like classes, interfaces, attributes and so forth. Transactions using standard read/write locks are also supported (see Subsection 3.4.1).

The OQL is similar to SQL. However, update operations are replaced by operations provided by the objects. Objects can be retrieved in an associative (like in SQL) or a navigational fashion. OQL supports quantifiers with membership testing and SQL-like SELECT statements.

Due to the alignment of the OMs, the mapping of a conceptual UML model to an ODMG model is straightforward. A UML class is mapped to an ODMG class, including attributes and methods. Multi-valued attributes are mapped to collection types, an extent is defined and inheritance is realized using the extend concept. Binary UML associations are mapped to relationship properties, which also allow for the definition of inverses (i.e, counterpart ends of the same relationship). Multiplicity is realized using collection types. $N$-ary relationships are mapped to separate classes with binary relationships to all end types.

### 3.1.4 Object-Relational Databases

ORDBs (Object-Relational Databases) and their management systems (ORDBMSs (Object-Relational Database Management Systems)) were developed as an alternative to pure OO-DBMSs. They extend standard RDBMSs with object-oriented concepts to support the aforementioned novel database applications [42]. Besides the name's focus on objects, they also comprise other novel features like multimedia data types. They have the advantage to be based upon well-established and sophisticated RDBMSs, which they complement with missing OO (Object-Oriented or Object-Orientation) features. Then again, while weakening the theoretical relational background they also lack to provide object-orientation in a traditional sense.

Although there is no standard metamodel for ORDBs, the general ideas can be derived from the SQL:2008 [95] standard. A core concept is the UDT (User Defined Type) also known as ADT (Abstract Data Type). A UDT (more precisely, a structured UDT) comprises attribute definitions and routine declarations, similar to a class in the traditional OO sense. UDTs provide encapsulation using auto generated getter and setter (called observer and mutator) as well as constructor methods, all of which can be manually overwritten. Inheritance (single) between UDTs is supported including substitutability, i.e., usage of subtype instances where a supertype is expected. A UDT may be instantiable or abstract. Besides normal attributes, so-called virtual attributes are supported, which derive data upon access.

A UDT can be used as the data type of a table's column to support complex-valued, non-1NF relations. Moreover, it can be used to instantiate typed tables. Only in the latter case a table's rows are considered to be objects. Object identity is guaranteed by specifying an additional column whose OID values can be auto generated by the DBMS. Based on this column and using a so-called reference type in another table, rows (i.e., objects) can be referenced by rows of the other table. The reference type is bound to the target table as well as its UDT. This mechanism, similar to OODBMS, provides an alternative to conventional relationships based on primary and foreign keys. For referential integrity a separate constraint definition is still needed (in contrast to ODMG references).

Typed tables can themselves establish an inheritance hierarchy parallel to those of their UDTs. However, as a prerequisite, typed tables in an inheritance relationship must also have UDTs in direct or indirect inheritance relationship. When inserting a row in a subtable, a copy is also inserted into all supertables. Each copy is reduced to those columns inherited from that supertable. This makes subtable objects also supertable objects. When updating an object, all copies in supertables or subtables are automatically updated, too. Apart from that, multiple independent table hierarchies can be instantiated from the same UDT hierarchy.

In [42], the authors argue that SQL:2008 compliant ORDBMSs support nearly all the same concepts as OODBMSs, including object-oriented concepts like object identity, encapsulation, or inheritance.

### 3.1.5 XML and Databases

Although the XML (Extensible Markup Language) itself was not originally developed as a metamodel for databases, it is a widespread format for data modeling and exchange. As such, it is also used in the database context. According to [4], the top element in XML is the document. Primarily, a document is built of elements and attributes. Other than in the database context, an XML attribute provides additional information to an XML element. In the well-known XML notation, elements are represented with tags in angle brackets (Listing 3.1). Simple elements directly contain a simple data value, e.g., a number or a string. Complex elements contain other elements. Altogether, XML data builds a tree-like hierarchical structure with complex elements as inner nodes and simple elements as leaf nodes. There are three types of XML documents. Data-centric documents are used to model and exchange amounts of data items. They are either structured, i.e., adhering to some predefined schema defining allowed tags, or semistructured, i.e., the data has a nonuniform structure and tags are used in an ad-hoc manner. Document-centric documents contain huge amounts of text and only very few or no structure. Finally, hybrid documents mix both the other formats. In context of this work, data-centric documents are of particular interest.

**Listing 3.1:** *Simple XML example.*

```
<Robot id="i4711">
  <name>KUKA LBR</name>
  <color>
    <red>255</red>
    <green>140</green>
    <blue>0</blue>
  </color>
</Robot>
```

To generically process XML documents, two common methods exist. Using DOM (Document Object Model), an XML document is completely parsed into a tree structure in memory where it can be accessed and manipulated using a standard API (Application Programming Interface). While this approach is convenient, it may not be applicable for large documents that do not fit into main memory. Another method avoiding this problem is SAX (Simple API for XML). It uses an event-based streaming approach where the calling program is notified of each start or end tag.

Documents fulfilling the syntactical requirements of the XML standard are called well-formed. Given a schema description, an XML document is called valid if it is well-formed and its contents comply with the schema. Common methods for describing an XML schema are DTDs (Document Type Definitions) and XSDs (XML Schema Definitions) (also see [96]). For various reasons, including their non-XML syntax, DTDs have been superseded by the more powerful yet more complex XSDs. The XML Schema Definition Language for describing an XSD is based on XML itself providing the advantage of tool reuse and rich modeling features. An XSD can define root elements for documents, complex types with complex or simple content models, simple types, child elements and attributes of complex types (including their type and multiplicity), inheritance of types (by extension or restriction), substitutability between elements, and abstractness of elements and types. Similar to relational databases, constraints can be declared. When defining an element, the values of a (simple type) child element or attribute can be declared unique. Alternatively, they can be declared a key (like a primary key in RDBs (Relational Databases)). The latter can be used in the declaration of a so-called keyref, which is similar to a foreign key in RDBs, to maintain referential integrity.

Different approaches exist to store and extract XML documents in and from databases. First of all, a document can be stored in a text field of a (relational or object-oriented) database. This is especially applicable for semistructured or unstructured documents and DBMSs with document processing capabilities. Regarding structured documents, however, the XML schema can be used to derive a relational or object-oriented database schema. An additional module is required to translate XML documents to database structures and vice versa. However, this approach also suffers from an impedance mismatch, as will be shown in Section 6.6. A third alternative are Native XML DBMS, whose database metamodel itself is based on XML. Finally, preexisting data from widespread relational databases can be extracted as XML documents for data exchange.

There are two main query languages in the XML context. XPath (XML Path Language) allows to specify expressions that select elements or attributes in an XML document. An expression consists of a path description based on the tree-like XML structure. Using pattern matching, a collection of satisfying elements, attributes or leaf values are returned. The second language is the more general XQuery, which in turn uses XPath, but adds more powerful constructs. A basic "FLWR" expression consists of a FOR clause iteratively assigning variables to elements from a collection expression, a LET clause assigning variables to expressions, a WHERE clause giving additional conditions, and a RETURN clause for specifying result expressions based on the selected items. Each combination of FOR variable bindings and the LET variable bindings is tested against the WHERE clause. Each (remaining) combination of bindings is then used to retrieve a part of the result.

### 3.1.6 Other Database Approaches

Finally, to complete this list, legacy and emerging database metamodels and concepts shall be presented here. According to [4], two noteworthy historically important metamodels are the network and the hierarchical metamodel. In the network metamodel, record types and set types are used to model networks of data. Set types model $1 : n$ relationships. Record instances are connected by instances of these relationships using a pointer-like mechanism. The network model supports a query language to navigate through the network one record at a time. It must be embedded into programming languages and was developed as an extension to COBOL (Common Business-Oriented Language). The hierarchical metamodel uses hierarchical tree structures where each hierarchy represents a set of related records. Several variations of the hierarchical metamodel exist.

There are several emerging concepts for database metamodels as presented in [97]. They are often subsumed under the term "NoSQL" databases to emphasize their renunciation of the prevalent relational model and its query language. Their field of application often lies in web applications and "big data." They can be roughly categorized into key-value stores, and columnar, document, and graph databases. As their name implies, similar to hashtables in programming languages, key-value stores store key-value pairs. They are especially advantageous for unrelated data like storing session data in web applications. Columnar (or column-oriented) databases are similar to relational databases. However, they store like data by columns instead of rows. Rows are flexibly build on arbitrary sets of columns on a row-by-row basis. Adding new columns is very easy (horizontal scalability) simplifying distribution to cluster nodes for "big data" scenarios. In document databases, objects are stored as so-called "documents." A document is identified by a key and contains an arbitrary number of fields including nested documents. Thus, such databases handle semistructured object data very well. Finally, graph databases store data with a focus on the interrelation of nodes. Values can be stored as key-value pairs at nodes or at the edges in between. For example, graph databases are used in social networking applications.

## 3.2 Model-Driven Engineering

A field of work substantially using (meta)models and providing different standards and techniques is MDE (Model-Driven Engineering). The following overview is mainly based upon [98]. The basic idea of this methodology is derived from the human's tendency towards abstraction, i.e., to generalize, classify, and aggregate. In science, this kind of abstraction is called modeling. As the human mind always works with abstraction it can be said that "everything is a model" [98]. To make this modeling explicit and to formalize it is one of the main goals of MDE.

There are different notions in this area. MBE (Model-Based Engineering) is the most general term including all activities that in the broadest sense use models for engineering tasks. In MDE, engineering processes are actually driven by modeling tasks. It comes in different forms like MDSE (Model-Driven Software Engineering) or MDPE (Model-Driven Product Engineering). MDD (Model-Driven Development) is a subtask of MDSE engaged in development tasks (MDSE in general also comprises system evolution or reverse engineering of legacy systems). Finally, the MDA (Model-Driven Architecture) is an implementation of MDD by the OMG using their standards.

### 3.2.1 Models, Modeling Languages and Metamodels

Reasons for using models in software engineering are increasing system complexity and pervasive usage, few IT (Information Technology) experts, and the need for exchange with non-IT professionals (e.g., managers). Models can be used as pure sketches for communication, for detailed system specification, or even for direct execution. The basic concept in MDSE is to model a system and to subsequently transform it into other models or code. The corresponding transformations themselves are also represented using models. Models are specified using modeling languages, which are called transformation languages in case of transformation models.

Modeling languages can be distinguished by their field of application. While a DSL (Domain-Specific Language) is tailored to a specific domain of applications, a GPL (General-Purpose Language) can be used in different domains. Well-known DSLs are HTML (HyperText Markup Language) or SQL, and well-known GPLs are UML or XML. Modeling languages themselves are also defined by a model – the metamodel, specifying its abstract syntax. The corresponding metamodeling language in turn is defined by a meta-metamodel.

Meta-metamodeling languages for defining the meta-metamodel, in turn, are usually reflexively defined by themselves to end the metaization. The levels of this metamodeling hierarchy (Figure 3.6) are usually called M0 for the real world system that is modeled by a model on level M1. The model's metamodel resides on level M2. Finally, the corresponding meta-metamodel is defined on level M3. Thus, the M2 level provides the modeling concepts for the M1 level and the M3 level provides the (meta)modeling concepts for the M2 level. An example is the MDA metamodel hierarchy with real world objects on level M0, their UML model on level M1, the UML language specification on level M2 and the meta-metamodel of OMG's MOF (Meta-Object Facility [99]) on level M3.

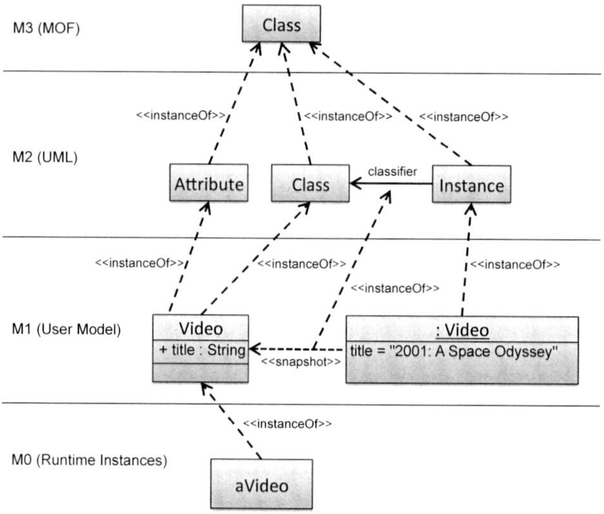


**Figure 3.6:** *An example of OMG's four-layer metamodel hierarchy (adopted from [8]).*

A modeling language is not only specified by its abstract syntax (i.e., its metamodel), but also by its concrete syntax and its semantics. The abstract syntax defines the logical structure and combination of language primitives. The used metamodeling languages usually provide a minimal object-oriented set of modeling concepts to represent metamodels in terms of metaclasses, metaattributes, and metaassociations. A concrete syntax defines a mapping of these primitives to a graphical or textual representation. However, instead of using a language's concrete syntax, a model can also be represented in terms of an object diagram corresponding to the metamodel (Figure 3.7). The language's semantics define the meaning of primitives and combinations thereof. Semantics can be defined in different ways: Denotational semantics are defined by a model-to-model transformation to an existing formal language with known semantics, operational semantics are defined by using a model simulator, and translational semantics by a model-to-text translation to produce executable code.

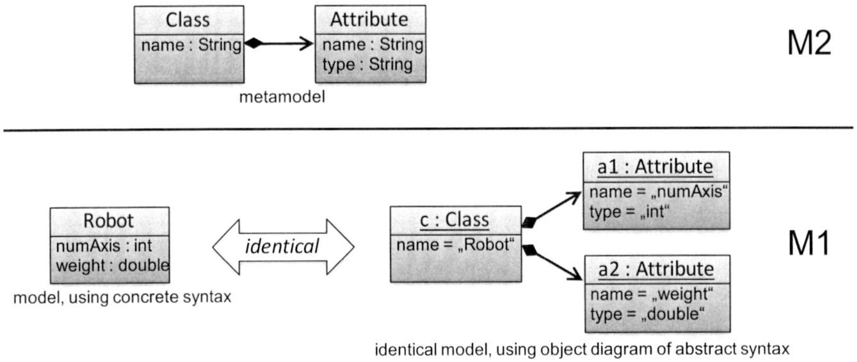


**Figure 3.7:** *An example of a simple object-oriented metamodel and a corresponding model, once represented with its (likewise object-oriented) concrete syntax and once as an object diagram.*

Instead of creating one's own modeling language, an existing language can be used as a basis for modifications. UML, for example, provides different concepts like stereotypes to vary semantics of existing metaclasses, tagged values to provide stereotypes with attributes, or predicates to restrict the variation of an elements semantics. A UML profile can be used to integrate such modifications. Well-known examples of standardized UML profiles are SysML (Systems Modeling Language [7]) or MARTE (Modeling and Analysis of Real Time and Embedded systems [100]).

Modeling languages can be complemented by an additional language to express constraints on models. For example, typically only simple constraints like cardinalities of associations are directly supported. More sophisticated interrelations like the uniqueness of names cannot be expressed. A well-known example for an additional language is the declarative OCL (Object Constraint Language [101]). It allows to define invariants, i.e., constraints that shall be fulfilled at any time.

### 3.2.2 Model Transformations

Besides models, transformations of models are the second important aspect of MDE (Figure 3.8). A transformation converts a model into another model (model-to-model, M2M). Apart from that, model-to-text (M2T) transformations exist. First of all, a transformation itself is also specified as a model adhering to the transformation language's metamodel (MT Language), which, in turn, conforms to the common meta-metamodel. A concrete transformation (MT Definition) is specified once between metamodels (MMa, MMb) on level M2. It represents a mapping defining correspondences between metamodel elements. Its execution, however, is performed on models (Ma, Mb) on level M1. Here, it creates a mapping between the elements of models that correspond to the metamodels. These correspondences are also called the traces of the transformation. Thus, besides the target model, a transformation execution can also yield relationships between source and target elements within a so-called trace model.

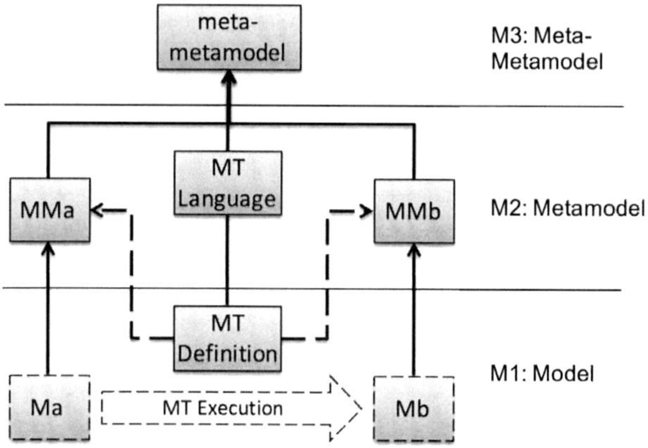


**Figure 3.8:** *Relation between models (*Ma, Mb*), transformation model (MT) definition and execution, and corresponding metamodels (*MT Language, MMA, MMb*), from [98] and [102].*

In the MDE context, M2M transformations are used to merge, align, refactor, refine, or translate models. In general, one or more models are transformed into one or more other models. One can distinguish between exogenous and endogenous transformations. An exogenous transformation is defined between different metamodels and can be vertical (e.g., from UML to Java) or horizontal (e.g., from UML to ER) regarding the degree of conceptualization. In contrast, an endogenous transformation is defined within the same metamodel. Furthermore, transformations can be out-place or in-place. An out-place transformation creates one or more completely new target models from the source model(s). This approach is usually used in the context of exogenous transformations. In contrast, in-place transformations rewrite an existing model, which is typically used for endogenous transformations. Endogenous, in-place transformations are, for example, used for refactoring models. Typically, they are realized using graph transformation approaches.

Exogenous, out-place transformations are, for example, used to translate a model represented in terms of one metamodel into another metamodel and are of interest in the context of this work. Two transformation languages are particularly prominent: ATL

(ATL Transformation Language [103, 104]) and QVT (MOF Query/View/Transformation [105, 98, 106, 107]).

According to [98], ATL (ATL Transformation Language [103, 104]) is a widespread transformation language used in academia and industry. Accordingly, an important practical aspect is its tool support. ATL is a rule-oriented language based on OCL, adding new language constructs for model transformation. It is declarative (like OCL) but also part imperative. ATL transformations transform one or more source models into one or more target models. ATL rules are unidirectional, i.e., back transformations have to be modeled separately. A transformation, also called a module, consists of a header with information on source and target metamodels and a body. The body contains rules and helpers. A rule can be automatically matched and executed, or can be "lazy" and called on demand from another rule. An example is given in Listing 3.2. Using this rule, any instance of "Member" from the source model "Families" that is female is transformed into an instance of "Female" in the target model "Persons." The rule is a "matched" rule, i.e., automatically applied by the ATL engine to any matching instance. In contrast, a "lazy" rule would have to be explicitly called on source model elements.

**Listing 3.2:** *Example of a (matched) ATL rule taken from [104]*

```
rule Member2Female {
    from
        s: Families!Member (s.isFemale())
    to
        t: Persons!Female (
            fullName <- s.firstName + ' ' + s.familyName
        )
}
```

In general, source models are treated as read-only and target models as write-only. ATL's engine is a virtual machine that executes the transformations. Transformation execution is divided into three phases. In module initialization (phase 1), among other things, a trace model for the links between source and target elements is initialized. It is used to determine the end of the transformation process (all source elements have a trace link) and for the later phases. In target element allocation (phase 2), source patterns and constraints of the rules are matched against source elements. For matched rules, the corresponding elements in the target model are allocated and a trace link is created. Finally, in target element initialization (phase 3), values are bound to target elements corresponding to the respective rules. Initialization is a separate phase so target elements created by other rules can be retrieved from their corresponding source elements using the previously build trace model.

QVT (MOF Query/View/Transformation [105, 98, 106, 107]) is an OMG transformation standard. The name derives from its functionality to query elements in source models, define a view for the appearance of the elements in the target model, and of course transformations. It comprises three different languages: The Relations, the Operational Mappings and the Core Language. QVT Relations is a declarative language. In contrast to ATL, it provides bidirectional transformations so models can be transformed in one way or the other with the same transformation. Furthermore, bidirectionality allows for model consistency checks and synchronization. QVT Operational is an imperative language for unidirectional transformations. It can be used in complex scenarios where declarative rules (i.e., QVT Relations) are to complicated. However, the advantage of bidirectionality gets lost. Finally, QVT Core is a low-level declarative language only intended as a compiler target for the other languages. Besides the three languages, the QVT BlackBox component allows for the integration of arbitrary other transformation languages.

Due to its widespread usage and tool support, the ATL transformation language has been chosen for the reference implementations of the presented approach. See Chapter 6 for more details.

### 3.2.3 Model-Driven Interoperability

The most common use case of MDSE is software development, i.e., MDD. Here, models are used throughout the development process from abstract, high level to increasingly detailed representations. The MDA process defines three levels of abstraction. A CIM (Computation-Independent Model) is used to specify the business view of the solution, independent of their implementation. The CIM is transformed into one or more PIMs (Platform-Independent Models) that include implementations, but in a generalized form without referring to concrete products or frameworks. Finally, the PIM is transformed into one or more detailed PSM (Platform-Specific Model) containing all necessary details for the system's realization. Subsequently, the PSM can either be transformed into code or may even be executed itself by a model interpreter. Another use case is reverse engineering, the "process of obtaining useful higher-level representations of legacy systems" [98]. Reverse engineering is used in the context of evolution or modernization of legacy systems.

A third use case is system interoperability. According to [98], this is defined by the IEEE (Institute of Electrical and Electronics Engineers) as "the ability of two or more systems or components to exchange information and to use the information that has been exchanged." One can distinguish between data- and operational-level interoperability. The first covers data and metadata of the systems, the latter their behavior. Previously, low-level approaches were used to realize interoperability manually using APIs, which is error-prone and tedious. In MDI (Model-Driven Interoperability), however, interoperability is realized on a higher level of abstraction using MDE techniques. Figure 3.9 gives an overview of a so-called generic interoperability bridge's basic structure. System *a* and *b* are represented by their formats to which two corresponding input files conform. To set up the MDI process, metamodels *MMa* and *MMb* representing the internal schema of each format have to be derived. A syntactic mapping is established between each system and the MDI world by defining injectors and extractors that transform input files *a* and *b* into models *Ma* and *Mb* conforming to the aforementioned metamodels and vice versa. These transformations can be realized in terms of text-to-model (injector) and model-to-text (extractor) transformations. Afterwards, a semantic mapping between the systems can be established within the MDI world by model-to-model transformations in between the models.

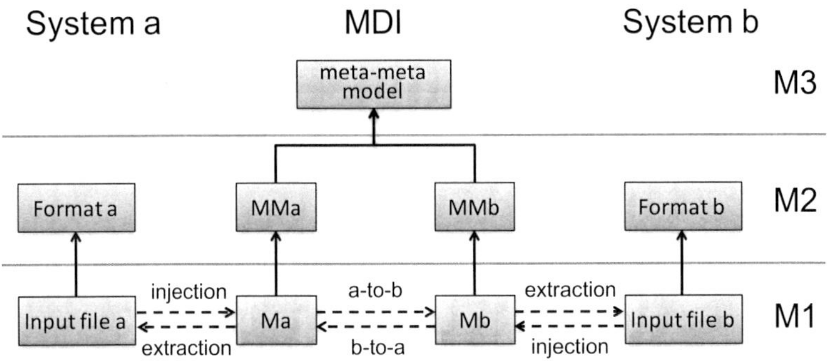


**Figure 3.9:** *Generic structure of a Model-Driven Interoperability bridge for System* a *and* b, *adopted from [98].*

### 3.2.4 Managing Models

For model interchange between different tools and other purposes, a serialization format is needed [98]. OMG provides a standard called XMI (XML Metadata Interchange [108]) (Figure 3.10). It can be used to (de)serialize models to (and from) XML. It allows to translate a MOF-compliant metamodel *A* into a corresponding XMI Schema in terms of an XML Schema Definition or Document Type Definition. A model *a* corresponding to this metamodel *A* can then be serialized into a corresponding XMI document that conforms to the XMI schema. The MOF 2 XMI Mapping specification contains rules for both levels. However, practical problems remain as the standard is not strictly followed by tool vendors. Furthermore, XMI does not include a model's graphical representation. An excerpt from an XMI file for the example used in Chapter 6 is shown in Figure 3.11 (a simple building model, here represented in terms of the VSD (Versatile Simulation Database) metamodel).

Other aspects of model management in the context of MDE are model persistence, model comparison, model versioning, model co-evolution, and global model management. In model persistence, database technology is used to manage very large models that are not feasible to handle in files anymore. Model comparison creates a difference model to compare models.

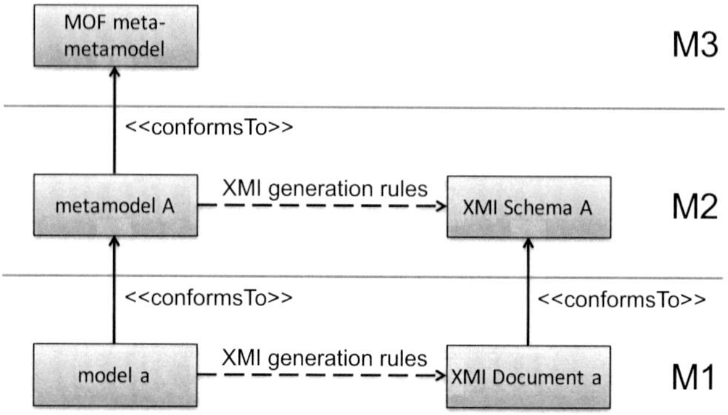


**Figure 3.10:** *Correspondence of models and XMI.*

```
<?xml version="1.0" encoding="ASCII"?>
<VSD:Database xmi:version="2.0" xmlns:xmi="http://www.omg.org/XMI"
              xmlns:VSD="platform:/resource/VSD2UML/SimpleVSD.ecore">
  <types xsi:type="VSD:MetaTypeValAtomicBasic" name="QString"/>
  <types xsi:type="VSD:MetaInstance" name="Building" isAbstract="true">
    <metaProperties name="name" metaType="//@types.0"/>
  </types>
  <types xsi:type="VSD:MetaInstance" name="House" baseClass="//@types.1">
    <metaProperties name="rooms" isAutoDel="true" metaType="//@types.3" kind="RefList"/>
  </types>
  <types xsi:type="VSD:MetaInstance" name="Room"/>
```

**Figure 3.11:** *Simplified excerpt from an XMI file for the example used in Chapter 6.*

Model versioning applies methods for version control known from software development to model management. Existing text-based systems like SVN (Apache Subversion) tend be unsuitable as they neglect the models graph-like structure so new methods are developed. Model co-evolution considers the interdependencies between models when one model changes. Finally, global model management is an approach for managing huge amounts of models within yet another model - a megamodel.

## 3.3 Unified Modeling Language

In this section, as mentioned above, a UML subset relevant to the presented approach is introduced. The UML language unit classes models the relevant metaclasses for object-oriented data. Without loss of generality, a simplified excerpt of this part of the UML (version 2.4.1) metamodel will be used throughout this work. It contains metaclasses needed for object-oriented data models with the relevant metaattibutes and the metaassociations between them. Figures 3.12–3.13 show the metamodel in two parts. The first contains those metaclasses to describe schemata, the second those to describe instances of schema components. The metamodel is described using the meta-modeling language and meta-

metamodel Ecore, which is similar to OMG's MOF meta-metamodel, from the EMF (Eclipse Modeling Framework [109]).

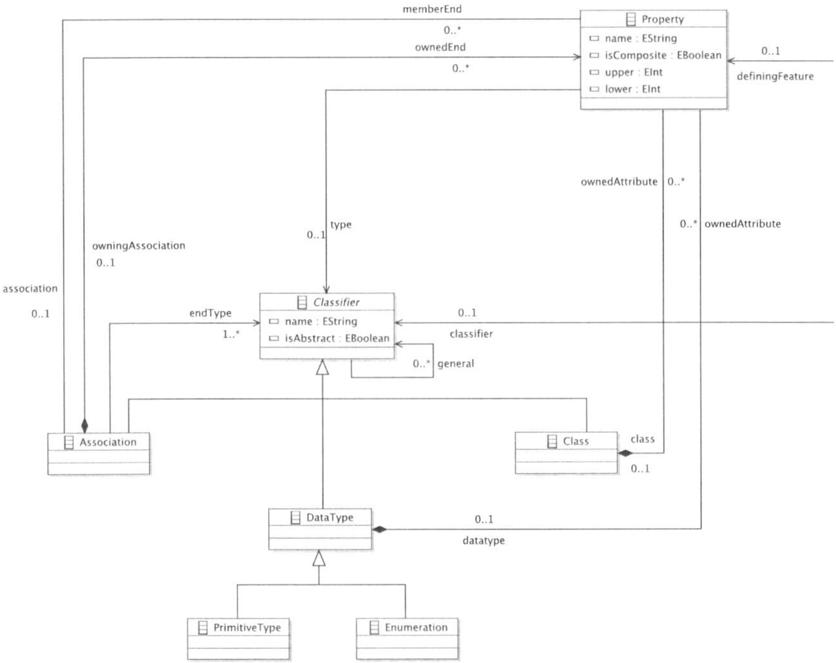


**Figure 3.12:** *A simplified metamodel of the UML language unit classes – Left part: metaclasses for schema description, continued in Figure 3.13.*

In Figure 3.12 the abstract metaclass `Classifier` is the base class for all kinds of data types. A `Classifier` may be abstract, has a name, and it can have zero or more generalizations. Thus, multiple inheritance is supported in UML. One specialization of `Classifier` is the UML `Class` for classifying objects. A `Class` can hold several `Properties` as attributes owned by the class using the metaassociation `ownedAttribute`. A UML `Property` holds a name, and upper and lower multiplicity bounds. Moreover, it has a `Classifier` as its type and its metaattribute `isComposite` represents ownership of referenced objects. Besides classes, simple `DataTypes` are also `Classifiers`. They can be further distinguished into `PrimitiveTypes` for simple data types (Bool, String, Real, Integer, and others) and `Enumerations`. In general, `DataTypes` can also hold `Properties` as owned attributes. Another kind of `Classifier` is the `Association` metaclass representing the concept of relationships between `Classes` (or `Classifiers`, in general). An `Association` has `Properties` as member ends to reference the objects it connects. However, the corresponding metaas-

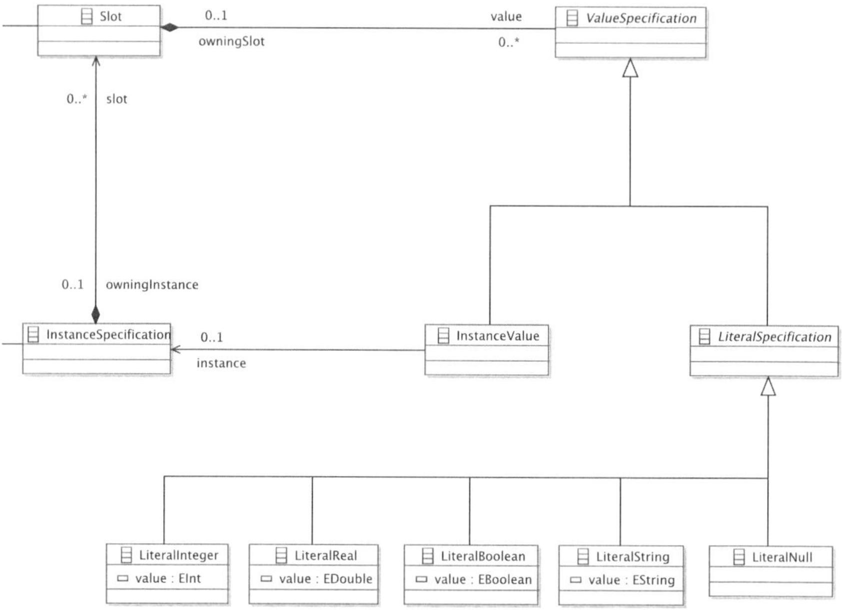


**Figure 3.13:** *A simplified metamodel of the UML language unit classes – Right part: metaclasses for instance data description, continuation of Figure 3.12.*

sociation `memberEnd` does not represent ownership of these properties. A common case is a binary association that has two properties as member ends, i.e., it connects two classes. Only in this case, an association's member end property can at the same time be an owned attribute of the corresponding class at the respective other end of the association. In all other cases, association ends must be owned members of their association using the metaassociation `ownedEnd`. Besides, the types of all member end `Properties` are collected with the metaassociation `endType`. For example, a binary association has either one end type (it connects a class with itself) or two end types (it connects two different classes).

In Figure 3.13, metaclasses to describe instances of UML schema components are modeled. An `InstanceSpecification` represents an instance of a `Classifier` using the metaassociation `classifier`. For a `Class`, such an instance is called an object, for an `Association` a link, and for a `DataType` a literal. An `InstanceSpecification` can own `Slots` representing its values. Each `Slot` has a defining feature, a corresponding `Property` of the instance's `Classifier` (using metaassociation `definingFeature`). A `Slot` aggregates one or more `ValueSpecifications` depending on the multiplicity of its defining feature. A -`ValueSpecification` can either be a `LiteralSpecification` for simple data types or an `InstanceValue` to reference another `InstanceSpecification`.

To simplify notation, in the context of this work the abbreviations listed in Table 3.6 are used.

**Table 3.6:** *Abbreviations for UML metaclasses.*

| abbreviation | UML metaclass |
|---|---|
| $CL$ | `Classifier` |
| $Cl$ | `Class` |
| $As$ | `Association` |
| $Pr$ | `Property` |
| $IS$ | `InstanceSpecification` |
| $Sl$ | `Slot` |
| $VS$ | `ValueSpecification` |

## 3.4 More Database Concepts

In this section, further basic database concepts are presented that are relevant in the context of this thesis.

### 3.4.1 Transactions, Recovery and Concurrency

Further important aspects of a DBMS include transactions, recovery, and concurrency control. According to [42], a transaction is "an action, or series of actions, carried out by a single user or application program, that reads or updates the content of the database." The ACID (atomicity, consistency, isolation and durability) properties are a set of desired transaction properties.

- Atomicity: Transactions shall be executed like a single operation, either completely or not at all.
- Consistency: A transaction should transform the database from one consistent state to another.
- Isolation: A transaction shall be executed without interference from or to other concurrent transactions.

- Durability: The effect of a committed transaction is permanent.

In general, a transaction can be begun, can execute read or write operations, can be ended, and then committed or aborted. All (write) operations are written to a system log. Different system failures or intervention by concurrency control can prevent a transaction from successful completion. A recovery component uses the log to undo operations of such non committed transactions, i.e., abort them. Likewise, operations that could only be written to the log but not to the database can be redone. A commit is only logged when all database operations as well as all (other) log entries were successful. Thus, the recovery component is responsible for atomicity and durability of transactions.

On multiuser DBSs, multiple transactions can be executed concurrently. Without control, different kinds of interference may occur. In this context, a database is represented as a collection of so-called data items of some granularity (e.g., a record or an attribute value).

- In the "Lost Update" problem, two transactions $T1$ and $T2$ read the same data item $X$. After $T1$ writes a new value for $X$, $T2$ does the same. Thus, $T1$'s update is lost for $T2$. This is particularly bad when $T2$'s update to $X$ is relative to its previous value (e.g., an increment).

- In the "Dirty Read" problem, an invalid, temporary value from an aborted but not yet recovered transaction is read by another transaction.

- In the "Incorrect Summary" problem, $T1$ adds up values while $T2$ changes one of them.

- Finally, in the "Unrepeatable Read" problem, the same value cannot be read twice by $T1$, as it is changed by $T2$ in between.

These examples justify the need for a concurrency control component. Its duty is to ensure transaction isolation.

As the central point of entry to a database, a DBMS controls the execution of all concurrent transactions. Here, a so-called schedule is used to order all associated operations. Regarding recoverability of uncommitted transactions, a schedule must fulfill increasing requirements to allow rollback at all (recoverable schedule), to avoid cascading rollback (cascadeless schedule), or to further simplify rollback (strict schedule). For concurrency control, a serial schedule executes all transactions consecutively. Here, no interference can occur but in practice it is too slow. A schedule equivalent to a serial schedule is termed serializable. Different definitions for equivalence exist, e.g., conflict equivalence. Here, the order of any two conflicting operations must be the same in both schedules. Operations are conflicting when they belong to two different transactions, access the same data item, and at least one of them is a write operation. However, in practice, serializability is hard or impossible to test, e.g., because the operating system decides on the effective execution order. Instead, concurrency control protocols are used to ensure that all resulting schedules are serializable.

In practice, most of these protocols use locking to restrict concurrent access. Here, each data item has a lock representing one or more operations' current access. When another operation cannot acquire the lock it has to wait in a queue until it is unlocked. Simple but impracticable is a binary lock, which can only be locked by one operation and unlocked by the same. Thus, it enforces mutual exclusion on its data item completely preventing concurrent access. More sophisticated is a read/write lock. A lock can be repeatedly acquired for reading, but only once for writing. This allows for a higher degree of concurrency and thus performance. Following the two-phase locking protocol (2PL), serializability can be proven. Here, each transaction is divided into two phases: The expanding phase only allows locking, the shrinking phase only allows unlocking. 2PL suffers from deadlocks where transactions mutually wait for the release of a lock. In practice, deadlocks are detected or timed out rather than using avoidance protocols. Detection is based on so-called wait-for graphs and cycle detection. For deadlock resolution, one or more transactions are forced to abort (victim selection) and restarted afterwards. As mentioned above, the recovery component takes care of the necessary rollback.

Besides locking, other concepts for concurrency control exist. In timestamp ordering techniques, conflicting operations must be executed in order of their transactions' running number. Otherwise, they are aborted, rolled back and restarted. As the approach does not use locking, deadlocks are avoided. On the downside, the produced schedules are not guaranteed to be recoverable. For that purpose, additional protocols must be incorporated. In multiversion concurrency control techniques, several versions of a data item can be maintained. Here, in some situations read operations may be presented an older version to keep up serializability. However, there are extra costs if data is not already versioned. In optimistic concurrency control techniques, serializability is checked only after all operations are executed but before commit. Write operations are cached to local copies of data items. While checking is reduced, the optimistic assumption is that only few transactions will interfere.

### 3.4.2 Distributed Databases

As presented in [4], a DDB (Distributed Database) can be defined as "a collection of multiple logically interrelated databases distributed over a computer network." A DDBMS (Distributed Database Management System) is defined as "a software system that manages a distributed database while making the distribution transparent to the user." As before, a DDBS (Distributed Database System) is the combination of both. Motivations for using a DDB are better performance (by load distribution, local data availability, and parallelized queries), availability and reliability, and scalability. However, drawbacks are the inherent complexity of distributed systems and a possible loss in write performance due to replication (see below). Examples in this context will be given for relational databases but can similarly apply to other systems.

Important concepts in DDBs are fragmentation, allocation and replication. Fragmentation means, data sets are split up in fragments to distribute them over several sites. Fragmentation can be horizontal, vertical, or mixed. In horizontal fragmentation, a relation's tuples are divided into tuple subsets according to some common property, typically an attribute's value. For example, a company's employees may be split up according to their office. In vertical fragmentation, a relation is divided into subrelations by splitting up its attribute set. The primary key has to be added to each subrelation to identify and reintegrate the original tuples (using a JOIN operation). In mixed fragmentation schemes, the two concepts are combined. Allocation is the mapping of these fragments to sites of the DDBs. Ideally, fragments should be assigned to those sites that use them most. In replication, the same fragment is assigned to multiple sites simultaneously. This improves performance as well as availability and reliability.

Another important aspect of DDBs or rather DDBMSs is transparency, autonomy and heterogeneity. Transparency includes hiding away details on network structure, storage location, fragmentation, and replication from the user. Autonomy describes the degree of independence of the individual sites taking part in the DDBMSs. It includes the site's ability to decide on a metamodel, a transaction management technique, on information sharing with other sites, query execution and so forth. Heterogeneity refers to the kinds of participating sites, i.e., whether they must all be identical or can differ in metamodels, query languages, constraints, schemata, and in particular semantics.

Based on the latter two characteristics, there are different categories of DDBS that can be compared to a standard DBS, which is not distributed, thus cannot be heterogeneous, and is fully autonomous. A pure DDBS is completely homogeneous and its sites themselves have no autonomy. In a Federated DBS, sites are heterogeneous and retain most of their autonomy. Multidatabase DBSs are nearly identical but retain full autonomy. The three approaches to DDBSs also differ in providing a common data schema for the distributed data. While this can be omitted for standard DBSs, a Distributed DBS needs to resolve this problem. In pure DDBSs, there is only one schema that exists at every site which is thus used as a global schema. In Federated DDBSs, each site has its own local schema, which is translated into a common data model of the federation and exported. Exported schemata can then be integrated into one or more federation schemata. In contrast, a Multidatabase provides a global schema only in an ad-hoc manner when the application requires it.

Some basic functionality of non-distributed DBMS has to be adapted for the distributed scenario. For example, queries have to be localized, i.e., split according to fragmentation and replication, and globally optimized. For transaction management a global transaction manager is needed (providing functions for transaction start, end, and so forth). To provide atomicity for global transactions, a global recovery manager can be used in combination with the so-called two-phase commit protocol (2PC). It splits the commit in two phases by issuing a command "prepare to commit" to all sites. Each site will force the writing of all log entries and confirm or decline the command. When the global manager received only confirmations (and no timeout), it sends the second command, the actual "commit" to all sites. Otherwise, it sends a rollback command. Furthermore, global recovery has to account for replication, individual site or communication failure, and distributed deadlocking. For distributed concurrency control, (distributed) locking needs to particularly account for replication. One approach is to choose a so-called distinguished copy that holds a representative lock for all its replicate copies. Different methods for the appointment of a distinguished copy exists.

As DDBSs are quite complex, a client-server architecture (Figure 3.14) is a common alternative using standard DBSs. In this three-tiered scenario, a client (providing the presentation layer) connects to an application server (providing the business logic), typically using HTTP (Hypertext Transfer Protocol). Only the application server accesses the database layer. It can integrate several databases to provide a form of distribution. However, it has to manage tasks like replication itself.

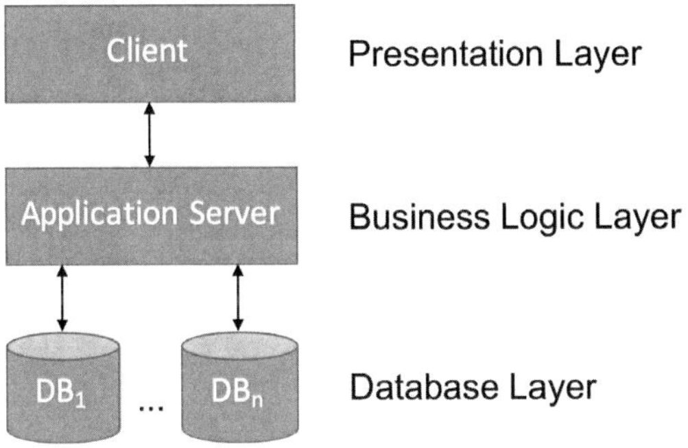


**Figure 3.14:** *Client-server architecture as an alternative to a real DDBS.*

According to [42], another alternative are so-called replication servers. They are provided as an additional service to standard DBMSs. Replication can be synchronous or asynchronous. In synchronous replication, all copies are immediately updated in a single global transaction when one is changed. This can, e.g., be realized using triggers (see Subsection 3.4.3). In asynchronous replication, the update of dependent copies can be deferred. This approach is used for mobile databases, which only connect to a network once in a while. When a connection is available, a snapshot is retrieved from a central DB using the replication server. In a subsequent phase without network connection the data may be read and updated in both databases. Upon reconnection to the network, changes within the databases can be replicated using the recovery logs. Conflicting updates can be detected by sending the old and new value of each update. For example, they can be resolved by comparing timestamps (e.g., taking the newest update as valid) or giving a site priority (e.g., to the central database's changes). On replication there are three modes for data ownership. In

Master/Slave mode, only one master site with writing rights exists per data item. While the master owns the master copy, slave sites may only read the value. Thus, no update conflicts can occur. Workflow mode works similarly, but master rights may be assigned to other sites. As only one site at a time can be assigned these rights, no update conflicts can arise, as well. Finally, in Update-Anywhere mode, any site may update any copy in a peer-to-peer-like approach. Here, the aforementioned update conflicts may arise. Thus, they must be detected and treated.

### 3.4.3 Active Databases

In the context of this work, an active database combines a passive data container with the entities' behavior (in particular, with respect to simulations) and the ability to actively provide notifications about changes. Traditionally, according to [4], an active database provides activity in terms of so-called triggers. These are active rules that usually comply to the ECA (Event Condition Action) model of rules. An event (E) is used to describe what triggers the rule. Usually, this is some kind of update to the database's data. It can also be time-based or some external event. An optional condition (C) can limit the events. Finally, an action (A) can be executed. Often, this is an SQL command, a transaction, or an external program call. As an example, an automatically derived total salary of a department can be considered. Here, the event is the change of an employee's salary, the condition is whether he works in the selected department, and the action would be a recalculation and update of the total salary (in terms of an SQL command).

Several aspects motivate active databases. Activity can be relocated from database applications to the central database. Complex integrity constraints can be checked. As shown before, derived data can be maintained. Besides updating aggregates, e.g., so-called materialized views can be kept up-to-date. Such views are cached into tables to optimize access performance. However, they must be updated, when the original data changes. As mentioned in Subsection 3.4.2, triggers can also be used to maintain replicate copies in distributed databases. Finally, they can also be used to implement a notification system to monitor changes in the database. Disadvantages of trigger usage may be a slowdown of the database system, difficult consistency checks for complex rule sets, and determination of their termination.

### 3.4.4 Temporal Databases

As described in [4, 110], in general, a temporal database combines "normal" data with temporal data. This can be explicitly modeled within the scope of the application schema, e.g., a date field "start of employment" for an employee's record. Here, application programs have to manage temporal data on their own, which can be a complex task for sophisticated scenarios. To cope with this complexity, different concepts have been developed generalizing the problem.

In the context of temporal databases, time is defined as "an ordered sequence of points in some granularity" [4]. Granularity is the temporal resolution, e.g., one second. In reality, these points are mapped to the corresponding intervals with a length equal to the granularity. Thus, events occurring in the same interval are said to be simultaneous with regard to the chosen granularity. A reference system for time values is called a calendar, e.g., the Gregorian calendar can be used. There are two types of events that can be mapped to time values. Point events are mapped to a single time point representing the occurrence of the event, e.g., a banking transaction. Duration events are mapped to time periods and represent the duration in which a value is valid, e.g., an employee's time of employment (from, to).

Furthermore, a time value must be interpreted. Such interpretations are called time dimensions [111]. The time associated with an event can represent its occurrence in the real world. This time dimension is called *valid time*, the corresponding database is called a *valid time database*. When time values refer to the point in time when the values were stored in the database, it is called *transaction time*, the corresponding database is called a *transaction time database*. A database combining both time dimensions is a *bitemporal database*. Besides these two most common time dimensions there can be more interpretations.

When using valid time, for each operation (read or write) the user has to supplement the point in real time corresponding to the event. This also allows to specify future or past events leading to so-called *proactive* or *retroactive updates*. When using transaction time, however, timestamps for writing operations are automatically derived from the database's system clock; proactive or retroactive updates are impossible. For reading operations omitting to specify a transaction time, the current (i.e., last written) value is returned. This can also be specified as a transaction time of *cur* (current). For other points in time, the corresponding historic value is returned.

When updating a data item in a temporal database, its previous state (i.e., version) is not lost. Rather, a new version with the new value is inserted and the previous version is closed becoming a so-called history version. Thus, every data item is represented by a set of $n>0$ versions. The state of a temporal database at a certain point in time (or a tuple thereof) is called a *snapshot*. Likewise, a non-temporal database is called a *snapshot database*.

A usual approach is to store start as well as stamps for each version and time dimension. While every version must have start timestamps, end times are only set to close a version. Deleting a data item is only performed logically by closing its current version. Inserting a new data item creates an initial version. Following this standard approach, in bitemporal databases, an update even creates two new versions. By updating a data item, its current version is closed concerning valid time by setting an end timestamp. The timestamp's update itself, however, leads to a new version regarding transaction time, but still holding the previous value of the data item. The second version is created with the actual new value and current timestamps.

In relational databases, this concept can be implemented by adding start and end timestamp attributes for each time dimension to every relation. This has the drawback of redundancy as changing a single attribute value of a tuple creates a new version duplicating all other attribute values. This can, for example, be reduced by dividing the relation into subrelations. In object-oriented or object-relational databases, a common approach is attribute-based versioning. Here, usually, an attribute version is stored as a tuple of start and end times for each time dimension and the corresponding value. Thus, for each of an object's attributes, a list of such tuples is stored. In addition, the object itself maintains so-called *lifespan* temporal attributes for each time dimension. They represent its overall lifetime from creation to deletion.

Following [112], the aforementioned approach of storing start as well as end times for each version is called an *interval representation*. In contrast, storing only start times is called a *time point representation*. Here, subsequent versions' start times close preceding versions. Consequently, each version has a certain *scope* comprising those points in time the version's value is "visible."

# Chapter 4

# System Requirements

This chapter defines basic requirements for the presented data management approach for eRobotics applications that build the basis for the methods introduced in the next chapter. The two main components of the approach are a 3D simulation system with a simulation database for its internal data management and an external database system. The former provides a real-time capable cache and drives the 3D simulation itself while the latter provides persistence and versioning, a common application schema, and an integrated communication hub for collaboration or distributed simulation.

For the sake of clarity of the following specifications, let *SimDB* be some simulation database system and let *ExtDB* be some external database system for which the requirements will be defined. The core idea of the approach's requirements is then shown in Figure 4.1: Map schema and instance data describing concepts of both databases' metamodels using appropriate model transformations as a precondition for the databases' conceptual compatibility.

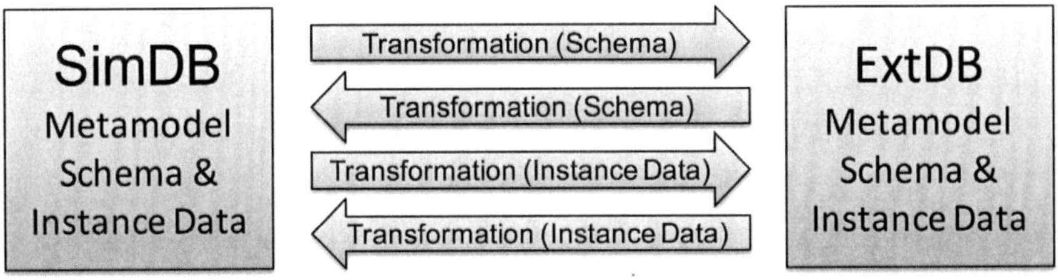


**Figure 4.1:** *Core idea of the approach's requirements: Map schema and instance data describing concepts of both databases' metamodels using model transformations.*

## 4.1 Metamodel-Based Requirements

A particularly important property for SimDB and ExtDB is how well these two database systems fit together regarding the representable data, i.e., schema structures and corresponding instance data. This property can be formalized using their metamodels. As presented in Chapter 3, a metamodel defines a modeling language, describing what can be modeled. Metamodels and hence modeling languages can be compared and matched using a model transformation language. However, before deducing the requirements, some comparable approaches are examined in the next section.

### 4.1.1 Comparable Approaches

Compared to the subsequent metamodel-based requirements definitions, similar approaches are used in the field of generic model management. According to [113], a model management system shall support various operations on schemata: match schemata, compose mappings between them, determine their difference, merge them, translate them into different metamodels, and derive transformations on data level from mappings on schema level. These operations shall be generic by supporting multiple metamodels and mapping languages. Here, a metamodel defines a language for expressing a schema, which itself defines a set of database states. Metamodels are usually SQL (Structured Query Language), XML (Extensible Markup Language) Schema (XSD (XML Schema Definition)), Entity-Relationship, or object-oriented like Java or ODMG (Object Data Management Group). However, the work concentrates on tool support for semi-automatic mappings.

The approach presented in this dissertation (both, for the requirements definition in the next sections as well as the runtime method that will be presented in Chapter 5) can be seen as an implementation of the so-called ModelGen operator [113] that automatically translates a schema from one metamodel into another, including the creation of a mapping between source and target elements. In contrast, for the so-called Match operator the emphasis is more on matching inherently different schemata presumably represented in the same metamodel.

Another implementation of the ModelGen operator is provided in [114]. In contrast to other authors, here, the notion of a model resides on level M2 describing schemata. In this work, a proprietary pivotal supermodel is used to transform schemata and also the corresponding data. However, the solution does not use standards for metamodeling and model transformations as presented in Section 3.2. In [115], the same system is extended to provide runtime transformation using views in the target database, supporting read-only access to translated schema and data. The authors of [116] take a similar approach using a proprietary pivotal graph-based representation. In [117], another approach for transforming schema and data is presented, but restricted to conversions between XML and SQL.

Regarding Requirement 3 in the next section, a similar problem is identified by the authors of [118]. Based on a frequent interpretation of the MOF (Meta-Object Facility [99]) hierarchy, they observe that the MOF standard does not specify the structure of M0-level instances of M1-level constructs. The instantation mechanism rather depends on the particular modeling language specified on level M2. This prevents the usage of transformation languages like ATL (ATL Transformation Language [103, 104]) or QVT (MOF Query/-View/Transformation [105, 98, 106, 107]) on level M0. But their solution does not work within the standards. They solve the problem by reorganizing the MOF standard using a uniform, level-independent representation of model elements. It is combined with a transformation language with instantiation and generalization functions implemented for each modeling language.

Besides its relation to generic model management, the approach presented in this thesis can also be seen as a variation of a generic interoperability bridge as defined within the MDI (Model-Driven Interoperability) concepts described in Subsection 3.2.3. Here, interoperability is achieved for SimDB and ExtDB on data level in general. That is, not specific application schemata are mapped but the general concepts for arbitrary schemata. Thus, the databases' metamodels are considered for the bridge. To guarantee a valid semantic mapping in between them, they must fulfill the subsequently presented requirements. All concepts for the actual data exchange are then conceptually specified based on the pivot UML (Unified Modeling Language [8]) metamodel in Chapter 5. This implicitly uses the semantic mapping in between UML and the databases' metamodels. Chapter 6 then presents how these concepts are implemented for actual databases. Here, an integrated approach combines syntactic and semantic mapping to allow for flexible online transformation of data during runtime.

### 4.1.2 Metamodels and Model Transformations

One level of the approach for coupling SimDB and ExtDB is a synchronization of the used schema descriptions. Here, correspondences between schema components are identified to build up a schema mapping. Such schema components are modeled as metaclasses of the respective database's metamodel. Instances of such metaclasses of ExtDB are either matched against existing counterparts within SimDB or are transferred, creating new metaclass instances in SimDB during runtime. When the metamodels are modeled using the same meta-metamodel like MOF, rules for these correspondences can be formally described using a transformation model written in a transformation language like ATL (Figure 4.2).

Thus, providing metamodels for both database systems (Requirement 1) and a transformation from ExtDB to SimDB (Requirement 2) is a precondition for schema synchronization.

**Requirement 1.** *Metamodels for SimDB and ExtDB.*

**Requirement 2.** *A model transformation from ExtDB's to SimDB's metamodel.*

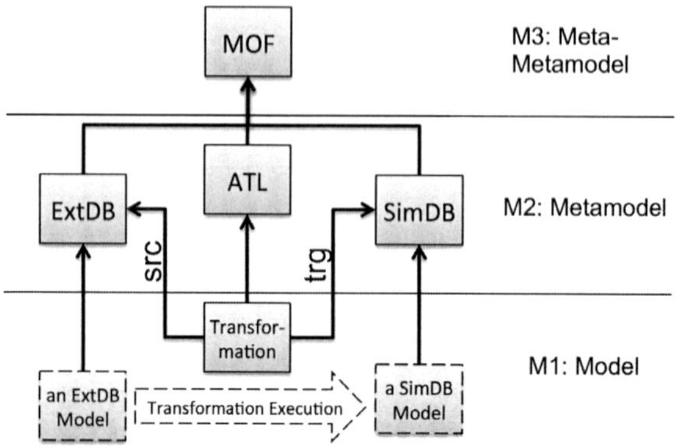


**Figure 4.2:** *Metamodels of ExtDB and SimDB and transformation in between (adapted from [102]).*

### 4.1.3 How To Model Instantiation

The next level of coupling SimDB and ExtDB is performed on instance data conforming to the synchronized schemata. Regarding schema synchronization, a metamodel containing only metaclasses for schema description suffices. Such are typically metaclasses describing classes, attributes, and associations in object-oriented or tables and columns in relational contexts. For data synchronization, however, additional information about instantiation concepts is necessary within a metamodel, i.e., how data conforming to a schema is instantiated.

In contrast to a frequent interpretation (see Figure 4.3), this instantiation should not be identified with the relationship between metalevel M1 and M0, as it is not part of the metamodel itself but part of the concept of the hierarchy. For example, frequently, a class "Satellite" residing on level M1 has an instantiation "Landsat 8" on level M0. The usual "instance-of" relationship in between, however, is not modeled in the corresponding metamodel and can thus not be used by a model transformation.

According to [119], this inter-level relation is rather a representation relationship (see Figure 4.4) between a model at level M1 and the modeled system at level M0, which may also be user data. Thus, the M1-level model represents or specifies an M0-level system under study [120]. Accordingly, relations crossing metalevels M2 to M3 and M1 to M2 are seen as linguistic instance-of relations [119], interpretations [120] or conforms-to relations [102]. They describe the application of a (meta-)modeling language to build (meta)models.

Compared to this, as part of the metamodel on level M2, ontological instance-of relations [119] model the relation between metaclasses for schema description and metaclasses for corresponding data, e.g., modeling objects and attribute values in object-oriented or rows and column values in relational metamodels. Thereby, both belong to the *theory* [120] of the specified meta-modeling language.

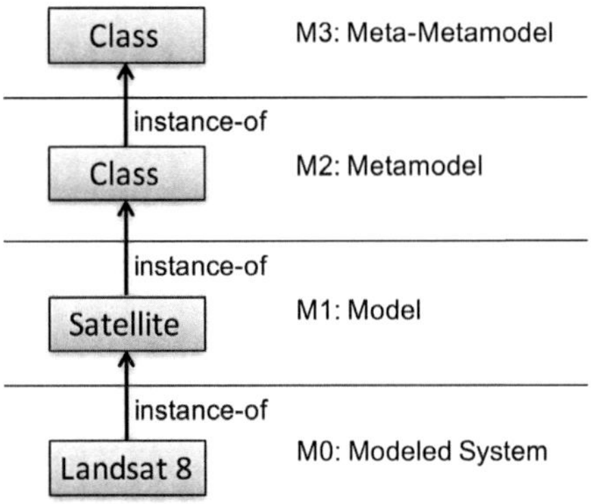


**Figure 4.3:** *Frequent interpretation of the metamodel hierarchy: The instantiation relationship is not part of the metamodel.*

Being part of the metamodel on level M2, these metaclasses and relations can also be taken into account within a transformation. This guarantees the modeling of correspondences between instantiation concepts within a transformation model for SimDB and ExtDB. Thus, appropriately designed metamodels are a requirement for data synchronization (Requirement 3).

**Requirement 3.** *Ontological instantiation concept in SimDB's and ExtDB's metamodel.*

### 4.1.4 UML as a Pivotal Metamodel

In principle, the previously defined Requirements 1–3 are sufficient as a precondition regarding the compatibility of SimDB's and ExtDB's modeling concepts. Nevertheless, a reasonable variation involves the usage of a pivotal metamodel as a mediator between the metamodels of SimDB and ExtDB, comparable to [121]. In this case, there is not one transformation defined between SimDB's and ExtDB's metamodels, but one transformation between SimDB's metamodel and the pivot metamodel and one between ExtDB's metamodel and the pivot metamodel (see Figure 4.5).

First of all, this results in linear instead of quadratic complexity with increasing number of considered database systems and thus metamodels. More importantly, a pivot metamodel can be used to guarantee certain modeling capabilities within SimDB and ExtDB. By choosing an appropriate pivot metamodel that provides the desired capabilities itself and by stipulating reasonable bidirectional (or two separate unidirectional) transformations to and from this metamodel, SimDB and ExtDB are constrained to also provide these capabilities.

As described in Chapter 3, in the context of 3D simulation, GIS (Geo Information System), CAD (Computer-Aided Design), or other 3D software, an object-oriented modeling is

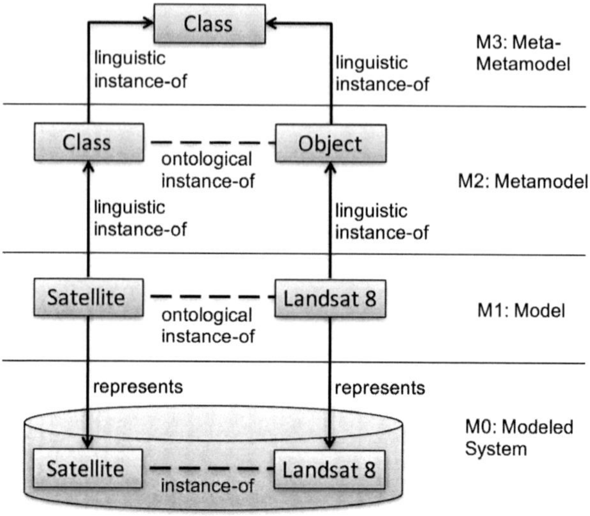


**Figure 4.4:** *Example for linguistic and ontological instantiation (adapted from [119]).*

advisable, as such data usually consists of a huge number of hierarchically structured parts with interdependencies. Thus, the UML is a reasonable choice for a pivot.

UML semantics of `InstanceSpecification` allow to specify the existence of an entity as part of a modeled system. However, regarding Requirement 3 and Figure 4.4, UML's semantics for meta-level M0 is slightly different. Standard UML semantics intend to use M1-level classes to *instantiate* M0-level objects (compare M1-class "Satellite" and M0-object "Landsat 8" in Figure 4.3). Following the approach modeled after [119], UML classes on M1 preferably *model* or *represent* runtime classes on M0 (compare "Satellite" on M1 as well

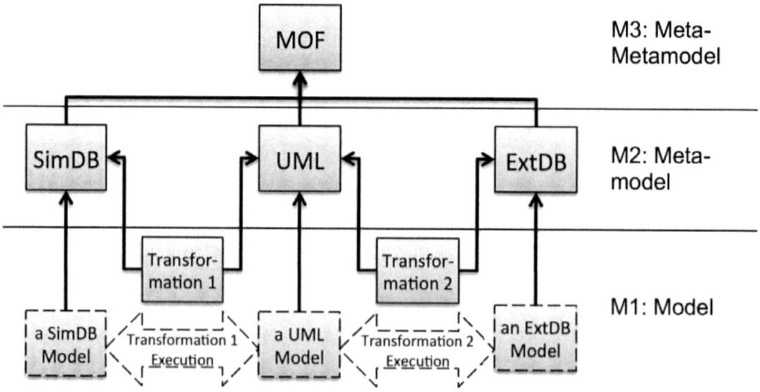


**Figure 4.5:** *UML as a pivot metamodel.*

as M0 in Figure 4.4). Accordingly, UML objects (M1) *represent* runtime objects (M0): In Figure 4.4 "Landsat 8" on level M1 represents "Landsat 8" on level M0. Concerning M1 and M0, instantiation relations are only defined within each level and not in between.

A pivot metamodel in general and the decision for UML in particular has another advantage. The previous requirement definitions postulated on SimDB and ExtDB do not give any insight on the individual metaclasses and their semantics. For example, it is unknown which of the metaclasses describe schema structures and which describe instances thereof. But to use the requirements as the basis for the approach of database synchronization in the next chapter, there has to be some knowledge about such semantics. A known pivotal metamodel with known semantics, i.e., a known *theory* [120], can resolve this lack of information. Adding the new Requirement 4 allows to make statements about SimDB's or ExtDB's metamodel components and their semantics by indirectly referring to the corresponding components within UML. As stated in Subsection 3.2.1, such semantics indirectly specified by a transformation to another metamodel are called denotational semantics.

Following this rationale, a UML metaclass can be used as a surrogate that represents those unknown structures within SimDB's or ExtDB's metamodel corresponding to it. To simplify nomenclature, the notion of a *pseudo metaclass* is introduced in this thesis. Figure 4.6 shows an example. Here, an excerpt of the UML metamodel is shown: The metaclasses `Classifier` and `InstanceSpecification`. The actual metaclasses of ExtDB or SimDB are unknown – at least their semantics are. However, indirectly by transformation, pseudo metaclasses ExtDB-`Classifier` and -`InstanceSpecification` as well as SimDB-`Classifier` and --`InstanceSpecification` can be defined. They represent whatever the UML metaclasses may be transformed to in either database. By use of this notion, the semantics of a UML metaclass can easily be transferred to the context of SimDB and ExtDB.

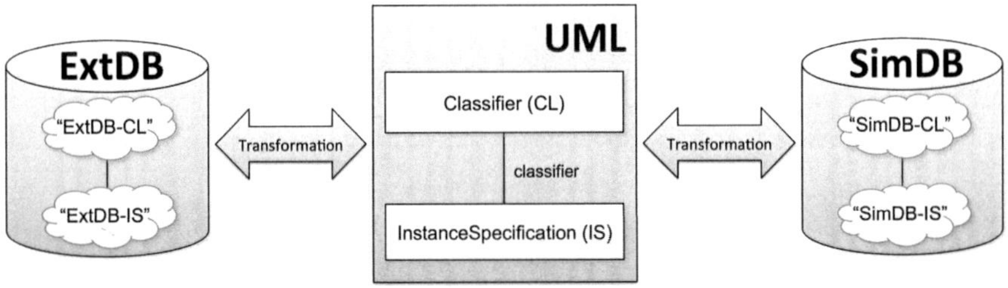


**Figure 4.6:** *Pseudo metaclasses ExtDB-`Classifier`, ExtDB-`InstanceSpecification`, SimDB-`Classifier`, SimDB-`InstanceSpecification` derived by transformation from the corresponding UML metaclasses.*

Altogether, this leads to Requirement 4. Due to the transitivity of model transformations it subsumes Requirement 2.

**Requirement 4.** *The UML metamodel as a pivot for SimDB's and ExtDB's metamodel.*

## 4.2 Database Runtime System Requirements

Besides the requirements concerning SimDB's and ExtDB's metamodels, there are some other requirements on both database systems concerning their runtime behavior.

Although these requirements refer to the runtime system and thus metalevel M0, they can be formulated in terms of instances of metaclasses. While metaclasses themselves are defined on metalevel M2, their (linguistic) instances populate level M1. Further following the rationale from Subsection 4.1.3, these instances on level M1 constitute a model of the system on level M0, representing (or specifying) its runtime structure. Based on this representation relation, it is legitimate to use the same notions for the system as for its model. Thus, while describing constraints for the runtime level, the following requirements are formulated in terms of pseudo metaclasses and instances thereof.

### 4.2.1 Reflection

For synchronization on schema level, SimDB and ExtDB must provide access to the schema description on runtime level M0. This is necessary to analyze the two systems, to map between them and to replicate their data. In the context of computational systems in general or programming languages in particular, such access methods are called *reflective*. According to [122], a reflective system contains structures representing aspects of itself, allowing to answer questions about and support actions on itself. A term used in this context is "reification" (verb "to reify") – the process of creating such structures for previously abstract concepts. As motivated above, such M0-level structures can exist in terms of reified versions of schema components from level M1. An example in Figure 4.4 would be the “Satellite” class on level M0 (accordingly, a “Satellite” table in a relational scenario) reifying the “Satellite” class modeled on level M1. Such M0 structures should be accessible providing the necessary schema information about name, type, inheritance (if applicable), and so forth.

For matching a schema from ExtDB that is already defined within SimDB, read-only schema access suffices. The more sophisticated approach for schema transfer additionally requires to create new schema structures within SimDB (but not within ExtDB) during runtime. Regarding the example from Figure 4.4, this corresponds to the creation of a new M0 class object, e.g., “Landsat 7”.

Additional reflective methods are required for data synchronization. During runtime, schema information has to be determinable from instantiated data. Thus, the instance-of relation within level M0 has to be resolvable. In the example, it must allow to identify the object “Landsat 8” to be of class “Satellite” (both on M0). Furthermore, new data has to be instantiated using schema structures. For example, given M0-level “Satellite”, create an additional runtime object “Landsat 7”. Another aspects of reflection in data synchronization is to query data, e.g., to retrieve all (ontological) instances of an ExtDB-Class.

Altogether, a substantial set of reflective methods to explore and create M0-level data, schema and the relationships in between them are needed inducing Requirement 5.

**Requirement 5.** *Reflection interface for SimDB and ExtDB.*

### 4.2.2 Instance Data Identification

Another requirement for data synchronization is the unambiguous identification of instance data entities on level M0 (Requirement 6). A mechanism must be provided so that data entities can be identified and managed within an instance data mapping, allowing to manage correspondences between both databases. For object-oriented or object-relational databases this may be an OID (Object Identifier), for relational databases an entity's PK (Primary Key).

**Requirement 6.** *Means in SimDB and ExtDB to unambiguously identify instance data entities.*

Besides identification, given such an ID (Identifier), it must also be possible to retrieve the corresponding instance data from the respective database.

### 4.2.3 Change Notification

Another prerequisite for synchronization on data level is a change notification service for M0-level instance data (Requirement 7). As described in the previous chapter, such notifications can be provided by an active database. Notifications from SimDB are necessary to detect, manage and synchronize local data changes. In a single user environment with one SimDB instance synchronized to an ExtDB instance, this is a sufficient requirement. In a multiuser environment, several SimDB instances are synchronized to a central ExtDB instance. Here, a notification service is also required for ExtDB so remotely synchronized changes of the global state in ExtDB can also be detected, managed and synchronized at every SimDB instance. Thus, a notification service for ExtDB is of vital importance for database-driven change distribution and therefore database-driven distributed simulation.

**Requirement 7.** *Notification service for SimDB and ExtDB.*

Table 4.1 lists the possible combinations for the availability of a notification service (N.S.) for SimDB or ExtDB and the consequential system configurations.

Table 4.2 gives the necessary types of notification for SimDB and ExtDB. Without loss of generality, insertions, removals, and changes shall only be notified for objects and links. Any alteration related to literals (instances of data types), however, shall be notified as a change of the corresponding object that holds the literal as the value of an owned attribute. This is because the UML specification states that literals are only identified by their value (or

**Table 4.1:** *System configurations depending on the availability of a notification service (N.S.) for SimDB and ExtDB.*

| | SimDB without N.S. | SimDB with N.S. |
|---|---|---|
| ExtDB without N.S. | single user read-only | single user read-write |
| ExtDB with N.S. | multiple users read-only (locally) | multiple users read-write |

value combination for structured data types). Thus, they will not be managed like objects or links (see Section 5.2). Altogether, any change to the structures representing an object property's value (the slot, the value specifications, etc.) shall be comprised by the single update notification for the object. For links, however, update notifications shall be omitted as their identity is derived from the linked objects. Thus, exchanging a link's member objects is removing the link and inserting a new link.

Databases may allow to insert prepared object subtrees of composite aggregation, which is a common operation for 3D data. In such scenarios, each object and link insertion shall be notified separately in a top-down manner, i.e., as if the instances would have been inserted one at a time. Accordingly, subtree removals shall be notified separately in a bottom-up manner.

**Table 4.2:** *Required notification types within a change notification service.*

| **notification** | **parameters** |
|---|---|
| object inserted | object or its ID |
| object removed | object ID |
| object updated | object or its ID & affected property |
| link inserted | link, its ID, its member end objects, or their IDs |
| link removed | link ID or member objects' IDs |

A summary of the system requirements is given in Figure 4.7. Both databases need metamodels (Requirement 1) including a concept for ontological instantiation (Requirement 3). Model transformations are needed from and to the UML metamodel (Requirement 4, subsuming Requirement 2). The databases' runtime level must contain a reified schema description (Requirement 5), provide ids for instances (Requirement 6) as well as a notification service (Requirement 7).

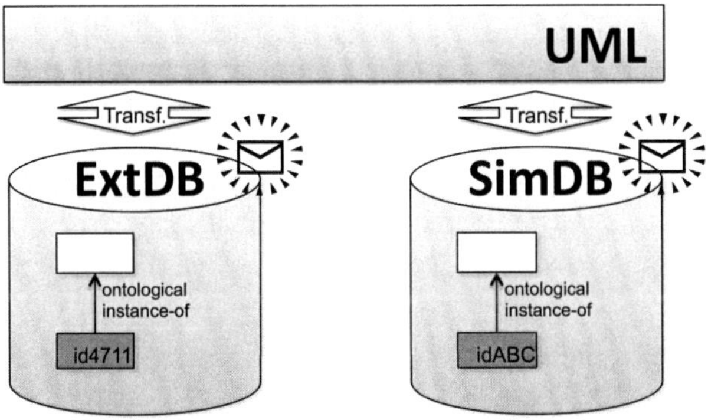


**Figure 4.7:** *Summary of the system requirements.*

# Chapter 5

# Synchronization

In this chapter, the new concept for generic database synchronization at runtime is specified in detail. For that purpose, the architecture introduced in Chapter 1 (Figure 1.7 on page 6) is substantiated as an initially three-tiered approach shown in Figure 5.1 where each tier manages synchronization on a different level:

1. synchronization on *schema level*, yielding a schema mapping
2. synchronization on *data level*, yielding an instance mapping
3. synchronization on *functional level*, yielding a functional mapping

The *version level* is a fourth level of synchronization residing underneath.

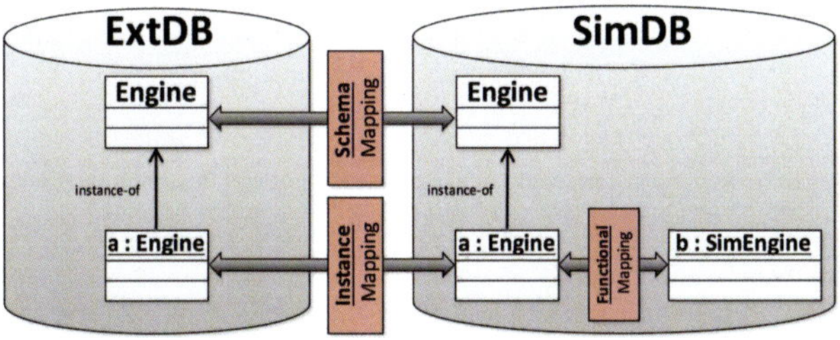


**Figure 5.1:** *Overview of the three-tier database synchronization approach.*

Synchronization is performed between each pair of SimDB instance and a central instance of ExtDB. Using schema synchronization (schema sync), SimDB is adapted to ExtDB's schema so both databases "speak the same language". In the example in Figure 5.1, an `Engine` class in ExtDB is synced to its counterpart in SimDB. There are two approaches to schema sync: By transfer and by matching. The former creates new schema components in SimDB on-demand, the latter matches a preexisting schema. Either approach builds the basis for data synchronization (data sync) where instance data from ExtDB is replicated to

SimDB to make it transparently available for the simulation system. In the example, the instance `a:Engine` is replicated to SimDB. Replicated data is kept in sync to make changes persistent and centrally distribute them to other instances of SimDB. Finally, functional data synchronization (functional sync) is used to map functional interpretations, i.e., semantics of instance data. In Figure 5.1, the class `Engine` might have no immediate meaning for the simulation system. Thus, `a:Engine` needs to be translated to the `SimEngine` class whose semantics might instead be known. Altogether, this multilevel approach shows great flexibility towards changes in instance data and even in schema by adapting to the participating databases at runtime.

One core concept of the architecture is decoupling the simulation system from ExtDB, hiding it from all its internal components. ExtDB's schema as well as its instance data can only be accessed by means of replicas within SimDB. Besides a general separation of concerns, this transparency makes SimDB work as an "intelligent" cache for ExtDB. It provides real-time data access for simulation as well as visualization and speeds up repeating access patterns, which would otherwise lead to repetitive queries to ExtDB.

Moreover, in Section 5.4, the usage of temporal databases on version level is described in detail.

The descriptions in the next sections also follow the rationale from Section 4.2, using the notion of (pseudo) metaclasses and instances thereof to describe concepts on runtime level. As mentioned before, to denote UML (Unified Modeling Language [8]) metaclasses or their pseudo-counterparts, abbreviations are used, e.g., within pseudo code listings.

## 5.1 Schema Synchronization

On the first level of the synchronization architecture, a schema from ExtDB is synchronized to SimDB. Schema sync provides a common data schema for the whole distributed system consisting of one or more instances of SimDB and a central instance of ExtDB. For schema description, important UML metaclasses (or their respective pseudo counterparts in SimDB and ExtDB) are `Class`, `Property`, `Association`, `DataType`, `Enumeration` and `PrimitiveType`.

Without loss of generality, the following specifications will always assume a *full* schema synchronization, meaning *all* of ExtDB's schema components are synchronized to SimDB. In practice, synchronization can be limited to a schema subset, e.g., for databases with multiple application schemata.

### 5.1.1 Schema Mapping

Once during system startup, ExtDB's schema is analyzed using its reflection interface giving access to the reified instances of metaclasses describing the schema. The schema sync process then yields a schema mapping between the two databases. This mapping is a basis for data synchronization, the next level in the architecture. Compared to model transformations, the mapping corresponds to the combined trace model (see Subsection 3.2.2) of applied model transformations from ExtDB's to UML's and from UML's to SimDB's metamodel.

### 5.1.2 Schema Synchronization by Transfer

Schema synchronization by transfer (schema transfer) dynamically creates a schema within SimDB. This transfer of the schema from ExtDB to SimDB is entirely performed at runtime. Provided write access, it uses the reflective methods to instantiate metaclasses of SimDB's metamodel appropriately. The concept is similar to *enforce domain* rules in QVT (MOF (Meta-Object Facility [99]) Query/View/Transformation [105, 98, 106, 107]) model transformations.

When considering ExtDB to define a common schema for the distributed system, transferring its schema to every SimDB is reasonable. An alternative would be to inversely transfer SimDB's existing schema to ExtDB. A use case for this scenario could be if an empty ExtDB is provided as a persistence layer for a single SimDB. However, the scenario is symmetrical to the presented direction (ExtDB $\rightarrow$ SimDB).

Algorithm 1 gives a conceptional overview using pseudo metaclasses. All of ExtDB's classifiers are iterated. A classifier is an instance of a non-abstract metaclass derived from `Classifier`. In UML, these are `Class`, `Association`, `DataType`, `Enumeration`, and -`PrimitiveType`. For each of these, a corresponding SimDB classifier is created, values of all metaattributes like name or `isAbstract` are copied, and a mapping is inserted. For each property of ExtDB that represents a class's or data type's owned attribute, or an association's owned end, a property in SimDB is created, metaattribute values like name or `isStatic` are copied, the ownership is set, and a mapping is inserted. In a postprocessing step, especially non-owned member ends of associations and direct generalization relations are adopted. As before, the usage of pseudo metaclasses implicitly covers the necessary transformations to the actual metaclasses of SimDB and ExtDB.

The result of this process is a set of newly created runtime schema components within SimDB and a schema mapping containing their correspondences to schema components in ExtDB. As described in the "Satellite" example in Subsection 4.2.1, the new schema components are reified (linguistic) instances of metaclasses from SimDB's metamodel. For this approach, use cases are

- schemata previously unknown to the simulation system,
- rapid prototyping or
- frequently changing schemata.

**Algorithm 1** Schema transfer

```
Define schema mapping M_S from ExtDB to SimDB
for all classifiers CL_Ext with type T ∈ {Cl, As, ...} do
    CL_Sim ← new SimDB-T
    Copy all metaattribute values of CL_Ext to CL_Sim
    M_S(CL_Ext) ← CL_Sim
    for all owned attributes/ends Pr_Ext of CL_Ext do
        Pr_Sim ← new SimDB-Property
        Copy all metaattribute values of Pr_Ext to Pr_Sim
        Add Pr_Sim to owned attributes/ends of CL_Sim
        M_S(Pr_Ext) ← Pr_Sim
    end for
end for
for all classifiers CL_Ext with type T do                          ▷ post-processing
    if T is Association then
        for all member ends Pr_Ext of CL_Ext do
            Add M_S(Pr_Ext) to members ends of M_S(CL_Ext)
        end for
    end if
    for all direct generalizations CL_Ext^gen of CL_Ext do
        Add generalization M_S(CL_Ext^gen) to M_S(CL_Ext)
    end for
end for
```

### 5.1.3 Schema Synchronization by Matching

In schema synchronization by matching (schema matching), SimDB already contains a predefined version of the schema, which only has to be matched against ExtDB's schema. Matching does not imply any translations between generally different schemata. For example, it does not match a name attribute as one string value ("John Doe") in ExtDB to separately modeled first ("John") and last ("Doe") name attributes in SimDB. It only applies to identical schemata represented using the different metamodels of SimDB and ExtDB.

Algorithm 2 illustrates the process of schema matching. While the basic procedure resembles Algorithm 1, instead of creating new classifiers or properties, equivalents are searched within SimDB and the postprocessing only verifies association ends as well as generalizations. The only result is the schema mapping (or failure). The procedure does not alter SimDB itself. It resembles *checkonly domain* rules in QVT model transformations where only the existence of the counterparts that hold a relation is checked.

**Algorithm 2** Schema matching

Define schema mapping $M_S$ from ExtDB to SimDB
**for all** classifiers $CL_{Ext}$ with type $T \in \{Cl, As, ...\}$ **do**
  $CL_{Sim} \leftarrow$ find equivalent to $CL_{Ext}$
  $M_S(CL_{Ext}) \leftarrow CL_{Sim}$
  **for all** owned attributes/ends $Pr_{Ext}$ of $CL_{Ext}$ **do**
    $Pr_{Sim} \leftarrow$ find equivalent to $Pr_{Ext}$
    $M_S(Pr_{Ext}) \leftarrow Pr_{Sim}$
  **end for**
**end for**
**for all** classifiers $CL_{Ext}$ with type $T$ **do** ▷ post-processing
  **if** $T$ is `Association` **then**
    **for all** member ends $Pr_{Ext}$ of $CL_{Ext}$ **do**
      Add $M_S(Pr_{Ext})$ to members ends of $M_S(CL_{Ext})$
    **end for**
  **end if**
  **for all** direct generalizations $CL^{gen}_{Ext}$ of $CL_{Ext}$ **do**
    Add generalization $M_S(CL^{gen}_{Ext})$ to $M_S(CL_{Ext})$
  **end for**
**end for**

Schema matching is less flexible than schema transfer. But when used with a static schema predefined at compile time of the simulation system (where applicable), it can have the advantage of static type safety. In contrast, dynamically created schemata can only be accessed using reflection, implying runtime type checking. Thus, use cases for schema sync by matching are

- stable (rarely changed) schemata, statically predefined in SimDB,
- a SimDB implementation that only provides read-only reflection or
- schemata dynamically defined in SimDB by another process (e.g., an XMI (XML (Extensible Markup Language) Metadata Interchange [108]) import).

### 5.1.4 Combined Synchronization

The two principles of schema synchronization can also be mixed. For example, schema matching can be performed by default while schema transfer is used as a fallback approach to dynamically add parts of a schema missing in SimDB. Thus, a combination of Algorithm 1 and Algorithm 2 first searches for an existing equivalent classifier in SimDB and otherwise creates a new one. Equally, properties are first searched and otherwise created. A particular use case is

- a more or less static core schema with changing extensions (profiles), e.g., for different applications.

## 5.2 Data Synchronization

The second level in the synchronization architecture is data synchronization. Based upon the established schema mapping, it is used to manage instance data between SimDB and ExtDB. It comprises data loading, unloading, change management and resynchronization. In contrast to schema sync, data sync spans the whole runtime of the distributed system.

Without loss of generality, the approach for synchronization on data level will consider *all* instances within SimDB and ExtDB. But in practice synchronization might only be of interest for a subset of instances, e.g., for a subtree of hierarchically structured 3D data. However, such restrictions can easily be realized by adding appropriate filtering mechanisms, especially to loading and change management.

### 5.2.1 Data Loading and Instance Mapping

One of the core features of the presented approach is making ExtDB's data transparently accessible to components of the simulation system by means of SimDB. Therefore, requested data is replicated from ExtDB to SimDB. For each pair (original and replica) a mapping is stored. In this context, the UML (and thus pseudo) metaclass `InstanceSpecification` is relevant. As previously mentioned, it represents an (ontologically) instantiated `Classifier`. Thus, the notion of an instance or instance data here usually refers to an `Instance-Specification`. When its classifier is a UML-`Class`, an instance is called an object, when it is a UML-`Association` it is called a link, and for all kinds of UML-`DataTypes` it is called a literal. For the special case of an UML-`Enumeration` there is even a separate metaclass `EnumerationLiteral` derived from `InstanceSpecification`. Furthermore, UML metaclass `Slot`, representing an instantiated `Property`, and `ValueSpecification` as the abstract base metaclass for miscellaneous types of values are of particular interest.

The methods for data loading presented below can be divided into two categories: While basic operations for data loading are used internally by the presented approach, interface methods provide data access to other components of the simulation system. To maintain transparency[1], the latter shall not expose ExtDB's nature, its pseudo metaclasses, or its runtime interface.

#### 5.2.1.1 Basic Operations

A basic operation in data loading is to load a single object. Here, the instance specification $IS_{Ext}$ (with a class-type classifier) is replicated from ExtDB to SimDB with all its (non-reference) values. The correspondence is stored as an entry in the central instance mapping $M_I$. In contrast, literals are only loaded implicitly in terms of values of object attributes. Other than objects, they lack an identity on their own and are only distinguishable by their value. Structured data types are treated as one combined value. In particular, no instance mapping is performed for literals. The treatment of links is discussed separately in the context of hierarchical loading.

Algorithm 3 illustrates the operation. It pre-checks whether the object given as an ExtDB-`InstanceSpecification` is already mapped, i.e., already loaded. Otherwise, its classifier is retrieved, which is a class. This ExtDB-`Class` $Cl_{Ext}$ is translated into the corresponding SimDB-`Class` $Cl_{Sim}$ using the schema mapping. $Cl_{Sim}$ is (ontologically) instantiated to get a new SimDB-`InstanceSpecification` $IS_{Sim}$. For each slot $Sl_{Ext}$, its property $Pr_{Ext}$ is retrieved and translated. Properties that reference other objects, i.e., with class type, are not handled here and thus skipped. Otherwise, using the translated property, a new SimDB-`Slot` is created for the object in SimDB. The slot's values are retrieved, replicated, and attached to the new SimDB slot. Finally, the pair of objects is stored in the instance mapping.

Algorithm 4 describes a value's replication in more detail. UML provides derived types of value specifications. One of them is `LiteralSpecification`, which in turn has several derivatives for simple literal values like integer, string or real values. These are handled generically in the first if-clause. Here, a new value specification $VS_{Sim}$ of the corresponding type in SimDB is created. For example, when $VS_{Ext}$ is a ExtDB-`LiteralReal`, a SimDB--`LiteralReal` $VS_{Sim}$ is created. Subsequently, the value – e.g., the floating point value in case of a real literal – is copied from the ExtDB to the SimDB value specification.

[1]Note again that *transparency* is always used in its information hiding meaning.

**Algorithm 3** Data loading: load a single object.

```
function LOADOBJECT(IS_Ext)
    if IS_Ext ∈ M_I then
        return M_I(IS_Ext)
    end if
    Cl_Ext ← classifier of IS_Ext
    Cl_Sim ← M_S(Cl_Ext)
    IS_Sim ← instantiate Cl_Sim
    for all Slots Sl_Ext of IS_Ext do
        Pr_Ext ← defining feature of Sl_Ext
        if Pr_Ext's value type is an ExtDB-Class then
            skip Pr_Ext                                          ▷ object reference
        end if
        Sl_Sim ← create SimDB-Slot for IS_Sim with M_S(Pr_Ext)
        for all VS_Ext ∈ Sl_Ext do
            add REPLICATEVALUE(VS_Ext) to Sl_Sim                 ▷ Algorithm 4
        end for
    end for
    M_I(IS_Ext) ← IS_Sim
    return IS_Sim
end function
```

Another kind of value specification is an instance value, which is used to reference other instances, i.e., other literals or objects. Referenced literals of possibly structured data types are replicated. While further details are omitted in the pseudo code, the replication works similar to object loading in Algorithm 3. It differs in also replicating an instance specification's own value (apart from its slots) and omitting instance mapping (as values lack identity). Furthermore, this process may recursively replicate other referenced literals. Referenced objects are not considered in this context. Finally, two other kinds of value specifications, i.e., expressions and opaque expressions, are not within the scope of this work.

**Algorithm 4** Value replication.

```
function REPLICATEVALUE(VS_Ext)
    T ← type of VS_Ext                        ▷ T may be LiteralBoolean, InstanceValue, ...
    if T inherits ExtDB-LiteralSpecification then                    ▷ simple data type
        VS_Sim ← instantiate SimDB's counterpart of T
        value of VS_Sim ← value of VS_Ext
        return VS_Sim
    else if T inherits ExtDB-InstanceValue then                  ▷ structured data type
        VS_Sim ← replicate data type value VS_Ext
        return VS_Sim
    end if
end function
```

The following basic operations incorporate links. Like literals, links are only identified by their current values. For each member end of an association, a link holds a slot with a single instance of the corresponding target type as a value. It is defined and identified only by this tuple. In case of binary associations, this is a pair of instances. However, in contrast to literals, links "belong" (not in the sense of ownership) to multiple instances. So, a separate management based on instance mapping is advantageous. In the context of this work, links are assumed to be unique and non-ordered. Otherwise, some additional data management would be necessary. Without loss of generality, associations shall only be defined for classes as end types, not data types. Thus, in the context of this thesis, links shall only connect objects, not literals.

For structured 3D data, a superimposed *hierarchical* loading function can be used to load an object and all of its ancestors. Here, an ancestor is recursively defined as another object aggregating this object or one of its other ancestors using an association with composite aggregation. A direct ancestor is called a parent, its counterpart is called a child. An object without a parent is a root object. According to the UML specification, a part object may only be included in at most one composite at a time. Thus, an object may have at most one parent at a time. Furthermore, associations with composite aggregation must be binary associations. Therefore, only associations with a multiplicity of $0..1 : n$ are considered here.

To preserve parent-child-relations and consistency within SimDB, it is a reasonable approach to load a part object only with its composite object. Therefore, Algorithm 5 can be used to recursively load an object including all its ancestor objects from ExtDB into SimDB. The approach is applied to a designated child object $IS_{Ext}^{child}$. After loading the object itself using Algorithm 3, a parent link is searched using Algorithm 7. When it lacks a parent link, it is returned as a root object. Otherwise, the parent object $IS_{Ext}^{parent}$ is retrieved from the other end of the link $IS_{Ext}^{link}$. After recursively loading $IS_{Ext}^{parent}$ with all its ancestors, the link itself $IS_{Ext}^{link}$ is loaded using Algorithm 6. Finally, the child object is returned as a result. Note that without loss of generality, the approach assumes that every connection between objects is realized using an association. However, for purely attribute-based object referencing, an implicit association could be assumed.

**Algorithm 5** Recursively load an object with all its ancestors.

**function** LOADOBJECTWITHANCESTORS($IS_{Ext}^{child}$)
    $IS_{Sim}^{child} \leftarrow$ LOADOBJECT($IS_{Ext}^{child}$) ▷ Algorithm 3
    $IS_{Ext}^{link} \leftarrow$ FINDPARENTLINK($IS_{Ext}^{child}$) ▷ Algorithm 7
    **if** $IS_{Ext}^{link}$ exists **then**
        $IS_{Ext}^{parent} \leftarrow$ parent object at other end of $IS_{Ext}^{link}$
        LOADOBJECTWITHANCESTORS($IS_{Ext}^{parent}$) ▷ recursion
        LOADLINK($IS_{Ext}^{link}$) ▷ Algorithm 6
    **end if**
    **return** $IS_{Sim}^{child}$
**end function**

The helper function described in Algorithm 6 is used to load a link. As previously mentioned, a link is identified by its tuple of end objects. When testing the instance mapping for an already loaded replicate of the link, implicitly this tuple is used as an ID (Identifier). When an identical link is already loaded it is returned. A prerequisite for link loading is that all participating member objects have to be already loaded into SimDB. Therefore, the tuple $t_{Ext}$ of linked objects is retrieved and checked for instance mappings. When all member objects are mapped, i.e., loaded, a new SimDB link is instantiated, registered in the instance mapping, and slots are created for each member end with instance values from the tuple.

In case of binary UML associations, an association's member end may also be an attribute owned by a class that specifies one of the association's end types. Otherwise, it is an owned end of the association. This can be defined independently per member end. In the former case, the target object is added to the source object's slot for the owned attribute.

Algorithm 7 gives a more detailed insight into the search for the necessary parent link at the beginning of Algorithm 5. It iterates over all binary links that have the designated child object as a member. For each such link, it determines the property $Pr_{Ext}^{child}$ used by the association for referencing the child object and checks the metaattribute `isComposite`.

**Algorithm 6** Load an ExtDB link between objects into SimDB.

**function** LOADLINK($IS_{Ext}^{link}$)
  $IS_{Sim}^{link} \leftarrow M_I(IS_{Ext}^{link})$
  **if** $IS_{Sim}^{link}$ exists **then**
    **return** $IS_{Sim}^{link}$
  **end if**
  tuple $t_{Ext} \leftarrow$ member objects of $IS_{Ext}^{link}$
  **if** $\exists\ IS_{Ext} \in t_{Ext} : M_I(IS_{Ext}) =$ undefined **then**
    **return** null
  **end if**
  $As_{Sim} \leftarrow M_I($ classifier of $IS_{Ext}^{link})$
  $IS_{Sim}^{link} \leftarrow$ instantiate $As_{Sim}$
  $M_I(IS_{Ext}^{link}) \leftarrow IS_{Sim}^{link}$
  **for all** $IS_{Sim} \in M_I(t_{Ext})$ **do**
    $Pr_{Sim} \leftarrow$ member end for $IS_{Sim}$
    add new $Sl_{Sim}$ for $Pr_{Sim}$ with instance value for $IS_{Sim}$ to $IS_{Sim}^{link}$
  **end for**
  **if** $As_{Sim}$ is binary **then**
    $IS_{Sim}^{a}, IS_{Sim}^{b} \leftarrow$ member objects of $IS_{Sim}^{link}$
    $Pr_{Sim}^{a}, Pr_{Sim}^{b} \leftarrow$ member ends of $As_{Sim}$
    **if** $Pr_{Sim}^{b}$ is owned attribute of $IS_{Sim}^{a}$'s class **then**
      add $IS_{Sim}^{b}$ to $IS_{Sim}^{a}$'s slot for $Pr_{Sim}^{b}$
    **end if**
    **if** $Pr_{Sim}^{a}$ is owned attribute of $IS_{Sim}^{b}$'s class **then**
      add $IS_{Sim}^{a}$ to $IS_{Sim}^{b}$'s slot for $Pr_{Sim}^{a}$
    **end if**
  **end if**
  **return** $IS_{Sim}^{link}$
**end function**

If it is set to true, the property is a part end of a composite aggregation and thus the link is returned as the current parent link of the child object. If no such link is found, a null is returned.

**Algorithm 7** Find the parent link of a given object.

**function** FINDPARENTLINK($IS_{Ext}^{child}$)
  **for all** binary links $IS_{Ext}^{link}$ with member $IS_{Ext}^{child}$ **do**
    $Pr_{Ext}^{child} \leftarrow$ property of $IS_{Ext}^{link}$'s slot for $IS_{Ext}^{child}$
    **if** $Pr_{Ext}^{child}$ `isComposite` **then** ▷ true for **part** end
      **return** $IS_{Ext}^{link}$
    **end if**
  **end for**
  **return** null
**end function**

#### 5.2.1.2 Interface

The previously introduced methods allow to load given objects from ExtDB. Yet, components of the simulation system have only indirect access to ExtDB's contents via the replicated data in SimDB. Thus, appropriate query mechanisms have to be provided, which must be transparently accessible from the simulation system. Using reflection is a way to provide data access without exposing ExtDB's characteristics. Internal data requests of the simulation system can transparently be formulated in terms of (reified linguistic instances of) SimDB's pseudo metaclasses. In the context of the example from Subsection 4.2.1, such a request could be to load all (ontological) instances of "Satellite", a reified instance of SimDB-`Class`. By applying the schema mapping from the previous level of synchronization, such requests can be translated into corresponding requests in terms of ExtDB's pseudo metaclasses. Algorithm 8 depicts this approach. Furthermore, such requests may also be filtered, e.g., relative to slot values.

**Algorithm 8** Load all objects of a class.

**function** LOADALLOBJECTSOFCLASS($Cl_{Sim}$)
  $Cl_{Ext} \leftarrow M_S^{-1}(Cl_{Sim})$
  **for all** $IS_{Ext}$ with classifier $Cl_{Ext}$ **do**
    LOADOBJECTWITHANCESTORS($IS_{Ext}$) ▷ Algorithm 5
  **end for**
**end function**

Another approach is to load all child objects of a given parent object $IS_{Sim}$ (Algorithm 9). After translating the SimDB object into its ExtDB counterpart, all child links of $IS_{Ext}$ are retrieved from ExtDB using Algorithm 10 and iterated. For each (binary) link, the ExtDB object at the other end is retrieved and loaded using Algorithm 3. Afterwards, the link itself is loaded using Algorithm 6. A more selective variation of this approach is to load only those child objects linked by a specific association (with composite aggregation).

**Algorithm 9** Load all child objects of a given parent object.

**function** LOADALLCHILDOBJECTS($IS_{Sim}$)
  $IS_{Ext} \leftarrow M_I^{-1}(IS_{Sim})$
  **for all** $IS_{Ext}^{link} \in$ FINDALLCHILDLINKS($IS_{Ext}$) **do** ▷ Algorithm 10
    $IS_{Ext}^{child} \leftarrow$ object at other end of $IS_{Ext}^{link}$
    $IS_{Sim}^{child} \leftarrow$ LOADOBJECT($IS_{Ext}^{child}$) ▷ Algorithm 3
    LOADLINK($IS_{Ext}^{link}$) ▷ Algorithm 6
  **end for**
  **return** all loaded $IS_{Sim}^{child}$
**end function**

A non-interface helper function to collect all child links of an object is presented in Algorithm 10. It iterates all links connected to the object, retrieves the property of the other end and checks the metaattribute `isComposite`. If its value is true, the other end – i.e., the end not referencing the given object – is a part end of a composition aggregation. In this case, the link is collected as a child link.

**Algorithm 10** Find all child links connected to a given object.

**function** FINDALLCHILDLINKS($IS_{Ext}^{parent}$)
  **for all** binary links $IS_{Ext}^{link}$ with member $IS_{Ext}^{parent}$ **do**
    $Pr_{Ext}^{child} \leftarrow$ property of $IS_{Ext}^{link}$'s other member end
    **if** $Pr_{Ext}^{child}$ `isComposite` **then**
      add $IS_{Ext}^{link}$ to result
    **end if**
  **end for**
  **return** result
**end function**

Recursively combining the previous approach, a subtree of objects can be loaded. Algorithm 11 gives an overview. It uses Algorithm 9 to recursively load all child objects of a given root object. Here, for a root object given in SimDB, an object subtree defined by composite aggregation is loaded from ExtDB into SimDB including all its descendants. Consistent with previous definitions, a descendant of an object is defined recursively as another object composed by this object itself or one of its descendants. Accordingly, a child is a direct descendant of an object. A variation of the proposed approach is to iterate all leaf objects of the subtree and apply Algorithm 5 to each.

**Algorithm 11** Recursively load a subtree of objects starting at a root object.

**function** LOADOBJECTSUBTREE($IS_{Sim}$)
  **for all** $IS^{child}_{Sim} \in$ LOADALLCHILDOBJECTS($IS_{Sim}$) **do** ▷ Algorithm 9
    LOADOBJECTSUBTREE($IS^{child}_{Sim}$) ▷ recursion
  **end for**
**end function**

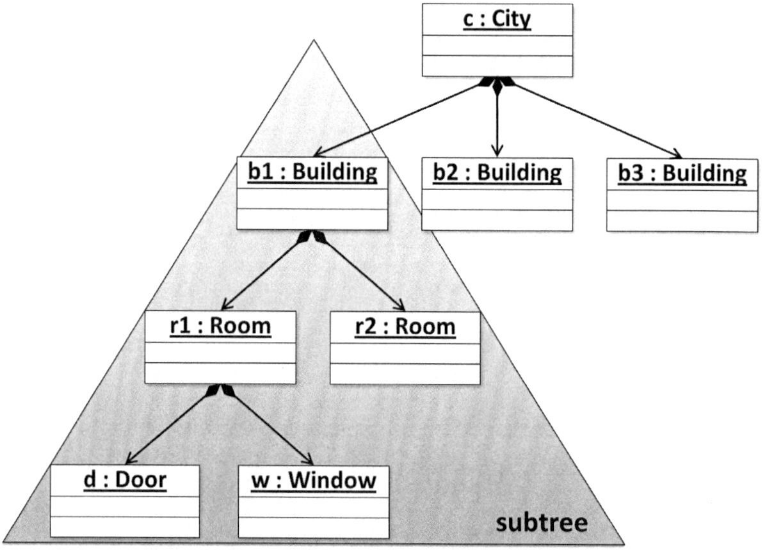


**Figure 5.2:** *Example of hierarchically structured 3D city data.*

An example for a subtree of hierarchically structured 3D city data is given in Figure 5.2. Building `b1` is its root object, the parent of Room `r1` and `r2` and an ancestor of all objects within the subtree (except itself). Door object `d` is a child of `r1` and a descendant of `b1` (and also `r1`). Calling `loadObjectWithAncestors` on `d` loads `d` as well as `r1`, `b1`, and `c` (when not already loaded). A call to `loadObjectSubtree` on `b1` loads the whole subtree starting at `b1`.

Besides associations with composite aggregation, general, $n$-ary links between objects may also be of interest. One possibility for an interface function is a generalization of Algorithm 9 which loads *all* objects connected with *any* link to the given reference object. This can be made more versatile by allowing to filter for links belonging to some given association. In either cases, each link's member objects are retrieved and loaded with their ancestors using Algorithm 5. Note that this iteration will include $IS_{Ext}$ itself but without any further effect. After loading all member objects, the link itself is loaded and connected to all the previously loaded members. Algorithm 12 presents the second variation (i.e., for links of a chosen association) in detail.

---

**Algorithm 12** Load linked objects of a given reference object.

---

**function** LOADLINKEDOBJECTS($IS_{Sim}$,$As_{Sim}$)
    $IS_{Ext} \leftarrow M_I^{-1}(IS_{Sim})$
    $As_{Ext} \leftarrow M_S^{-1}(As_{Sim})$
    **for all** $IS_{Ext}^{link}$ of $As_{Ext}$ with member $IS_{Ext}$ **do**
        **for all** $IS_{Ext}^{member} \in$ member objects of $IS_{Ext}^{link}$ **do**
            LOADOBJECTWITHANCESTORS($IS_{Ext}^{member}$) ▷ Algorithm 5
        **end for**
        LOADLINK($IS_{Ext}^{link}$) ▷ Algorithm 6
    **end for**
**end function**

---

#### 5.2.1.3 General Queries

Using the interface described above, data from ExtDB can be queried transparently from within the simulation system and loaded into SimDB. As described in Chapter 3, this can be called a navigational type of data access (navigation from one object to another). It is particularly well-suited for object-oriented data and thus for 3D simulation. Using reflection, queries like "load all instances of a class" are also possible. Both types of queries can be combined with filters on property values to restrict the number of loaded objects. For example, in spatial streaming presented in Subsection 5.2.3, only objects fulfilling some geometric property shall be loaded. For simple scenarios, such filters can be more or less explicitly integrated into the interface functions. For example, Algorithm 8 could be enhanced by providing a property, a value and an operator (equals, less than ...) to filter instances.

More complex filters and queries require the usage of a query language. In the proposed approach, this can currently be realized by using the native query language of ExtDB within the simulation system. In this scenario, queries are passed through to ExtDB. This, however, limits transparency as details of ExtDB's nature, i.e., the utilized query language, must be revealed to the simulation system. Besides the query language, queries themselves have to be expressed in terms of ExtDB's and not SimDB's schema and structure, also limiting transparency. For systems similar to each other (e.g., the VSD (Versatile Simulation Database)–SGJ (SupportGIS Java [123]) reference implementation presented in Chapter 6), this may not be bothersome. In general, however, a generic approach for mapping between query languages would be desirable. In analogy to the metamodel-based requirements presented in Chapter 4, the mapping may possibly also be formalized using MDE (Model-Driven Engineering) methods. Likewise, a pivotal query language that can operate on UML structures may be advisable for generalized method specifications as well. The OCL (Object Constraint Language [101]) might be a candidate for such a language. A further elaboration of this topic, however, is beyond the scope of this thesis.

### 5.2.2 Change Management

Following the definition in Subsection 3.4.2, the presented scenario (i.e., the combination of SimDB and ExtDB) would be a DDB (Distributed Database). Figure 5.3 depicts a classical DDB structure. Several databases build a virtual database that is transparently accessed via the DDBMS (Distributed Database Management System). In the example, a set of Tree objects is horizontally fragmented, allocated to the different databases and thus partially replicated. Similarly, the presented approach aims at transparency of the distribution. In Figure 5.4, it is depicted correspondingly. However, it is a special case, in which SimDB is a cache for ExtDB. Simulation clients access the shared Semantic World Model only via SimDB. The nature and (for the most part) the existence of ExtDB are hidden away. The master copy of the Semantic World Model is stored in ExtDB. An exception are local changes in a SimDB instance that are not yet synchronized to ExtDB, thus residing only at that client. In contrast, a conventional DDB is accessed as a whole from the outside and the DDBMS hides away its distributive nature.

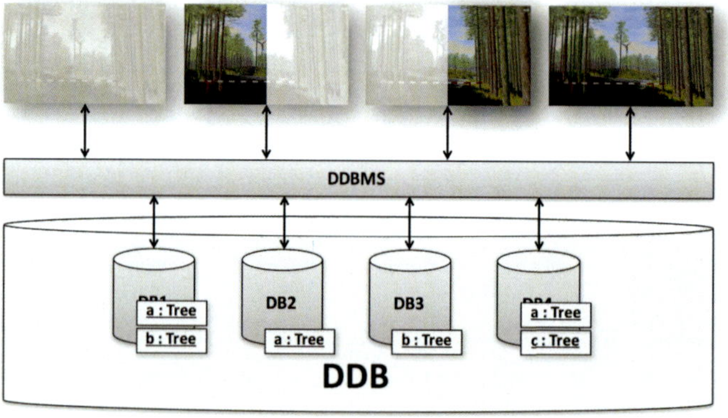


**Figure 5.3:** *Conventional distributed database with a centralized DDBMS.*

Important DDB concepts are fragmentation, allocation and replication, as well as autonomy and heterogeneity. For the presented approach, horizontal fragmentation is used, splitting up object sets (but not objects themselves) between the central ExtDB and the connected SimDBs. All fragments are allocated to ExtDB. Further allocation, i.e., replication, is realized on-demand for the different SimDB instances as shown in the previous sections. Thus, in the example in Figure 5.4, all Tree objects are allocated to ExtDB and

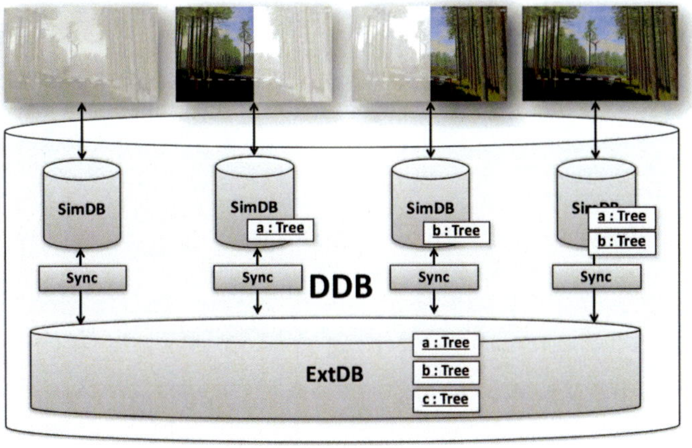


**Figure 5.4:** *The presented approach can also be interpreted as a distributed database consisting of the central ExtDB and several SimDB instances.*

some of them are also allocated (i.e., replicated) to the connected SimDBs. While ExtDB is fully autonomous, SimDB is limited to the schema adopted from ExtDB. As both databases usually are different systems – e.g., SimDB is a runtime database – the assumed DDB is heterogeneous.

One ore more instances of SimDB have a star-shaped connection to one instance of ExtDB. Changes are synchronized independently between each pair of SimDB and ExtDB. In the example in Figure 5.4, there are four SimDBs connected with their respective synchronization component to the central ExtDB. Differences in between such a pair are resynchronized periodically but not synchronously. Thus, we have a similar scenario as described in Subsection 3.4.2 for replication servers with asynchronous replication. However, in contrast to mobile databases, the connection is always kept alive and resynchronization is typically short-term. Furthermore, there is no global transaction or recovery manager. Changes to ExtDB by any client or to SimDB by any client component are committed without control of the synchronization component, which can merely monitor such changes. Thus, following durability (as in ACID (atomicity, consistency, isolation and durability)) they cannot be undone. Durability is important as an online (i.e., live) 3D simulation cannot be reset in the middle of a run.

One way to treat concurrent changes is an active concurrency control using locks. For distributed concurrency control, one approach is to choose a so-called distinguished copy, which holds a representative lock for all its replicate copies as shown in Subsection 3.4.2. In our case, the master copies in ExtDB could be adopted for this purpose as they are shared among all clients. However, locking is not recommendable here as acquiring locks would be time-consuming (as an ExtDB access would be necessary each time) and possible deadlocks may interrupt a running simulation.

Therefore, a lock-free approach using notifications was developed. For each pair of SimDB and ExtDB, the mechanism monitors changes by listening to the notifications. For resynchronization, it schedules transactions of the respective database. Due to the monitoring approach, they can only comprise a single data operation. The approach is somewhat similar to optimistic concurrency control (see Subsection 3.4.1). However, transactions cannot be rolled back when changes are conflicting. Instead, conflicts are only implicitly resolved: The last client changing a value is given precedence. Altogether, it is crucial that the synchronization component always knows about the state of synchronization for each copy. However, besides resynchronization and passive monitoring, the mechanism cannot and must not intervene, e.g., by rejecting changes as mentioned above.

#### 5.2.2.1 Change Tracking

For each pair of SimDB and ExtDB, a change tracking component connects to the notification services of SimDB for so-called *internal* notifications and of ExtDB for so-called *external* notifications. Notifications include insertions and removals of objects and links, as well as updates of object properties. A link between objects can only be removed or inserted but not updated, as its identity is only derived from the connected objects (and the corresponding association on schema level).

For the sake of simplicity, external notifications from ExtDB are abbreviated as extInsert, extUpdate, and extRemove, internal notifications from SimDB as simInsert, simUpdate, and simRemove, accordingly (Table 5.1).

**Table 5.1:** *Types and abbreviations of notifications from SimDB and ExtDB.*

| | internal (SimDB) | external (ExtDB) |
|---|---|---|
| property update | simUpdate | extUpdate |
| instance insertion | simInsert | extInsert |
| instance removal | simRemove | extRemove |

During runtime, these notifications are evaluated. Depending on the current state of the corresponding pair of master and replicate copy represented by an instance mapping entry, a transaction may be scheduled that can later be used to resynchronize the detected change from the one to the other database. A scheduled transaction comprises one data operation with its kind (insert, remove, or update), the affected instance (object or link) or its ID, and for updates the affected property. Table 5.2 gives an overview of the utilized transactions and their abbreviations. A transaction for transferring a change from SimDB to ExtDB is called an *out-bound* transaction and will be abbreviated with the prefix *sim2ext*. For example, when detecting an object insertion within SimDB by a simInsert notification, a new sim2extInsert out-bound transaction may be scheduled. Its (future) execution will insert an equivalent object of the corresponding ExtDB-`Classifier` (using the schema mapping) into ExtDB. Here, the current property values are retrieved from the SimDB object's slots and are replicated for the new ExtDB object. Finally, the new object complements the corresponding instance mapping entry with its identifier. This can be seen as the complementing operation to the loading of objects. Links are treated accordingly but without the need for property value replication. An instance's removal (object or link) from SimDB, notified by a simRemove notification, may lead to a sim2extRemove transaction whose (future) execution will remove the associated ExtDB instance. A simUpdate notification signals the change of a SimDB object's property and may be scheduled as a sim2extUpdate transaction to transmit the value change from SimDB to ExtDB. Similar to sim2extInsert transactions, a sim2extUpdate transaction's execution retrieves the current value of its corresponding property from SimDB and replicates it to ExtDB.

**Table 5.2:** *Types and abbreviations of transactions between SimDB and ExtDB.*

| | out-bound (SimDB → ExtDB) | in-bound (ExtDB → SimDB) |
|---|---|---|
| property update | sim2extUpdate | ext2simUpdate |
| instance insertion | sim2extInsert | ext2simInsert |
| instance removal | sim2extRemove | ext2simRemove |

Accordingly, external notifications may lead to the scheduling of *in-bound* transactions for resynchronizing global changes from ExtDB to SimDB. They are prefixed by *ext2sim*: ext2simInsert, ext2simRemove, and ext2simUpdate. Responses to external notifications are mostly identical to their internal counterparts. However, due to the nature of SimDB being a cache for ExtDB, a variation applies when treating external insertions. New objects or links within ExtDB may be handled by different strategies. They may be ignored or subsequently taken into account by a loading transaction (ext2simInsert).

Figures 5.5–5.8 show the basic idea of the notification-based distributed synchronization using an example with a central ExtDB and two SimDB clients. A tree object is replicated to two simulation databases. One client changes the tree's state (i.e., fells it) indicated by a notification. The change is synchronized to the central database where another notification is issued. The latter causes another synchronization of the change to the second client.

Altogether, instance mapping entries (i.e., pairs of master and replicate copy) can be seen as to reside in a certain state of synchronization. Some examples are given in Figure 5.9: An object `a:Tree` may exist in the central ExtDB without being loaded (i.e., replicated) to SimDB (i.e., no mapping exists), a replicated object `b:Tree` may be unchanged (in sync), an object `c:Tree` may only exist in SimDB (a transaction for its insertion in ExtDB is pending), a previously replicated object `d:Tree` may be deleted in SimDB (a transaction

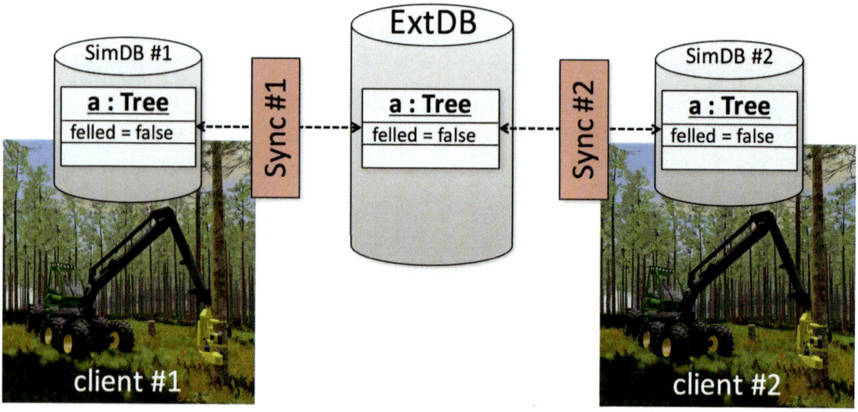


**Figure 5.5:** *1st step: Initial situation of a distributed synchronization example: all databases in sync.*

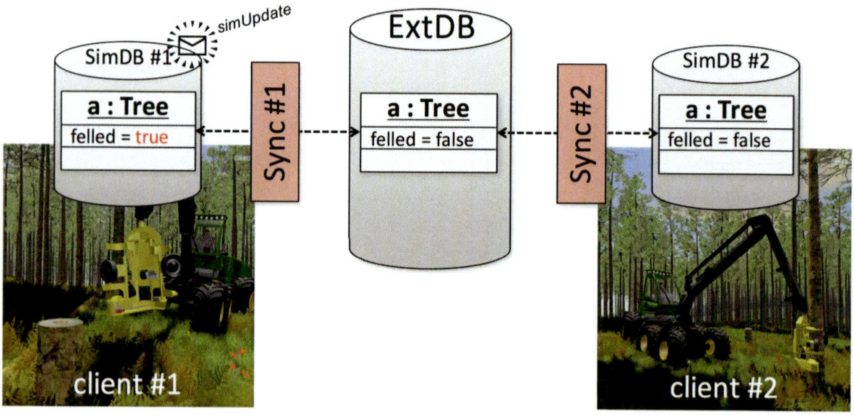


**Figure 5.6:** *2nd step: Client #1 changes the tree's state; its SimDB issues a simUpdate notification.*

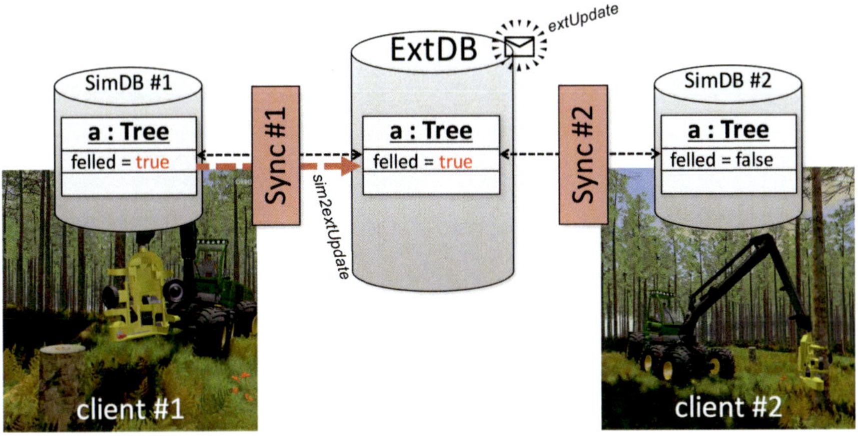


**Figure 5.7:** *3rd step: Sync component #1 responds using an out-bound sim2extUpdate transaction to synchronize the change to ExtDB, which in turn issues an extUpdate notification.*

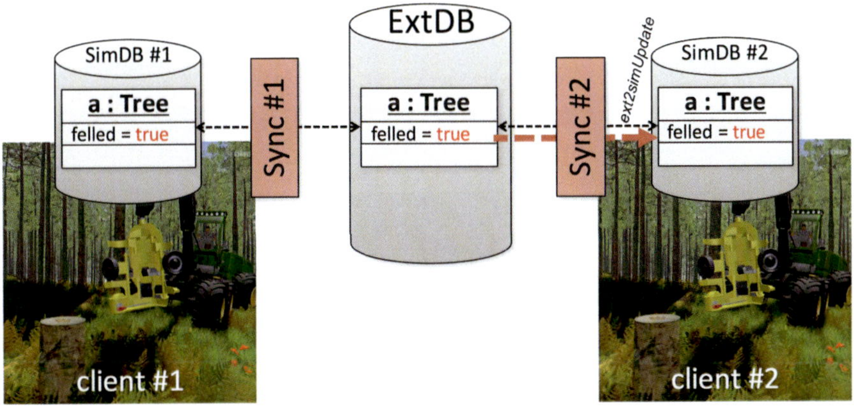


**Figure 5.8:** *4th step: Sync component #2 uses an in-bound ext2simUpdate transaction to adopt the change from ExtDB to SimDB #2.*

for its deletion within ExtDB is pending), or a replicated object `e:Tree`'s property may be changed within SimDB (a transaction for synchronization to ExtDB is pending).

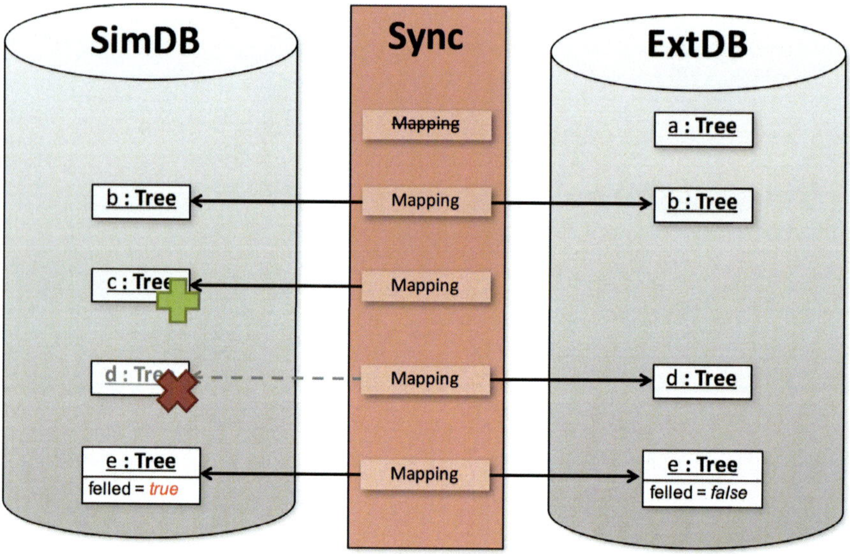


**Figure 5.9:** *Exemplary mapping states between pairs of master and replicate copy.*

This can be modeled as a state machine in statechart notation [124] for each object's or link's instance mapping entry. For objects, this state machine is given in Figure 5.10, for links in Figure 5.11. It may be in a synchronous state (*Synced*), a *Loading* or *Unloading* state, a state representing its absence or non-management (*NonManaged*), or a state of pending transaction (*ext2simInsertPending*, *ext2simRemovePending*, etc.). For update transactions, the synchronization states of an object's properties are concurrently modeled in the sub states of state UpdatesPending shown in Figure 5.13.

In these state machines, events comprise internal and external notifications, as well as some management events for object loading and unloading, failure thereof, and update completion. To simplify the state machine diagrams, any event undefined for a state shall trigger a transition to an omitted error state. Notification events are also implicitly filtered based on the related instance to match the considered instance mapping. That is, the state machine for a certain instance mapping will only receive notifications for the corresponding instances from ExtDB or SimDB. Note that transitions depicted with italic text are special conditions dealt with in the Subsection 5.2.2.2.

An exemplary chain of events depicted in Figure 5.12 would be the insertion of a new tree object into SimDB leading to a transition guarded by simInsert from the initial state NonManaged to state sim2extInsertPending. Here, a sim2extInsert transaction is scheduled

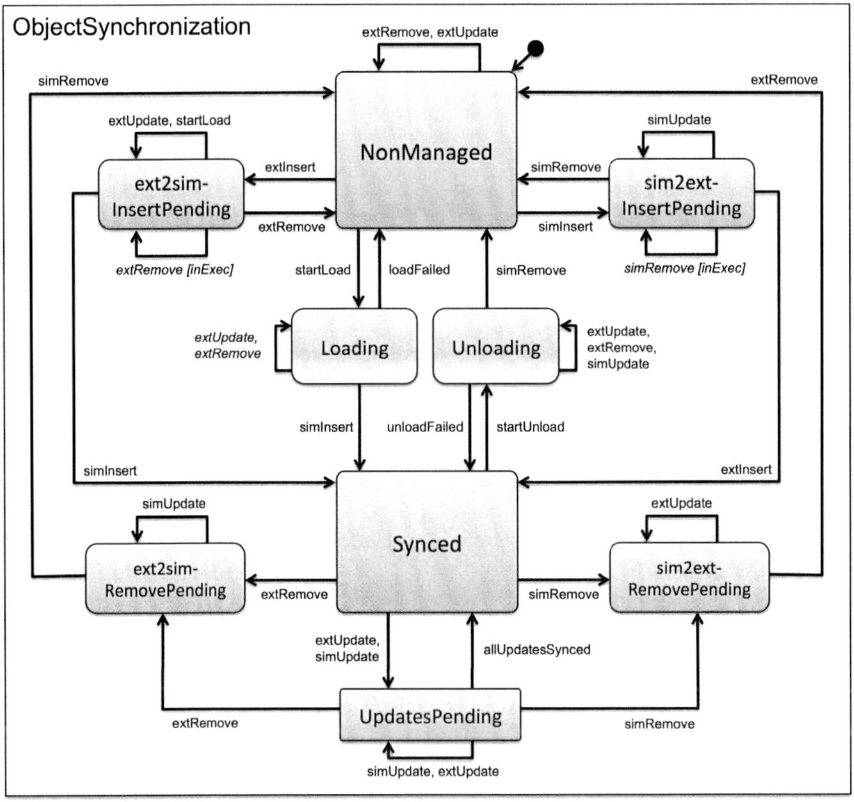


**Figure 5.10:** *Synchronization states of an object's instance mapping.*

for the new object. When the transaction is executed (see Subsection 5.2.2.3), an equivalent object is inserted into ExtDB eventually causing the database to issue an extInsert notification. In turn, this event triggers a transition from the sim2extInsertPending to the Synced state. Thus, the extInsert event confirms the insertion into ExtDB and is used as a receipt to acknowledge a transaction's successful execution. This is especially useful for handling concurrent changes within SimDB and ExtDB occurring during other transaction's execution as will be shown later.

The receipt handling mechanism is also used to handle mutual changes that cancel each other out. An example are mutual removals: If an instance is first removed from ExtDB and subsequently from SimDB by independent processes, a previously scheduled ext2simRemove transaction with pending execution (in state ext2simRemovePending) is canceled out by the incoming simRemove notification for the same instance. The event causes a transition to the NonManaged state.

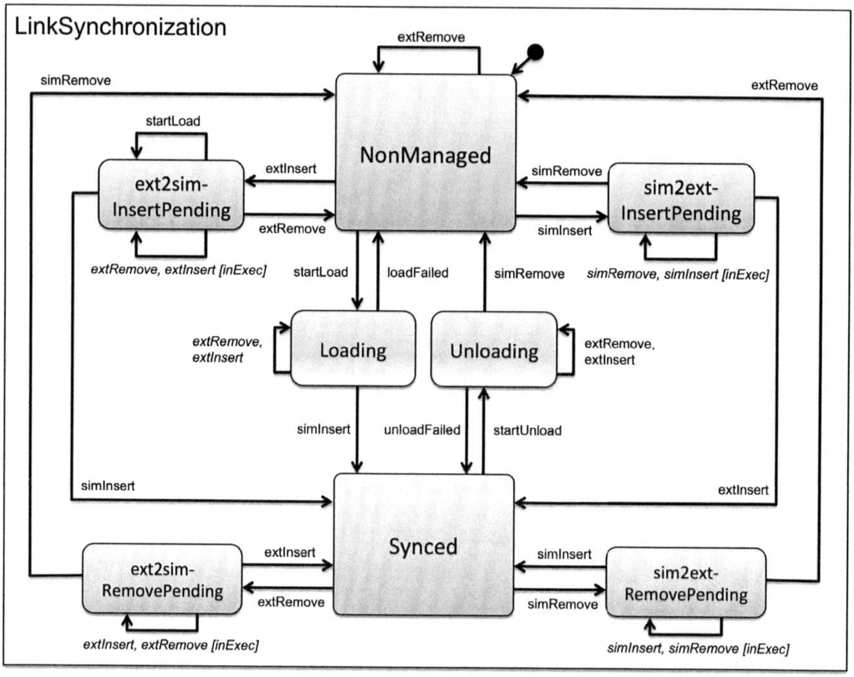


**Figure 5.11:** *Synchronization states of a link's instance mapping.*

The same effect can be observed for the insertion of links. As before, links identify only by their member objects. In contrast to objects, they can be inserted identically but independently into both databases. In the state machine for links, this is represented by a transition from, e.g., sim2extInsertPending to Synced triggered by an extInsert for the identical link without having executed the scheduled transaction.

The state machines for objects and links are very similar. The latter allows an additional transition from the pending remove states back to the Synced state. In contrast to objects, an identical link can be reinserted after its removal. The former includes an additional update management for objects. The UpdatesPending state encapsulates a sub state structure for managing property updates (Figure 5.13). Primarily, it contains a super state UpdatesPr with concurrent regions for each of the object's properties, e.g., region UpdatesPr$_i$ for the object's $i^{th}$ property. A region for `Property` $Pr_i$ has three states representing an unchanged property value (SyncedPr$_i$), a property value changed within SimDB (sim2extUpdatePendingPr$_i$), and a property value changed within ExtDB (ext2simUpdatePendingPr$_i$). Internal transitions are triggered by update notifications (simUpdate and extUpdate) filtered for the corresponding property. To simplify modeling, the update event that caused the transition to UpdatesPending shall be repeated

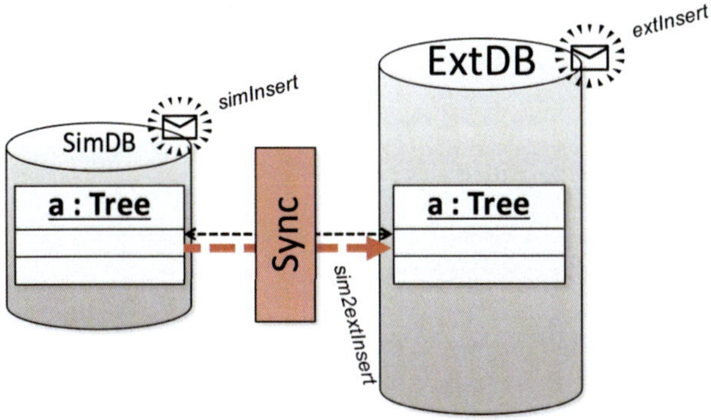


**Figure 5.12:** *Exemplary insertion of a tree object into SimDB and subsequent synchronization to ExtDB using a sim2extInsert transaction.*

to initially activate the appropriate sub state, e.g., activate sim2extUpdatePending$\text{Pr}_i$ by repeating a simUpdate event. Further updates to the object's value for $Pr_i$ can be ignored when they stem from the same database (i.e., both SimDB or both ExtDB). For example, in state ext2simUpdatePending$\text{Pr}_i$, further extUpdate notifications for $Pr_i$ can be ignored as the new value has to be transferred to SimDB, anyway. However, a subsequent update to the same property from within SimDB causes a change conflict (see Subsection 5.2.2.2). The modeled strategy is to give precedence to the more recently notified change. Thus, a transition to sim2extUpdatePending$\text{Pr}_i$ is triggered. When the transaction implicitly scheduled on entering one of the update states is executed, a notification is needed as a receipt. However, in contrast to insert or remove transactions, there is no "natural" counterpart for update transactions. An executed ext2simUpdate transaction causes a simUpdate notification that is indistinguishable from any other third party change. Thus, before execution, an "inExec" flag is set. For ext2simUpdate, the next simUpdate notification for $Pr_i$ will trigger a transition back to the synced state of this property (the inExec flag will be reset). When all concurrent regions are in their respective synced state, a synchronized (in terms of concurrency) transition to the Done state is triggered (modeled by the vertical bar). On entering this state, the allUpdatesSynced event is raised triggering a transition from the super state UpdatesPending to the Synced state (see Figure 5.10).

In some situations, events may also be ignored. Within the state machines, this may be modeled as self-transitions. For example, in sim2extRemovePending, further extUpdate events from ExtDB can be ignored as the corresponding object will be removed from ExtDB, anyway. The same applies to pending insertions as property values will be replicated on execution time. For a pending ext2simInsert, the startLoad event has to be ignored, which will be emitted by the loading process used by the transaction. For non-managed instances within ExtDB, remove and update notifications can be ignored as they are of no interest

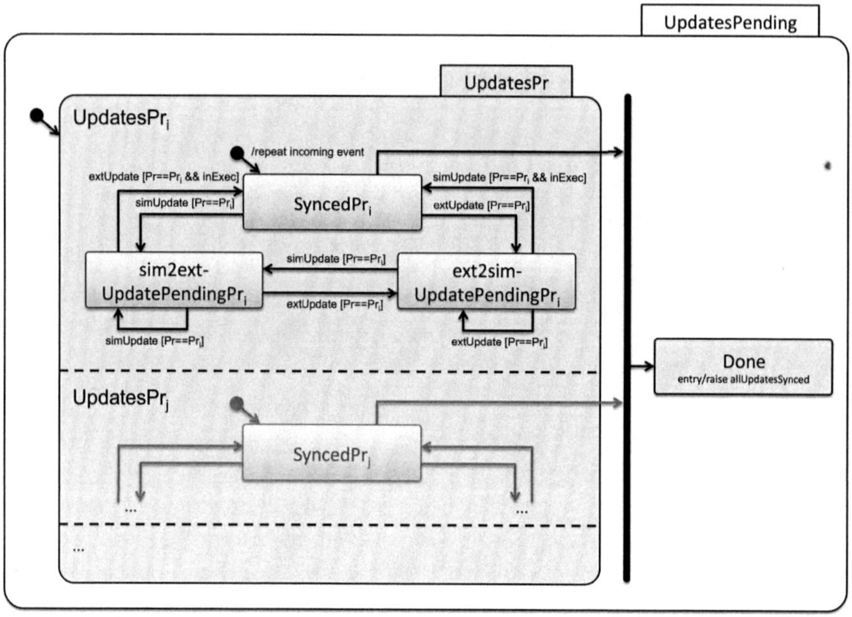


**Figure 5.13:** *Sub structure of state UpdatesPending from Figure 5.10 for property updates.*

to SimDB. Note that the sub regions in Figure 5.13 do not explicitly model ignored update events for properties $Pr \neq Pr_i$. Nevertheless, they shall be ignored and not cause a default transition to the omitted error state.

Besides change tracking, both state machines also contain states for the loading and unloading of objects or links. To announce a currently non-managed instance's loading, the methods presented in Subsection 5.2.1 shall raise an additional startLoading event. The instance remains in the Loading state either until its insertion into SimDB is acknowledged by an appropriate simUpdate receipt event or until the load process fails. Accordingly, before unloading a synchronized instance, a startUnload event shall be raised and the Unloading state is activated. Reaching this state, subsequent changes to the instance are ignored and consequently get lost. A simRemove notification serves as a receipt to acknowledge the unloading process and triggers a transition to the NonManaged state. Failing this, an unloadFailed event is raised to return to the Synced state.

#### 5.2.2.2 Change-Conflict Handling

As mentioned above, changes (insertions, removals, and updates) from ExtDB and SimDB may conflict when they occur to the same instance (and property) before executing the corresponding transaction. For example, in a city scenario, a building's street number is locally changed within SimDB causing a sim2extUpdate transaction. Before this change is made persistent and globally available within ExtDB by executing the transaction in a resynchronization run, the very same number is changed within ExtDB (e.g., by another simulation client). Following the strategy modeled above, the previously pending sim2extUpdate is omitted and instead a new ext2simUpdate transaction is stored.

In general, different strategies exist to handle such conflicts. First of all, conflicts can be avoided beforehand by giving only mutual exclusive write access to instances. This approach could be used in distributed simulation scenarios where separate objects are simulated by different clients without interaction. This can be managed by a superordinate simulation control. Avoiding the occurrence of conflicts could also be realized by explicitly locking changed instances or their property value in the respective other database. However, this may stall or even reset a simulation run as mentioned above.

Thus, a monitoring (i.e., reactive) handling of change conflicts as mentioned above is inevitable. The presented methods' strategy is embedded in the given state machines. For change conflicts, two scenarios can be distinguished: A conflict may either occur *before* or *during* a transaction's execution. Before executing a transaction, conflict handling can be realized straightforward. It is modeled with simple transitions within the state machines. One example is the precedence for more recently notified updates as shown above. Another strategy is that object removals are final and thus "always win". That is, a pending remove transaction for an object precedes all update events for the object. For pending object insertions, conflicts cannot occur as the corresponding object does not exist in the respective other database. In the context of links, the behavior slightly differs. Again, as a link identifies only by the objects it connects, one and the same link can be independently inserted and removed from both databases. Here, the same strategy as for the update of an object's property value applies: the more recently notified change precedes previous changes.

As long as a transaction is still pending, incoming events can always be processed by state transitions to reflect the relation between SimDB and ExtDB. In a resynchronization run, the current state of each state machine is evaluated (see Subsection 5.2.2.3). If a state with pending transaction $T1$ is determined $T1$ is executed. However, this decision is made independently at each client. A notification from a previously committed, conflicting transaction $T2$ may arrive just after $T1$'s execution is started. In some cases, $T1$ may still be abortable. But the notification may just as well arrive when $T1$ commits. So, while native transactions of the utilized DBMSs (Database Management Systems) themselves are usually isolated the decision to start a pending transaction is not. This limits transaction isolation (i.e., ACID properties) in the distributed system.

The same applies to the reading of property values. Objects can be removed, and links can be removed and inserted based only on the information from the corresponding notification. For object insertions and property updates, however, the current state of the respective source database has to be retrieved as notifications themselves do not contain the corresponding values. Thus, when such a transaction is executed the source values may have already been changed by subsequent transactions whose notifications may either have not yet arrived or transaction execution may already have started as described above. This also limits transaction isolation.

Thus, a strategy had to be found for dealing with such situations. Otherwise, scenarios where a change in one database is neither reflected within the other database nor within the instance mapping's state machine may occur. For example, a property value is changed in ExtDB, but its instance mapping's state machine is in state Synced although SimDB still holds the previous value.

The primary instrument to handle such interfering changes is the aforementioned usage of notifications as receipts. For that purpose, they must have the following features:

1. A notification's arrival guarantees the corresponding operation to be executed, i.e., committed.
2. The order of arrival of a single database's notifications is identical to the execution order (commit order) of the corresponding operations.
3. Between one running instance of SimDB and ExtDB there is at most one transaction being executed at a time (see Subsection 5.2.2.3).

Based only on these assumptions, a conflict management can be stable. However, one should keep in mind:

1. A notification not yet received does not imply that the corresponding operation is not yet executed (notifications may be delayed).
2. On arrival of a notification, the *current* state within the database must not be consulted for further state transitions. By time of arrival it may already have been changed several times.
3. The order of arrival between notifications from ExtDB and notifications from SimDB is arbitrary.

Based on these considerations, a special event handling can be implemented to process the queued events after a transaction's execution. As stated above, the main problem are notifications arriving between the start of a transaction's execution and the arrival of the corresponding receipt notification. For a proper event handling, these events must sometimes be reordered. To be precise, they are captured and reinserted into the event queue just after the receipt event. This ensures their correct processing in terms of state transitions. The procedure is necessary for object or link insertions, link removals, object updates, and object or link loading. In the state machines, transitions with italic text particularly model this case.

In the sub states of UpdatesPending, this highlighting is omitted as the same transitions are needed for standard and for this special event handling.

One example are updates (Figure 5.13). A property's update transaction can be examined separately as updates of different properties are independent of each other. Table 5.3 lists an exemplary sequence of events for some integer property and the associated actions, state machine states, values in SimDB and ExtDB, and emitted notifications. In the example, the local property's slot value in SimDB is updated several times even while changes are replicated to ExtDB. Notifications are used to ensure that all updates are reflected within the state machine's current state.

Initially (step #1), SimDB and ExtDB are in sync at value 10. The value in SimDB is changed to 20 (#2) and the corresponding simUpdate notification (a) triggers a state machine transition (#3). At some point in time, the client starts the resynchronization process (#4). Then, a first interfering update (#5) changes the value to 30. As property update notifications do not contain a value it must be retrieved from the respective database at transaction execution time (#6). Afterwards, a second interfering update (#7) changes the value to 40. In #8, the read value 30 is replicated to ExtDB. As mentioned above, the order in which notifications from SimDB and ExtDB are received is arbitrary. Thus, notifications simUpdate (a) and (b) may be processed first (#9, #10). As the "inExec" flag is set, all notifications are stored (instead of ignored without the "inExec" flag being set) until the corresponding receipt notification extUpdate is processed in #11. Subsequently, the flag is reset and both stored notifications are reinserted into the event queue. While the receipt notification eventually yields a transition back to the Synced state (#12), notification reinsertion causes the necessary transition back to the state of pending updates (#13) to replicate the value of 40 from SimDB to ExtDB. The additional simUpdate notification (c) only yields a self-transition (#14) as an update is already pending. Another resynchronization run would replicate the value to ExtDB starting at #15.

This approach to capture and reinsert notifications is needed as it is unknown whether an interfering update was done before (#5) or after (#7) reading the current value from SimDB in #6 to execute the sim2extUpdate transaction in #8. Note that when only interfering updates of the first type occur, the additional simUpdate notifications are in fact redundant. However, this is acceptable to guarantee that no updates are lost between SimDB and ExtDB. In case of interfering updates from other clients to ExtDB, additional extUpdate (instead of simUpdate) notifications are emitted. Here, notifications need not be stored as the first extUpdate notification is simply interpreted as the expected receipt and subsequent extUpdates yield normal state transitions. Finally, the same store-and-reinsert strategy is used similarly in the other use cases mentioned above (object insertions, link removals, and object or link loading).

Another example is a pending link insertion from SimDB to ExtDB (sim2extInsertPending) in Figure 5.11. After starting the transaction's execution, the link may concurrently be

**Table 5.3:** *Example of a local interfering update of some integer property within a single SimDB.*

| # | action | state machine | SimDB val. | ExtDB val. | notification |
|---|---|---|---|---|---|
| 1 | (initial state) | Synced | 10 | 10 | |
| 2 | update 10 → 20 in SimDB | | 20 | | simUpdate (a) |
| 3 | process event simUpdate (a) | → UpdatesPending / sim2extUpdatePending$Pr_i$ | | | |
| 4 | start resync | inExec := true | | | |
| 5 | update 20 → 30 in SimDB (1st interference) | | 30 | | simUpdate (b) |
| 6 | read current value from SimDB | | | | |
| 7 | update 30 → 40 in SimDB (2nd interference) | | 40 | | simUpdate (c) |
| 8 | execute transaction sim2extUpdate | | | 30 | extUpdate |
| 9 | process event simUpdate (b) | [inExec=true] ⇒ store simUpdate (b) | | | |
| 10 | process event simUpdate (c) | [inExec=true] ⇒ store simUpdate (c) | | | |
| 11 | process event extUpdate | → UpdatesPending / Synced$Pr_i$ → Done<br>inExec := false<br>reinsert simUpdate (b) in event queue<br>reinsert simUpdate (c) in event queue | | | allUpdatesSynced |
| 12 | process event allUpdatesSynced | → Synced | | | |
| 13 | process event simUpdate (b) | → UpdatesPending / ext2simUpdatePending$Pr_i$ | | | |
| 14 | process event simUpdate (c) | (self-transition) | | | |
| 15 | start resync ... | ... | | | |

removed and reinserted into SimDB several times by different components of the simulation system. It may also be inserted into ExtDB from a third party client. In this case, sim2extInsert's execution will have no further effect. Subsequently, the link may even be removed and reinserted again within ExtDB. However, after the execution process, all corresponding (possibly queued) events are processed until the receipt arrives. As the first extInsert notification is the receipt, no other extInsert and thus no extRemove notification can precede it. Hence, only simRemove and simInsert events have to be captured. They represent the current state of the link within SimDB. When the extInsert event arrives, these captured SimDB notifications are reinserted into the state machine's event queue just after the extInsert receipt. After the extInsert triggers a transition to the Synced state, the reinserted notification events are processed regularly. Note that it is irrelevant whether the link insertion in ExtDB actually originates from the successful execution of the sim2extInsert transaction or from a third party's operation. In both cases, the link is established and an extInsert notification is emitted.

Regarding change tracking and conflicts, dependencies between different operations could also be a problem. Inserting an object usually also causes a parent link's insertion and removing an object causes a removal of all corresponding links and all (hierarchically) descendant objects. However, all these operations – dependent or not – cause the same kind of notifications and all interdependencies are resolved by the respective database itself. Thus, such dependent changes can be treated by the standard mechanisms and need no special handling.

Altogether, as mentioned above, this approach cannot avoid or fix conflicts but only detect them and react on them. However, the utilized SimDB and ExtDB themselves are not corrupted as they provide safe standard database access methods. Thus, only the distributed synchronization state must be kept free of corruptions. This is ensured by the presented approach.

#### 5.2.2.3 Resynchronization

In resynchronization, all scheduled transactions are executed to bring the two databases back in sync. This process can be triggered in several ways. When the approach is applied in a collaborative scenario, it can be initiated manually. For immediate response from and to other users, it can also be automatically triggered after each transition to a state with pending transaction. In distributed simulation, typical access patterns include constantly repeated changes of the same few property values, e.g., a moving car and a moving helicopter. In such scenarios, transactions can be aggregated within short but arbitrary periods to lower the impact on traffic. However, this includes a trade-off between traffic and update rate.

Transactions are processed in groups of the same type to gain advantage from dependencies and optimize execution performance. An overview is given in the list below.

1. ext2simRemove and sim2extRemove for objects (in reverse order of occurrence)
2. ext2simInsert and sim2extInsert for objects
3. ext2simChange and sim2extChange (for objects)
4. ext2simRemove and sim2extRemove for links
5. ext2simInsert and sim2extInsert for links

At first, all ext2simRemove and sim2extRemove transactions for objects are executed to remove deprecated objects. As an optimization measure, this is done in reversed order of occurrence of the corresponding notifications. System requirements for the notification services specify the removal of object subtrees to be notified in bottom-up order (see Subsection 4.2.3). Additionally, subtrees may be removed manually in terms of further subtrees piece by piece. Thus, the transaction for a removal of the ExtDB root object of a completely removed subtree will always be preceded by all its descendant objects. Processing transactions in reversed order, the corresponding root object within SimDB will be deleted first and its instance mapping entry is removed. Due to the semantics of composite aggregation, this deletion will recursively delete all SimDB descendant objects in one operation (typically optimized by SimDB). Pending ext2simRemove transactions for descendant objects receive a notification for the removal of their target object, which serves as a receipt triggering a transition to the NonManaged state.

Next, all ext2simInsert and sim2extInsert transactions for object insertions are processed. For each ext2simInsert, the standard loading mechanism is used, including replicating current property values from the corresponding slots. Loading an object also includes loading all the object's ancestors to provide parent-child-relations within SimDB. Upon their loading, a startLoad event will be emitted to provoke a transition into the Loading state (for objects and parent links). Only for the object to be inserted itself and its parent link this event will be ignored. sim2extInsert transactions for objects make new objects globally available within ExtDB. The necessary operations can be seen as the counterpart to the loading operations.

Performing all object removals and insertions first assures further link operations are executed optimally. Beforehand, all ext2simUpdate and sim2extUpdate transactions are executed applying the current property values from ExtDB to SimDB and vice versa. In the next step, links are removed from SimDB and ExtDB by executing all corresponding ext2simRemove and sim2extRemove transactions. As with dependent object removals, each link already removed receives a receipt notification causing a transition to the NonManaged state. All remaining pending link removals are executed normally.

Finally, all ext2simInsert and sim2extInsert transactions are executed. The former are treated like their counterparts for objects by loading the corresponding link into SimDB using standard mechanisms (see Subsection 5.2.1). For parent links previously inserted in conjunction with an object insertion, receipt notifications may already have triggered a transition to the Synced state. As with link removals, all other link insertions are executed normally. When a designated link lacks a member object within the target database, the transaction will (detectably) fail to execute, reset the inExec flag, and stay in pending state. This may occur although object insertions are executed before link insertions. For example, an object and a link may be inserted while the resynchronization process has already executed all other object insertions. Likewise, a member object may be removed in the target database. However, the next resynchronization cycle will take care of this.

### 5.2.3 Data Unloading and Streaming

Besides loading instance data it can also be unloaded. Unloading an instance denotes its controlled removal from SimDB to reduce the amount of memory occupied during runtime. For objects, this removal includes all descendant objects and the corresponding links. Unloading a parent link is identical to unloading the child object (and its descendants). Unloading any other link just unloads the link itself.

A prerequisite for unloading an instance from SimDB is the absence of pending out-bound (sim2ext) transactions. In this case, the SimDB instance is called *clean*. Otherwise, it cannot be unloaded as the corresponding changes would be lost. In-bound transactions can be ignored as global changes are only of interest if the related data is still loaded. Thus, an instance does not have to be entirely synced before being unloaded. All corresponding descendant objects must not have out-bound transactions as well. They cannot be unloaded themselves and without their ancestor their connection to their subtree of composite aggregations is broken. For example in Figure 5.2, if Room `r1` was to be unloaded, Door `d`, Window `w` and `r1` itself must be without pending out-bound transactions. The same applies to dependent links connected to the object or its descendants. Likewise, they can only be safely removed from SimDB when they are clean.

Algorithm 13 illustrates a depth-first search to check a subtree rooted at object $IS_{Sim}$ with parent link $IS_{Sim}^{plink}$ for the prerequisites mentioned above. $IS_{Sim}$ is considered *recursively clean* when all its child objects are recursively clean and its parent link, all its non-composite links, and itself are clean. While checking this, the algorithm collects all recursively clean objects and their respective parent and non-composite links in the set $S_{clean}$. Note that links already removed within SimDB with a pending sim2extRemove transaction do not have to be checked. They can be handled independently from their (previous) member objects.

Algorithm 14 implements a strategy to remove a recursively clean subtree from SimDB. If Algorithm 13 determines the subtree to be completely clean, the startUnload event is raised for each instance in the subtree (from $S_{clean}$) to prepare the unloading process of the respective instance. Afterwards, the subtree's root object is removed from SimDB, which includes the removal of all descendants and their links. Note that to simplify matters the startUnload event – although omitted from Figures 5.10–5.13 – shall also trigger transitions from all states with pending in-bound transactions (ext2simRemovePending, ext2simInsertPending, ext2simUpdatePr$_i$).

**Algorithm 13** Check if an object can be unloaded: Recursive search for out-bound transactions.

**function** SUBTREECANBEUNLOADED($IS_{Sim}$, $IS_{Sim}^{plink}$, $S_{clean}$)
  $ok \leftarrow true$
  **for all** $IS_{Sim}^{link} \neq IS_{Sim}^{plink}$ with member $IS_{Sim}$ **do**
    **if** $IS_{Sim}^{link}$ is child link **then**
      $IS_{Sim}^{child} \leftarrow$ object at other end of $IS_{Sim}^{link}$
      **if** not SUBTREECANBEUNLOADED($IS_{Sim}^{child}$,$IS_{Sim}^{link}$,$S_{clean}$) **then**
        $ok \leftarrow false$
      **end if**
    **else**
      **if** $IS_{Sim}^{link}$ has out-bound transaction **then**
        $ok \leftarrow false$
      **else**
        add $IS_{Sim}^{link}$ to $S_{clean}^{link}$
      **end if**
    **end if**
  **end for**
  **if** $ok$ and ($IS_{Sim}$ and $IS_{Sim}^{plink}$ have no out-bound transaction) **then**
    add $IS_{Sim}$, $IS_{Sim}^{plink}$ to $S_{clean}$
    $S_{clean} \leftarrow S_{clean} \bigcup S_{clean}^{link}$
    **return** true
  **else**
    **return** false
  **end if**
**end function**

**Algorithm 14** Unload a whole subtree.

```
function UNLOADSUBTREE(IS_Sim)
    S_clean ← ∅
    IS_Sim^plink ← parent link of IS_Sim
    ok ← SUBTREECANBEUNLOADED(IS_Sim, IS_Sim^plink, S_clean)
    if not ok then                                            ▷ Algorithm 13
        return
    end if
    for all IS_Sim^clean ∈ S_clean do
        raise event startUnload(IS_Sim^clean)
    end for
    remove IS_Sim
end function
```

A variation of this approach is given in Algorithm 15. Here, the subtree is pruned, i.e., all recursively clean sub subtrees are unloaded to free as much space as currently possible. Algorithm 13 is used to determine all recursively clean instances. In a pre-run, the startUnload event is raised for all these instances before removing them from SimDB in a second run.

**Algorithm 15** Unload a subtree with pruning.

```
function UNLOADPRUNESUBTREE(IS_Sim)
    IS_Sim^plink ← parent link of IS_Sim
    SUBTREECANBEUNLOADED(IS_Sim, IS_Sim^plink, S_clean)       ▷ Algorithm 13
    for all IS_Sim^clean ∈ S_clean do
        raise event startUnload(IS_Sim^clean)
    end for
    for all IS_Sim^clean ∈ S_clean do
        remove IS_Sim
    end for
end function
```

Based upon loading and unloading, streaming strategies can be realized. They allow the simulation system to access huge data sets stored within ExtDB piece by piece, i.e., of which only parts are needed at a time within SimDB. These instance sets are usually determined by applying a filter on a property and varying its parameters. Below, three types of streaming are presented: spatial streaming, hierarchical streaming and streaming for data processing.

To move through a huge virtual environmental model like a city or a forest model, a spatial filter can be used to select only those buildings around a user's current position. If he moves, previously loaded sets of buildings can be unloaded and new sets can be loaded, based on the new position. Thus, this is a *spatial streaming* approach. A simple approach to discretize data management in such scenarios with movement over a 2D surface is to use a filter based on bounding rectangles. The area is uniformly subdivided into tiles (squares). For each tile the user approaches, all objects are loaded and logically associated with the tile. Objects may be associated to several of these tiles, depending on their geometric features. Nevertheless, they will only be loaded once into SimDB (see exit condition in Algorithm 3). When a tile is left behind by the user, objects are disassociated from it. Objects without remaining tile associations can be unloaded. Note that using spatial filters and geometry representations need to be supported by the respective databases. Mapping between semantic concepts like "geometry" is introduced in Section 5.3.

Another use case for streaming is to navigate through hierarchically structured data, e.g., in a user interface for SimDB. In an industrial context one may want to explore a factory model's structure by navigating from a factory root object via the corresponding links to the associated factory floors, from one of the factory floors to its associated working cells, and so forth. In user interfaces, this can be presented using a so-called tree view. On opening a branch in such a view, all associated objects can be loaded, on closing the branch they can be unloaded. This implements *hierarchical streaming*.

A third type is *streaming for data processing* purposes. This approach is used when large amounts of data in ExtDB shall be processed in smaller subsets within SimDB. The idea is similar to an iterator in programming languages or a database result cursor. Each subset is loaded, processed in some way, resynchronized if necessary, and unloaded. Resynchronization is only applied when either the subset itself is changed or additional instances are created by data processing. In the latter case, such newly created instances may be unloaded as well. Streaming for data processing can use different iteration strategies. It may apply spatial streaming to process data spread over an area, hierarchical streaming to process a subtree of objects, or other specialized approaches. For example in an annual process, tree instances from a forestal inventory database are loaded in tiles by a spatial filter, processed by simulating their growth, resynchronized, unloaded, and so forth.

### 5.2.4 Retain-And-Release Strategy

So far, data loading and unloading is considered to be used by one mechanism of the simulation system at a time, e.g., only by spatial streaming or only by hierarchical streaming. When multiple mechanisms are used in combination, repeated attempts to load the same instance always yield the same single replicate within SimDB. However, unloading an instance can only be done once. Thus, a conflict of interest may arise when the same instance is loaded by several mechanisms and at some point unloaded by one of them. For example, one component of the simulation system initially loads a building instance using spatial streaming.

Another component also loads it using hierarchical streaming yielding the identical replicate. When the first component unloads the building it is no longer available to the other, too.

To avoid this problem, it is necessary to retain an instance from being unloaded as long as it is required by some component of the simulation system. Likewise, the instance has to be released when it is no longer required. In short, an instance can be retained or released. Different retain-and-release strategies are possible, which are typically based upon methods like reference counting. One approach is to provide loading and unloading requests with an optional identifier of the invoking component. Instance mapping entries maintain a state for load requests of each component, i.e., a boolean flag per component. Each loading request sets the flag of the provided identifier. Unloading requests accompanied by an identifier unset the corresponding flag and proceed only when all flags are unset. In this approach, it is easy to retrace which component retained an instance. However, each component can retain an instance only once. This is a drawback when a single component requires the same instance several times. An alternative approach is generic reference counting. Instance mapping entries maintain a single reference counter. Each loading request for an instance increments its counter, each unloading request decrements it. Unloading itself is only pursued for a zero reference counter. Counting may also be optional per load or unload request. While this approach allows for a more flexible retaining and releasing of instances, it is not as easy to retrace why an instance is retained from being unloaded. A combination of both approaches is reference counting per identifiable component, providing traceability and multiple retaining of the same instance per component. This approach is used in this work.

The approach for spatial streaming in the previous subsection already employs a retain-and-release management by associating loaded objects with corresponding tiles. However, using the integrated strategy presented above, loading objects for a tile retains them once and unloading releases them once. Again, only completely released objects are really unloaded.

Instead of unloading immediately, it can be deferred by scheduling a kind of garbage collection for completely released instances. This way, unload tasks are accumulated and processed later. This strategy can be used when memory in SimDB is not essential. It may also be advantageous when instances are required shortly after being released. Retaining an instance once again will preserve it from garbage collection. Furthermore, the point in time for unloading may be chosen depending on the current work load to optimize overall system performance.

## 5.3 Functional Data Synchronization

Synchronizing SimDB and ExtDB on schema and data level provides a basis for data management and exchange. It allows all connected simulation clients to speak the same language. Reflection and inheritance from built-in base classes can be used to generically access unknown data so, e.g., standard user interfaces are able to read and write objects and their attribute values. However, the actual semantics of the data may be unknown to the simulation system, i.e., the language is spoken but not understood. This may occur in particular when using standardized data schemata like CityGML [24, 25] or SEDRIS [125] instead of a proprietary format of the simulation system. Such standards usually foster the accessibility of the shared Semantic World Model within ExtDB. They should be preferred to pursuit an open approach to data management.

Thus, there have to be certain mechanisms to translate parts essential to the functioning of the simulation into the simulation system's own representation. In this thesis, this process is called *functional data synchronization* and serves as a third layer of synchronization. It is used for mapping data like geometry representations, transformations or physical parameters so their functional meaning can be decoded and used by simulation algorithms. For example, the internal renderer needs an appropriate geometry representation to be able to process and display geometry data.

This translation is realized entirely within SimDB. It also creates a mapping – a functional data mapping – between the original data and its functional equivalent. However, this does not have to be a one-to-one mapping on object or attribute value level. Whole object sets representing more complex structures can be supported, too. In contrast to schema and data synchronization, only few methods are generic.

## 5.3.1 Categories

In general, methods for functional data synchronization can be categorized into these orthogonal classes:

- *schema-aware* versus *schema-unaware*
- *bidirectional* versus *unidirectional*
- *substituting* versus *supplementing*

### 5.3.1.1 Schema-aware Versus Schema-unaware

When simulation data is encoded in some format, the specific classes and attributes have to be interpreted and mapped to an equivalent representation in SimDB. Thus, functional data synchronization needs to be aware of its schema and semantics – it cannot be completely generic. For example, a specific representation for transformations (rotation, translation) needs to be known by a mechanism mapping such structures to the simulation system's own. Such application specific or rather schema specific methods shall be called *schema-aware*. The opposite are *schema-unaware* and thus generic mapping approaches. Schema-unaware mappings can be used for mapping built-in core types of the utilized databases. An important example are basic data types for geometry representations within 3D simulation or geo databases. Usually, such types are independent of a concrete schema, thus, making the corresponding mapping schema-unaware.

#### 5.3.1.2 Bidirectional Versus Unidirectional

Independent of schema-(un)awareness, the direction of functional data synchronization is relevant. In the simplest cases, synchronization is done one-way, i.e., *unidirectional*. Data encoded in the schema shared between SimDB and ExtDB is kept in sync only in direction of the translation. This means, newly loaded data or updates are reflected within the functional equivalent. This is sufficient for scenarios where the latter is used, e.g., only for rendering or collision detection, and at most the former – the original data – may be changed. Thus, an example for unidirectional functional data synchronization may be the translation of physical parameters for dynamic objects into a representation known by the simulation system. The counterpart is a *bidirectional* approach where changes to the functional equivalent within SimDB are also synchronized back to the original encoded representation. An example are transformations within dynamic objects represented in an application schema. Their functional equivalents are not only read (e.g., for rendering) but also written, e.g., to simulate a joint movement in a robot model. To make such changes globally available within ExtDB, they have to be reflected in the original data within SimDB, first.

#### 5.3.1.3 Substituting Versus Supplementing

Finally, the translated structures can either *substitute* or *supplement* the original data within SimDB. Substituting functional data synchronization needs to be integrated with data and schema synchronization to replace the original structures with their functional equivalent. To keep these mechanisms generic, this approach should be used in the schema-unaware case. It can particularly be applied for mapping the aforementioned integrated, schema independent core types like geometry representations. It also allows for optional variations, like mapping an integer representation of a color value (think of $10526880 = \#A0A0A0$) in ExtDB to a native color data structure ($(160, 160, 160)$) provided by SimDB. In the supplementing approach, functional equivalents are created as separate structures within SimDB. This is usually done in a mechanism separate from and independent of schema or data synchronization. Note that these structures are of temporary nature and shall not be managed by data synchronization, which can be achieved by appropriate restriction mechanisms. The approach is usually chosen for the non-generic (i.e., schema-aware) case, when both the original representation and the functional translation are needed within the simulation system, or when specialized translations are needed in between.

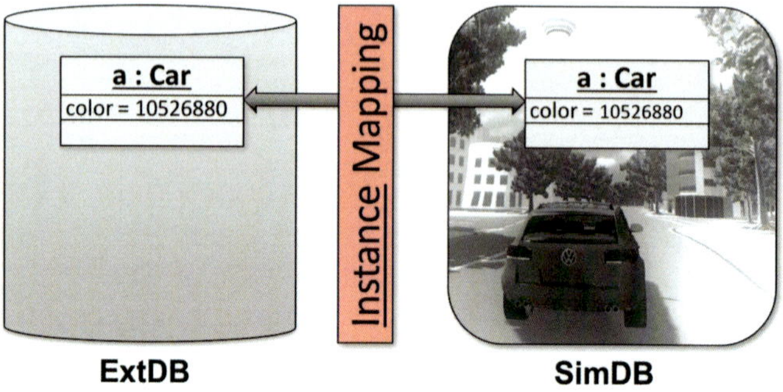


**Figure 5.14:** *Example scenario without functional data synchronization.*

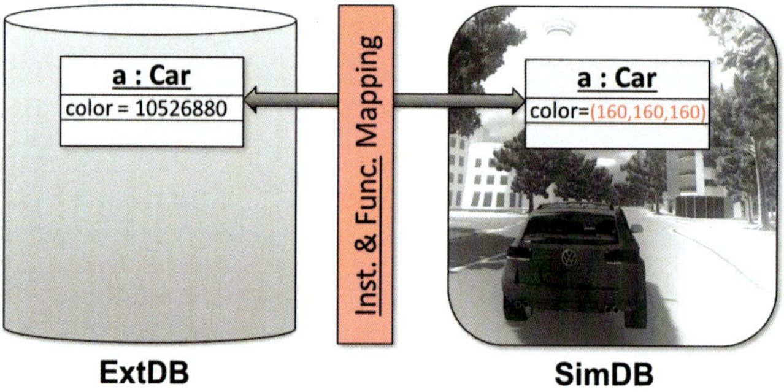


**Figure 5.15:** *Example scenario with schema-unaware, substituting, and bidirectional functional data synchronization.*

## 5.3.2 Examples

Figure 5.14 exemplifies the basic problem in a scenario without functional synchronization. A car object in ExtDB is modeled with a color value encoded as an integer. Using schema and data synchronization, an identical car object is replicated to SimDB. However, the color value cannot be identified and thus appropriately visualized by the simulation system.

In Figure 5.15, the color value is translated into a native color representation within SimDB. It uses a substituting, schema-unaware approach integrated into schema and data synchronization. The actual integer-type attribute of the Car class is replaced by and translated into a color-type attribute in SimDB. Changes can be handled by standard change management (see Subsection 5.2.2) making the mapping bidirectional.

In the next example (Figure 5.16), the encoded color value is replicated into SimDB without modifications. A mechanism for supplementing functional data synchronization creates an additional Material object holding the translated color representation usable by

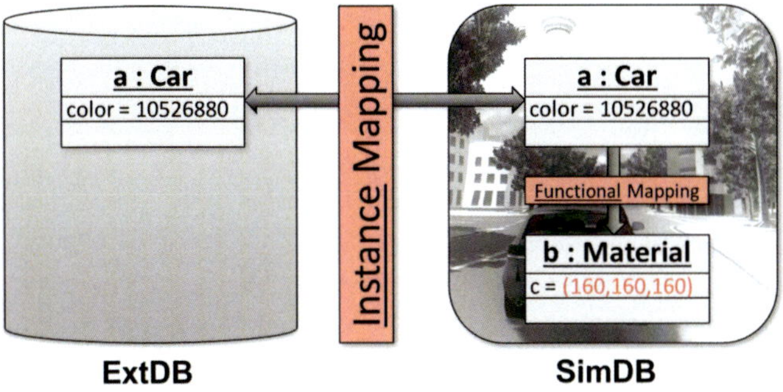


**Figure 5.16:** *Example scenario with schema-unaware, supplementing, and unidirectional functional data synchronization.*

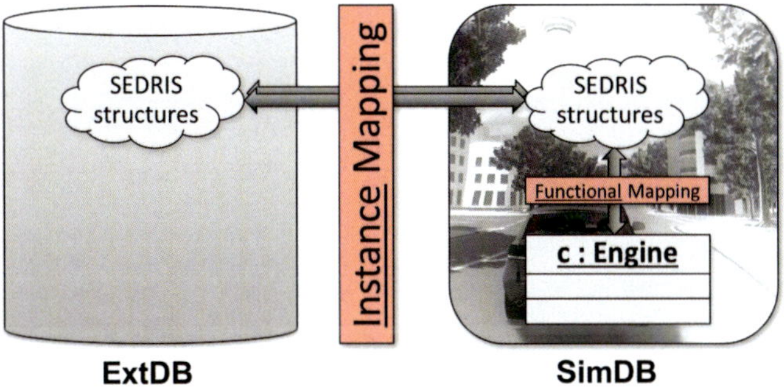


**Figure 5.17:** *Example scenario with schema-aware, supplementing, and bidirectional functional data synchronization.*

the simulation system. In this example the color may be static and thus a unidirectional approach suffices. Furthermore, it is also schema-unaware.

Finally, in Figure 5.17, a schema-aware example is given. Here, some SEDRIS object structure representing an engine is loaded into SimDB. A mechanism aware of the applied SEDRIS encoding rule creates an additional Engine object that can be interpreted by the simulation system. Changes to the engine, e.g., its current speed, are resynchronized to the SEDRIS structures within SimDB and from there to ExtDB.

### 5.3.3 Best Practices

Typically, schema-unaware methods are integrated into the mechanisms for schema and data synchronization. This implies a substituting and usually also a bidirectional approach as this is the standard behavior of schema and data synchronization. First, schema sync needs to take the mapping into account. As mentioned above, this can either be the standard mapping for special data types, e.g., geometry type in SimDB on geometry type in ExtDB. It may also be a variation that should be configurable on a per schema component basis, e.g., the integer-on-color scenario. During runtime, data sync must adhere to these mappings and translate the data accordingly – usually in both directions.

In case of generic but very special translations, a dedicated realization may be better for separation of concerns. This can only be done supplementing, which is also the type of choice for the schema-aware case. It is realized as a downstream process on top of schema and data sync. A basic approach is to use SimDB's notification service. A functional data sync manager responds when a new object of interest is inserted. This can either be by loading from ExtDB or by creation from some other component of the simulation system – the origin is indistinguishable for the manager. In both cases, it spawns a new handler responsible for the synchronization of the original data and the functional equivalent. The latter is created on initialization of the handler. The handler also connects to SimDB's notification service to detect changes of the original data and the functional equivalent. The latter is only needed for bidirectional synchronization, the former for both cases.

On an incoming change notification for the original data, the handler applies the change to the functional equivalent accordingly and vice versa. However, the handler's own changes need to be distinguished from third party changes. When the simulation system may block in the meantime, this can be realized by ignoring notifications during updates by the handler (see Algorithm 16). For concurrent synchronization, a receipt-based approach as in Subsection 5.2.2 can be realized.

## 5.4 Temporal Data Management

Simulation models in general and Semantic World Models in particular are inherently dynamic. During a simulation run, they are constantly being changed. Thus, not only their current state but also their history of states is of particular interest, i.e., how the simulation developed and the model changed over time. Therefore, persistence should not only be provided for the model's current state but also for the whole history of states. This allows for analysis, archiving or debriefing of simulations or for version management in modeling processes. A separate logging component may be used to capture this development. Using a temporal database as introduced in Subsection 3.4.4 for ExtDB, however, such changes can automatically be versioned by the data management component itself [126].

### 5.4.1 Temporal Database Synchronization

Usually, SimDB itself is a snapshot database, i.e., non-temporal. Thus, replication from a temporal ExtDB must be performed with reference to a certain timestamp provided by the

**Algorithm 16** Sequential synchronization of original data and functional equivalent.

```
init ignore ← false
function onEventChangeOriginalData
    if ignore then
        return
    end if
    ignore ← true
    apply changes from original data to functional equivalent
    ignore ← false
end function
function onEventChangeFunctionalEquivalent
    if ignore then
        return
    end if
    ignore ← true
    apply changes from functional equivalent to original data
    ignore ← false
end function
```

user or an application component. To make the snapshot consistent, the entirety of replicate copies must always represent the same timestamp. Thus, on changing the reference time, replication has to be updated. A naive approach is to unload all instances and then reload them with the new reference time. A more efficient approach is to only reload data that changed in between the previous and the new reference time. For this purpose, however, ExtDB must be able to (quickly) provide a list of all changes between two reference times, e.g., by maintaining a queryable global change log.

Assuming a transaction time database for ExtDB with such a global change log and given a previous reference time $t_{i-1}$, a user requests a new time $t_i$. For $t_{i-1} < t_i$ (going forward in time), the log is queried for all entries within $[t_{i-1}, t_i]$. The list of changes contains all instances of ExtDB whose corresponding instances in SimDB have to be updated. To preserve the chronological sequence, changes are processed in ascending order. Each change from the log is used to update SimDB accordingly. Properties updated in ExtDB are updated in SimDB accordingly; the same applies to insertions and deletions. Repeating changes to the same property or operations that cancel each other out (e.g., inserting and deleting the same instance) should be aggregated. Altogether, the process is more or less identical to the update mechanisms presented in Subsection 5.2.2 for incoming change notifications from ExtDB. Thus, they may be reused for this purpose. For $t_i < t_{i-1}$ (going back in time), the log is queried for all changes within $[t_i, t_{i-1}]$. To update replicate copies in SimDB, the list must be processed in descending order. Furthermore, some meanings must be inverted. An instance deletion becomes an insertion and vice versa. Only property updates need not be adjusted. Finally, a global log may also be used by a client's user to browse and select those reference times with associated changes.

When data synchronization transfers changes from SimDB to ExtDB, previous value versions are preserved by ExtDB. Figure 5.18 gives an example. ExtDB manages an object `a-:Tree` in a forest data schema. Two clients have a replicate copy. Client #1 changed the value of the tree's `felled` property from `false` to `true`. Subsequently, the client resynchronizes its SimDB with the central ExtDB. Before updating its property value accordingly its previous state is archived by closing the value version. In this example, a transaction time database is used. Thus, the history version automatically receives a closing timestamp $t_{end}$ from the DBMS.

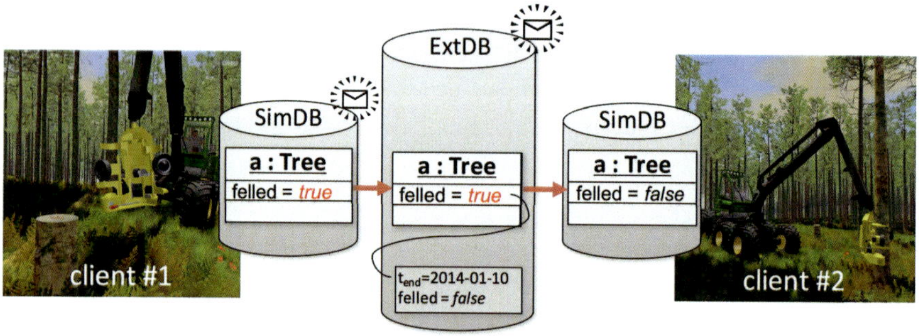


**Figure 5.18:** *Example: The central ExtDB database adopts a change from client #1. A history version is created by closing the previous value version.*

Instead of a transaction time, a valid time database might also be used. Here, clients must explicitly provide timestamps when resynchronizing changes. This allows to use different time values than the current system time of the DBMS. When SimDB is used in the context of data acquisition, data processing, or similar tasks, a user or an algorithm may provide timestamps representing corresponding real world changes or phenomena. For example, when deriving a forest model from airborne laser scanner data, the estimated age of each extracted tree can be used to timestamp the tree object's creation with the physical tree's supposed "birthday." Considering a simulation application, the simulation time can be used for valid time. Any change to the model can then be supplied with a corresponding timestamp from the simulation clock. These timestamps may have to be buffered in SimDB when resynchronization to ExtDB is asynchronous. When using valid time for simulation time in a distributed simulation, simulation clocks have to be synchronized (separately) so that clients update ExtDB with coherent timestamps.

Using a valid time database as ExtDB, the same reference time should always be used for loading data as well as for resynchronizing changes back to ExtDB. Otherwise, instances in

SimDB do not reflect the corresponding state of the Semantic World Model when applying the changes. For the same reason, with a transaction time database for ExtDB, SimDB should be considered read-only when accessing historic data. Here, any change would automatically be provided with ExtDB's current system time and thus can never be identical to the historic reference time.

Regarding the change management approach presented in Subsection 5.2.2, no immediate modifications are needed when using a transaction time database. Clients using the reference time "current" process incoming notifications as usual. Changes are automatically timestamped by the DBMS representing a consistent reference time for the distributed system. Clients in historic mode need not process any notifications. First of all, as mentioned above, such a client is always in read-only mode. No local changes will occur and thus no internal notifications will be created. Furthermore, a transaction time database does not allow retroactive updates. Other clients cannot change the historic state currently viewed by this client. Thus, any external notification can be ignored.

When using valid time, these restrictions do not apply anymore. Clients always have to work at a concrete reference valid time as their is no generic concept of "current" like in transaction time. Furthermore, there does not have to be a consistent reference time among the clients. For scenarios like data acquisition, different clients may concurrently work at different reference times. Finally, the usage of valid time allows for retroactive updates. Thus, altogether, there is no explicit historic mode. The usage of a separately synchronized simulation time for valid time can be seen as an exception. Simulation time behaves like transaction time as it is consistent among the clients and for causality reasons no retroactive updates should be allowed. Another exception are scenarios where clients only change disjoint instance sets.

For a general integration of valid time into a distributed scenario change management has to be extended. External notifications have to include corresponding valid timestamps. A client needs to compare them to its own current reference time. The synchronization state will then have to be updated accordingly. For example, a client may ignore notifications for (in regard to its own reference time) future changes as they cannot have an impact on its own replicate copies. In contrast, the client has to consider notifications with timestamps earlier or equal to its own reference time. This includes the usage of external notifications for receipts of its own changes. However, a detailed analysis of this evaluation process is beyond the scope of this thesis.

Similar considerations apply when using a bitemporal database, i.e., a database combining valid and transaction time. A reference valid time must always be provided. It is used to load the corresponding data from ExtDB to SimDB and to timestamp changes on resynchronization. Concomitantly, reference transaction time may either be "current" allowing for read-write-access or historic just allowing read-only access. When changing the reference time vector, data can be completely reloaded using the naive approach as mentioned above.

Also the more sophisticated global change log approach might be used. In the bitemporal case, this log is two-dimensional. The particular evaluation strategy for different combinations of previous and new reference transaction and valid time. As for the usage of valid time only, change management has to also be extended for the bitemporal case. Both aspects, however, are yet to be analyzed in detail.

### 5.4.2 *n*D-Versioning Concept

Besides valid and transaction time (e.g., combined in a bitemporal database), even more time dimensions can be thought of. One of these is the *effectivity* of a change, i.e., the time it becomes effective or valid in a formal sense. For example, in data acquisition for a forestry application (see Chapter 7), tree heights may be updated over a longer period of time. Each height value is associated with the appropriate valid timestamp (actual time of the measurement) and transaction timestamp (time of the database entry). The third timestamp represents the time a change becomes effective, e.g., the beginning of the next inventory period at the end of all measurements. This allows to decouple the description of real world phenomena with valid time from the effectivity of these values while modeling the more or less technical information about data storage with transaction time. While this scenario with three time dimensions shall be used to motivate and explain the following specification, the concept can be generalized to arbitrary kinds and numbers of time dimensions.

For this higher-order temporal database, a new concept for evaluating time point representations was developed. As mentioned in Subsection 3.4.4, in this case, historic versions are only implicitly closed by other versions' timestamps. Below, it is shown how this representation can be applied to all integrated time dimensions at the same time.

#### 5.4.2.1 One and Two Time Dimensions

To begin with, this approach can also be applied for one or two time dimensions. In the former case, every update is associated with a single (scalar) timestamp $t_i$ with associated version $v_i$. The interval $[t_i, t_j)$, where $t_j > t_i$ is the next timestamp, defines $v_i$'s scope (with $t_j = \infty$ if $t_i$ is the last timestamp). A retroactive update (e.g., in case of a valid time database) with timestamp $t_k$, $t_i < t_k < t_j$ splits the existing interval into $[t_i, t_k)$ and $[t_k, t_j)$.

In the bitemporal case (i.e., with the two time dimensions transaction and valid time), an update is associated with a timestamp tuple $(t_i^T, t_i^V)$ for transaction time $T$ and valid time $V$. Here, the two-time-dimensional scope of the associated version $v_i$ initially (without any other existing versions) is a quarter-plane restricted by the two rays emerging from $(t_i^T, t_i^V)$ parallel to and in positive direction of the respective axis (dotted area in Figure 5.19 left).

Inserting a new version $v_{i+1}$ with a timestamp tuple $(t_{i+1}^T, t_{i+1}^V)$ with $t_i^T < t_{i+1}^T$ and $t_i^V < t_{i+1}^V$ (Figure 5.19 center) reduces the scope of $v_i$ to two infinite "tubes" while the new scope of $v_{i+1}$ is again defined by a quarter-plane rooted at $(t_{i+1}^T, t_{i+1}^V)$. Thus, value version $v_{i+1}$ is only

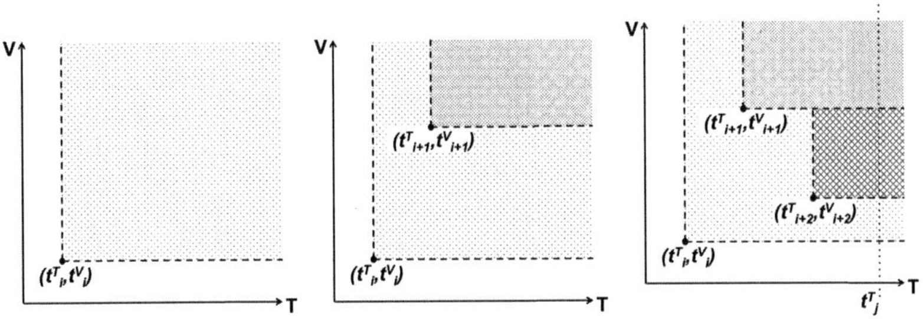


**Figure 5.19:** *Bitemporal example of the evaluation schema for the higher-order temporal database. Scopes for the versions associated with one, two, and three timestamp tuples of transaction time T and valid time V.*

visible when considering a reference time greater or equal in both timestamp components. As transaction time does not allow retroactive updates, $t_i^T < t_{i+1}^T$ must always be valid. However, valid time allows for $t_i^V > t_{i+1}^V$. An example is shown in Figure 5.19 (right). A new version $v_{i+2}$ with timestamp tuple $(t_{i+2}^T, t_{i+2}^V)$ is inserted where $t_{i+1}^T < t_{i+2}^T$ and $t_{i+1}^V > t_{i+2}^V$. While $v_i$'s scope is similarly restricted as in the previous example, $v_{i+2}$'s scope stops at $v_{i+1}$'s. This behavior is called the "Golden Rule": The expansion of a limiting ray stops at preexisting other scopes. In the exemplary scenario, the expansion of the ray in $V$-direction ($V$-ray) shall stop. This allows retroactive updates with regard to valid time to "slide in between" existing values. That is, for any $t^T \geq t_{i+2}^T$, the scope of $v_{i+2}$ is between $v_i$'s and $v_{i+1}$'s scopes. As a corollary, $T$-rays do *not* stop at existing $V$-rays. In particular, this makes the scope of new versions independent of their insertion's order regarding valid time. In Figure 5.19 (right), the order of the valid timestamp components is irrelevant to the resulting partitioning along the $V$ axis. Figure 5.20 gives an example for an alternate insertion order. The partitioning regarding valid time along any $t_j^T > t_{i+2}^T$ is identical to the prior case.

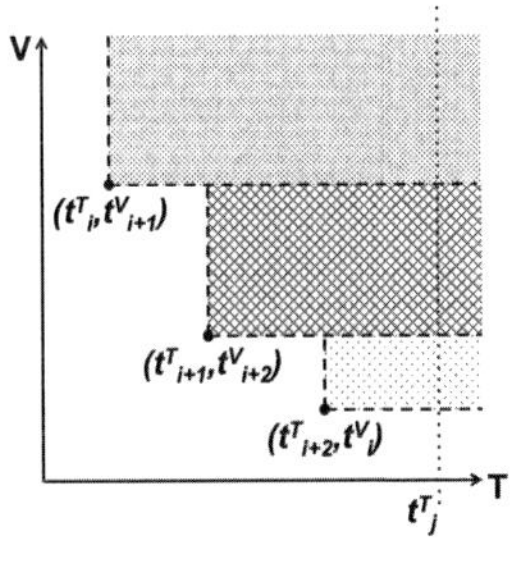


**Figure 5.20:** *Inserting versions in an alternate order (i.e., different transaction times) yields the same partitioning along a $t_j^T > t_{i+2}^T$.*

An example for accessing a bitemporal database using this concept with the synchronization methods mentioned above is given in Figure 5.21 (reading) and Figure 5.22 (writing). ExtDB contains a simple forest model comprising a `Tree` class with a `height` attribute. A snapshot of the object `a:Tree` is replicated to the client using reference time ($t^T$=cur, $t^V$=2012). By using transaction time $t^T$=cur (the default access mode for most users), the last written value for valid time $t^V$=2012 is replicated. Thus, the height of `a:Tree`'s snapshot within SimDB is $16.0m$.

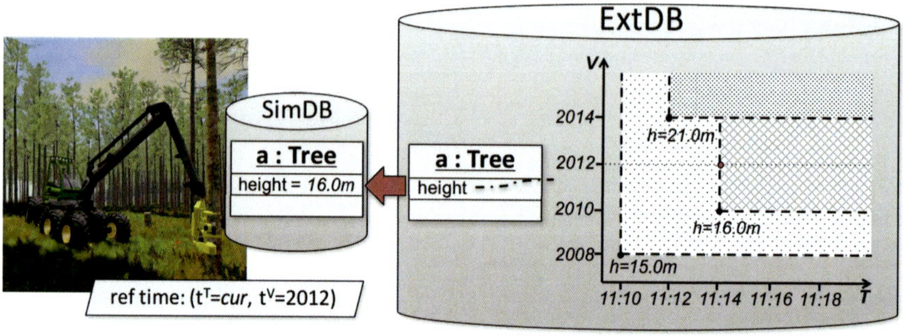


**Figure 5.21:** *Bitemporal synchronization example: Replicating a snapshot of a tree object from ExtDB with reference time* ($t^T$=*cur*, $t^V$=2012).

An example for updating the previously replicated `a:Tree` object is given in Figure 5.22.

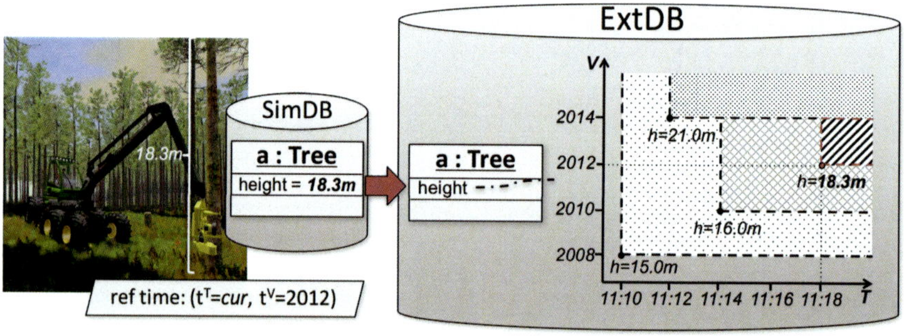


**Figure 5.22:** *Bitemporal synchronization example: Updating a tree object's height within ExtDB for reference time* ($t^T$=*cur*, $t^V$=2012) *(transaction executed at 11:18h).*

The tree's height actually measured $18.3m$ in 2012 so it must be updated. While keeping the same reference time ($t^T$=cur, $t^V$=2012), the new value is resynchronized to ExtDB. It is inserted with the chosen valid time $t^V$=2012 and the system's current time for transaction time – in this case $t^T$=11:18.

#### 5.4.2.2 Three Time Dimensions

The evaluation schema can now be extended to the three time dimensions as mentioned above: transaction time $T$, valid time $V$, and effectivity time $E$. This leads to three-dimensional timestamps $(t_i^T, t_i^V, t_i^E)$ for every version $v_i$. The resulting scope (to begin with, without interference of other timestamps) is a "cube" with infinite extent in direction of each axis. The simplest case can be compared to the 2D case in Figure 5.19 (center) and is shown in Figure 5.23: The scope for timestamp $(t_i^T, t_i^V, t_i^E)$ is reduced to (up to) three "walls" by a new version with timestamp tuple $(t_{i+1}^T, t_{i+1}^V, t_{i+1}^E)$ if $t_{i+1}^T \geq t_i^T, t_{i+1}^V \geq t_i^V, t_{i+1}^E \geq t_i^E$. Note that – as for the 2D case – the actual scopes infinitely expand in (positive) axis directions.

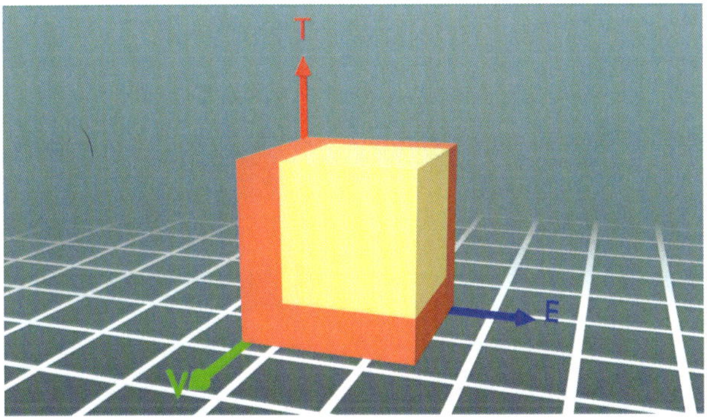


**Figure 5.23:** *Intersection of $i^{th}$ (orange) and $(i+1)^{th}$ (yellow) 3D time scope for $t_{i+1}^T \geq t_i^T$, $t_{i+1}^V \geq t_i^V$, $t_{i+1}^E \geq t_i^E$ ($T$ axis in red, $V$ axis in green, $E$ axis in blue). Actual scopes infinitely expand in (positive) axis directions.*

For other constellations, again, the "Golden Rule" resolves ambiguities. In the 3D case, the rays emerging from a timestamp tuple in each axis direction have to be tested against the orthogonal quarter-planes defined by the other two axes of other timestamps. An example is given in Figure 5.24. The $V$-ray of one timestamp (orange) is tested against the quarter-plane defined by the $T$- and $E$-rays ($T$-$E$-quarter-plane) of a second timestamp (yellow). To allow for retroactive updates relative to the $V$-axis to "slide in between" existing values as in the two-time-dimensional case, the $V$-ray has to stop at the $T$-$E$-quarter-plane.

In general, the rule has to state whether a $T$-, $V$-, or $E$-ray has to stop at the respective orthogonal $V$-$E$-, $T$-$E$-, or $T$-$V$-quarter-planes. Like in the 2D case, a desired property is that the partitioning shall be independent of the versions' insertion order, i.e., of their timestamps' $T$ component. Corresponding to the partitioning of the vertical line at $t_j^T$ in Figure 5.19 (right) and Figure 5.20, this is the partitioning of a "high enough" intersecting $V$-$E$-plane, i.e., for a $t_j^T$ greater than any occurring $t_i^T$. An example is given in Figure 5.25. Compared to Figure 5.24, the $T$ component $t_i^T$ of the $i^{th}$ timestamp (orange) is less than that of $t_{i+1}^T$ (yellow). In each case, the respective $V$ and $E$ components are identical. In both

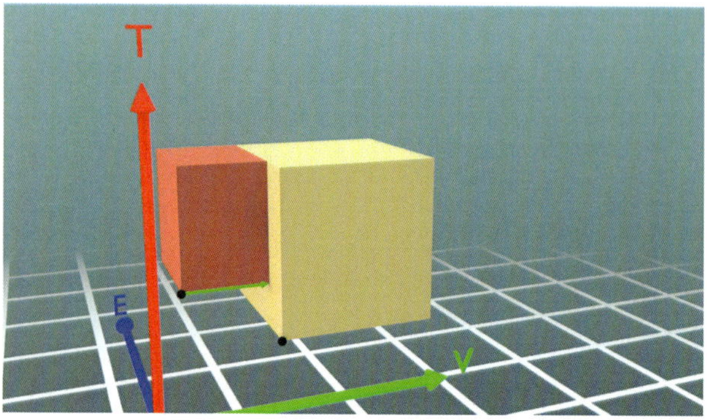


**Figure 5.24:** *Expansion in $V$-direction of one timestamp's scope (orange) stops at $T$-$E$-quarter-plane of other timestamp's scope (yellow) allowing retroactive updates relative to the $V$-axis to "slide in between" existing values.*

scenarios, however, the final (i.e., with regard to $T$) partitioning along an intersecting $V$-$E$-plane (depicted in purple in Figure 5.25) is equal. In the first scenario ($t_i^T > t_{i+1}^T$, Figure 5.24), a $V$-ray *must* stop at a $T$-$E$-quarter-plane. In the second ($t_i^T < t_{i+1}^T$), an $E$-ray *must not* stop at a $T$-$V$-quarter-plane. Otherwise, the partitioning would not be consistent.

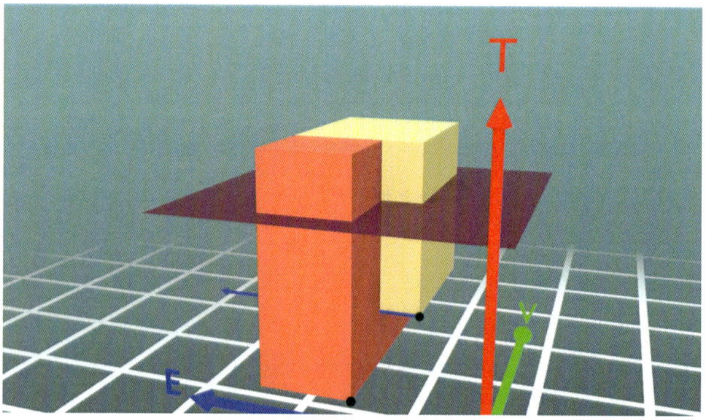


**Figure 5.25:** *Expansion of $E$-ray must not stop at $T$-$V$-quarter-plane to yield the same partitioning on a $V$-$E$-plane (purple) as in Figure 5.24.*

Figures 5.24 and 5.25 depict the case where $t_i^V < t_{i+1}^V$ and $t_i^E > t_{i+1}^E$. For reasons of symmetry, the same arguments apply to the case where $t_i^V > t_{i+1}^V$ and $t_i^E < t_{i+1}^E$. In fact, only the indexes ($i$ and $i+1$) and thus the colors of the two scopes (orange and yellow) need to be swapped.

The other distinct case is $t_i^V < t_{i+1}^V$ and $t_i^E < t_{i+1}^E$. For $t_i^T < t_{i+1}^T$ this is already depicted in Figure 5.23. Here, all coordinates of timestamp $i$ (orange) are less than those of timestamp $i+1$ (yellow). To achieve the same partitioning on a $V$-$E$-plane for $t_i^T > t_{i+1}^T$, $T$-rays *must not* stop at $V$-$E$-quarter-planes. Figure 5.26 shows an example. The $T$-ray emitted from the $(i+1)^{th}$ timestamp (yellow) does *not* stop at the $V$-$E$-quarter-plane defined by the $i^{th}$ timestamp (orange). The dashed ovals mark the yellow scopes expansion reducing the orange scope. Again, the same argument applies to $t_i^V > t_{i+1}^V$ and $t_i^E > t_{i+1}^E$ and can be depicted by switching colors (orange and yellow) in Figures 5.25–5.26.

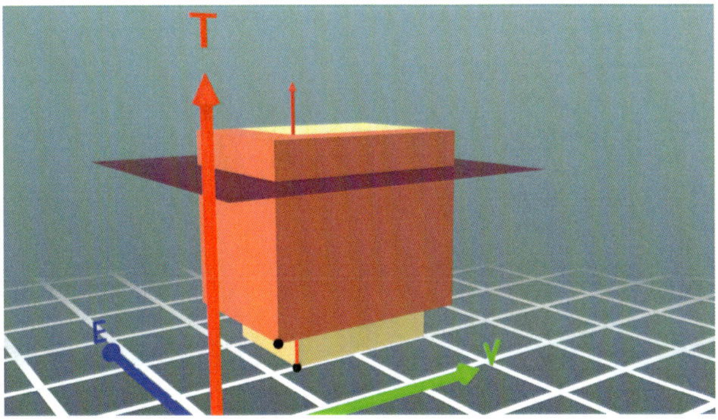


**Figure 5.26:** *Expansion of a $T$-ray must not stop at $V$-$E$-quarter-planes to yield the same partitioning on a $V$-$E$-plane (purple) as in Figure 5.23.*

Altogether, the Golden Rule for the case of three time dimensions states that

- $T$-rays *must not* stop at $V$-$E$-quarter-planes,
- $V$-rays *must* stop at $T$-$E$-quarter-planes, and
- $E$-rays *must not* stop at $T$-$V$-quarter-planes.

The constraints for the choice of these rules are

- partitioning on a "high enough" $V$-$E$-plane shall be independent of insertion order, i.e., transaction time $T$ and
- retroactive updates relative to the $V$-axis shall "slide in between" existing values.

# Chapter 6

# Reference Implementations

In this chapter, two reference implementations of the proposed data management approach for eRobotics applications are presented. Both are based on the 3D simulation system VEROSIM (Virtual Environments and Robotic Simulation [127]) and its simulation database VSD (Versatile Simulation Database) used as an implementation of SimDB (see Section 6.3). For ExtDB, two different systems are adopted. The first is SGJ (SupportGIS Java [123]), an object-oriented abstraction layer for standard relational database systems or other storage back-ends (see Section 6.4). As a second example, a combination of XML (Extensible Markup Language) Schema and instance documents is used as an ExtDB implementation (see Section 6.6).

To allow their usage in the proposed approach, each SimDB's and ExtDB's conformance to the requirements defined in Chapter 4 has to be evaluated. In particular, this means the specification of suitable metamodels as well as transformations from and to the UML (Unified Modeling Language [8]) metamodel. Figure 6.1 gives an overview. Here, the UML's position as a pivot metamodel becomes clear once again.

Combined with the methods from Chapter 5, these transformations could be used directly to realize the reference implementations. An example is given in Figure 6.2. In this scenario, schema and instance data is serialized to XMI (XML Metadata Interchange [108]) representations in the concrete SimDB or ExtDB metamodel (here: VSD). This model data is then transformed by applying the respective ATL (ATL Transformation Language [103, 104]) transformation to yield an XMI representation conforming to the UML metamodel. After deserializing this data, the *generic* synchronization methods from Chapter 5 can be applied for schema or data synchronization. Resulting model data (e.g., of a loading process) is then again serialized, transformed and deserialized to the respective other database (here: SGJ).

While this approach is possible, it does not provide the necessary performance for eRobotics applications. Therefore, the knowledge within the model transformations (i.e., the mapping) is used to build *customizations* of the generic method specifications for each considered pair of SimDB and ExtDB. In this chapter, these pairs are VSD–SGJ and VSD–XML as mentioned above.

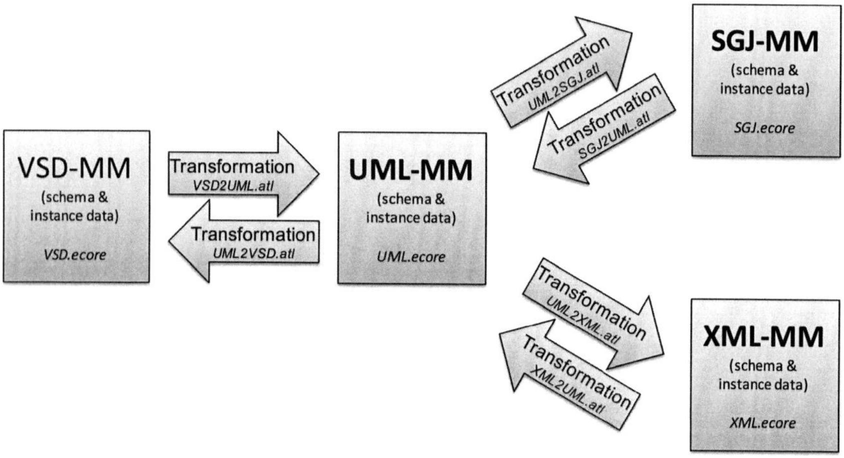


**Figure 6.1:** *Considered metamodels (MM) and transformations in between for the reference implementations.*

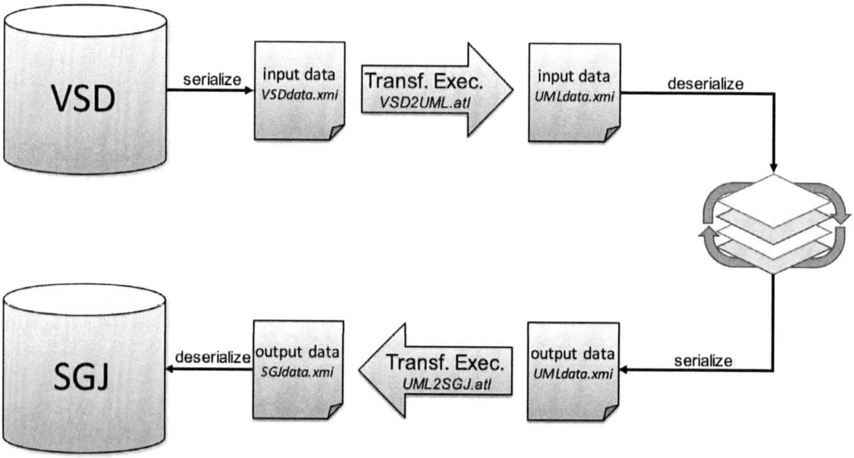


**Figure 6.2:** *Example for a possible reference implementation directly using the model transformations and the generic synchronization methods.*

Based on Requirement 5, these customizations directly use reifications of the metaclasses (of the respective SimDB and ExtDB) as well as instances thereof. The necessary direct mappings between the metaclasses of both systems can be obtained by chaining the model transformations given from and to the UML metamodel. The implementations directly use the respective database interfaces to connect the two systems following the presented approach. For example, in schema synchronization of the VSD–SGJ reference implementation, each SGJ class is directly mapped to its VSD metainstance counterpart. Likewise, in data synchronization, the SGJ objects of an SGJ class are mapped to VSD instances of the corresponding VSD metainstance.

## 6.1 Tools for Metamodeling and Model Transformation

Chapter 3 presented the fundamentals of metamodeling and model transformations. However, such techniques can only be employed with adequate tool support. According to [98], an important aspect of tools for (meta-)modeling is the difference to pure drawing tools, which indeed allow to build graphical models or metamodels but lack the conceptual representation behind. Due to its similarity to UML modeling, many CASE (Computer-Aided Software Engineering) tools provide metamodeling support. The interchange of model data between tools can in theory be realized using the XMI serialization format. However, different interpretations of the standard often lead to incompatibilities between the different vendors. Thus, an integrated tool for metamodeling and model transformations seems to be preferable.

Eclipse with the EMF (Eclipse Modeling Framework [109]) was identified as such a platform. In particular, it provides actively developed implementations of the model transformation languages ATL and QVT (MOF (Meta-Object Facility [99]) Query/View/Transformation [105, 98, 106, 107]). EMF uses the alternative meta-metamodel Ecore, which is similar to OMG (Object Management Group)'s MOF meta-metamodel. Despite QVT's standardization by OMG, the ATL implementation in EMF is more mature. Thus, also following [98], a combination of Ecore-compliant metamodeling and ATL model transformations was chosen for this work.

## 6.2 UML Metamodel

Reference implementations shall fulfill the requirements given in Chapter 4. To test Requirement 4, a representation of the UML metamodel is needed. To be precise, given the choice of tools presented above, it needs to be Ecore-based. In principle, such a metamodel is given by the UML2 EMF sub project [128]. However, as shown in Chapter 3, a simplified metamodel of the UML 2.4 language unit classes was constructed manually for the sake of simplicity. In particular, it contains those metaclasses used in Chapter 5. Figure 3.12 (on page 53) shows those parts of the metamodel for schema definition, Figure 3.13 (on page 54) those metaclasses for instance data definition.

### 6.2.1 Reference UML Model

Besides a metamodel of the UML, model transformations to and from this metamodel must be given to verify Requirement 4. To test (i.e., to execute) these transformations, concrete models conforming to the metamodels are needed. Therefore, an exemplary reference UML model for generic buildings was created. It consists of a schema part shown in Figure 6.3 and an instance data part shown in Figure 6.4. It was designed to cover many of the relevant modeling concepts: Abstract base classes, inheritance, value-typed attributes, or associations (with ownership).

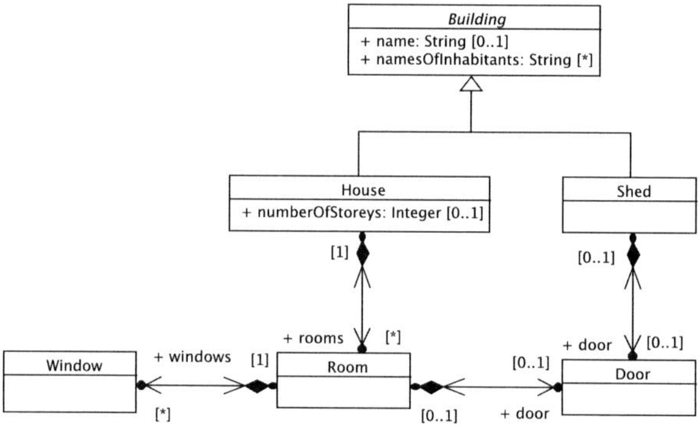


**Figure 6.3:** *The exemplary reference UML building model to test the model transformations – Data schema.*

## 6.3 SimDB: Versatile Simulation Database (VSD)

The 3D real-time simulation system VEROSIM was originally developed as a virtual reality and robot simulation system. Due to its flexible nature, it has become the basis for the development of various eRobotics applications in the fields of industrial automation, space robotics and environmental modeling (also see Chapter 7).

All its rendering and simulation techniques are based on an object-oriented, in-memory, runtime simulation database called VSD. Similar to the common scene-graph, VSD builds a graph-like structure by means of objects and references in between. However, unlike scene-graphs, it does not only support a fixed set of generic node types. VSD rather provides means to freely configure a schema for its objects. By offering views on its contents, time-critical components like rendering and simulation can still quickly access their respective

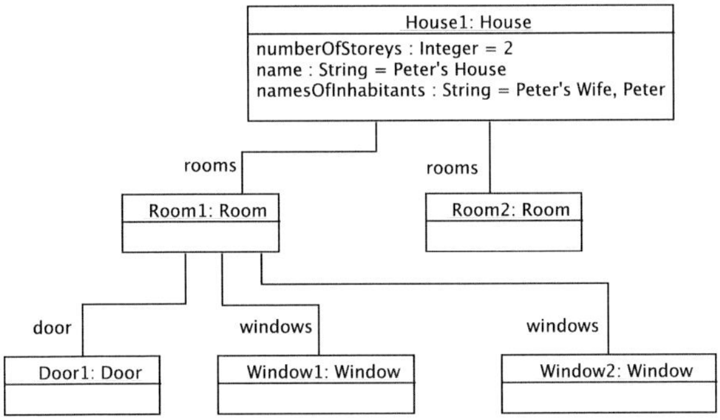


**Figure 6.4:** *The exemplary reference UML building model to test the model transformations – Instance data.*

part of interest without repetitively traversing the whole graph. A VSD schema describes the structure as well as the behavior of its objects. That is, the simulation logic is not externally applied to the Semantic World Model but is in fact part of the objects it comprises. For that reason, VSD can be called an active database.

In VSD, an object is called an instance. It can hold so-called properties representing its attribute values and outgoing references to other instances. A VSD schema defines so-called metainstances representing classes of instances and corresponding metaproperties representing their attributes. Metatypes in general, which comprise the metainstances, represent all other data types used for typifying metaproperties like character strings, integer values, or boolean values. More details are given below.

## 6.3.1 VSD Metamodel

Like UML, VSD's basic structure can be represented using an Ecore-based metamodel. In this section, a simplified metamodel including the aspects relevant for this thesis is given. As the metamodel is targeted at the presented approach for database synchronization, only the structural features of VSD are modeled, while behavioral aspects like metamethods are omitted. Figure 6.5 shows metaclasses used for schema descriptions and Figure 6.6 adds those needed for modeling instance data conforming to a schema.

In Figure 6.5, the abstract `MetaBase` metaclass is the root of all metaclasses describing VSD metadata providing a common name metaattribute. `MetaType` represents the abstract concepts of data type while `MetaInstance` corresponds to the object-oriented concept of a class as mentioned above. A `MetaInstance` can have one or no base class (multiple inheritance is not supported) and can be abstract, i.e., no corresponding (ontological) instances (objects) can be created. A `MetaInstance` can hold several `MetaProperties` corresponding

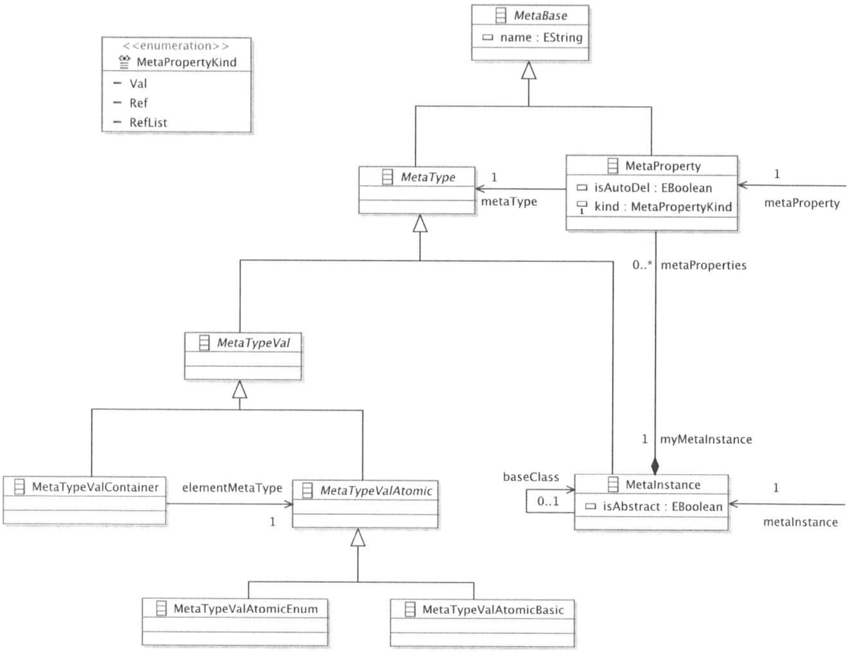


**Figure 6.5:** *A simplified VSD metamodel – Metaclasses for schema description.*

to the class's attributes. A `MetaProperty` itself has a type defining the domain of allowed values. Its kind additionally specifies whether the type is a value or a reference to another instance (either a single instance or a list of instances). The metaattribute `isAutoDel` specifies whether referenced instances are owned by the referring instance. VSD allows multiple ownership where reference counting is used to determine whether a target instance is deleted when all its referring instances (its "parents") are deleted. Besides, there are derivations of `MetaType` representing value data types. These can either be atomic (single) value data types modeled by `MetaTypeValAtomic` or multi-valued types represented by `MetaTypeVal-Container`, which themselves refer to a `MetaTypeValAtomic` representing their elements' type. In turn, `MetaTypeValAtomic` can be divided into basic and enum data types. Examples for basic data types are character strings or boolean, integer, and double values.

Figure 6.6 contains the Ecore metaclasses representing ontological instances of VSD metadata. All of these metaclasses hold an auxiliary metaattribute `_name` used for testing the transformations, only. Metaclass `Instance` models the concept of an object whose type is defined by the reference to its `MetaInstance`. Its attribute values are modeled by `Properties` representing ontological instances of `MetaProperty`. A `Property` has a `Variant` holding its

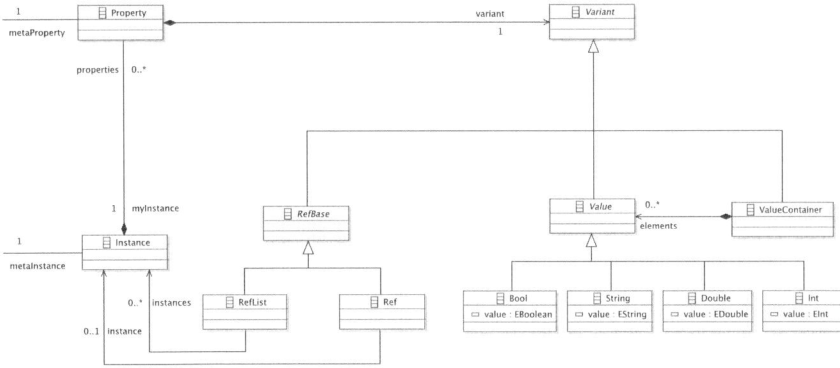


**Figure 6.6:** *A simplified VSD metamodel – Metaclasses for instance data description.*

value. Note that a `Property` in UML is used for schematic descriptions while a `Property` in VSD represents instance value data. Corresponding to the type of the `MetaProperty`, a `Variant` can be a simple `Value` like `Bool`, `String`, `Double`, or `Int` (in this simplification of the VSD metamodel only these types are included). Moreover, a `Value` can be a `ValueContainer` holding several atomic values or it can be a reference or list of references (`Ref`, `RefList`) referring to other instances. Altogether, this metamodel fulfills the SimDB part of Requirement 1 (existence of a metamodel) and Requirement 3 (metamodel including ontological instantiation) as defined in Chapter 4.

VSD can also be interpreted as a modeling language as described in Chapter 3 with the presented metamodel as its abstract syntax definition. It has different textual representations as a concrete syntax. One is source-code-based where C++ header files are decorated with additional informations to define metadata. Another concrete syntax allows to define data as well as metadata from within a proprietary file format for Semantic World Models or using a scripting language. Thus, semantics are either translational by code compilation or denotational by interpreting the model or script files.

### 6.3.2 Model Transformation VSD–UML

Given the metamodels for VSD and UML, a model transformation between them can be specified. As mentioned above, the ATL transformation language is used in the context of this work. As ATL is unidirectional, two transformations have to be build: from VSD to UML and vice versa.

An excerpt from the ATL transformation `VSD2UML` is given in Listing 6.1. A corresponding exemplary transformation input and result from the reference building model (Subsection 6.2.1) is given in Listings 6.2–6.3.

As a first example, the rule `VSDMetaInstance2UMLClass` is given, transforming a VSD `MetaInstance` into a UML `Class`. It is a matched ATL rule, so any metainstance that matches the source pattern given in `from` will be transformed using this rule. As its source pattern does not impose any restrictions it covers any metainstance. The created UML class adopts name, base class and the abstract flag directly from metainstance `mi`. Note that while `mi.name` and `mi.isAbstract` are both of basic Ecore data types (String and Boolean), `mi.baseClass` is an instance of VSD `MetaInstance` itself that cannot directly be assigned to the UML class's metaattribute `general`. However, the ATL engine interprets such assignments and searches for a matched rule to transform the element of the source metamodel (VSD) into an element of the target metamodel (UML). In this case, it is the rule `VSDMetaInstance2UMLClass` itself that will be applied to transform the base metainstance into a base class. Finally, the metaattribute `ownedAttribute` is assigned all UML properties created from the metainstance's own value-kind and reference-kind metaproperties as well as those created from the reverse direction of any metaproperty pointing at metainstance `mi`. To determine all value-kind metaproperties, ATL collection operator `select` is used. All these metaproperties are automatically transformed by another matched rule omitted in the example. In the second component of the `Set`, `collect` is used to apply a navigational expression on each collection element – in this case, ATL operator `resolveTemp`. It is used to determine elements of the target metamodel from elements of the source metamodel (here, iterator variable `e`) by referring to its name in a target pattern of another ATL rule. In this case this is necessary, as `propToTrg` is a non-default (i.e., not the first) target pattern of rule `VSDMetaPropertyRef2UMLAssociation`. In the third component of the `Set`, all instances of metaclass `MetaProperty` are retrieved and only those are selected, whose target type (`metaType`) equals the rule's metainstance `mi`. These are exactly those metaproperties pointing at `mi` from another (or the same) metainstance. For each of these, operator `resolveTemp` is used to determine the reverse direction UML property `propToSrc` also created by `VSDMetaPropertyRef2UMLAssociation`.

The rule `VSDMetaPropertyRef2UMLAssociation` transforms a VSD `MetaProperty` of kind `Ref` or `RefList` into a binary UML `Association`. This association connects those UML classes derived (by transformation) from the metaproperty's source (i.e., its owning metainstance) and target metainstance (i.e., its type). The rule's input is any VSD `MetaProperty` that has a non-value kind (i.e., a `Ref` or `RefList` kind). Such metaproperties are transformed into an instance of UML metaclass `Association` as well as two instances of UML metaclass `Property` for the association's member ends. The association's metaattribute `endType` is initialized with the source (`mp.myMetaInstance`) and target type (`mp.metaType`) of metaproperty `mp`, which are automatically transformed by the matched rule

**Listing 6.1:** *Exemplary excerpt from ATL module VSD2UML*

```
rule VSDMetaInstance2UMLClass {
    from
        mi: VSD!MetaInstance
    to
        cl: UML!Class (
            name <- mi.name,
            general <- mi.baseClass,
            isAbstract <- mi.isAbstract,
            ownedAttribute <- Set{
                mi.metaProperties -> select(e | e.kind=#Val),
                mi.metaProperties -> collect(e |
                thisModule.resolveTemp(e, 'propToTrg')),
                VSD!MetaProperty.allInstances() -> select(e | e.metaType = mi)
                    -> collect(e | thisModule.resolveTemp(e, 'propToSrc'))
                }.flatten()
        )
}
rule VSDMetaPropertyRef2UMLAssociation {
    from
        mp: VSD!MetaProperty (
            mp.kind<>#Val
        )
    to
        ass: UML!Association (
            endType <- Set{mp.metaType, mp.myMetaInstance},
            memberEnd <- Sequence{propToSrc, propToTrg}
        ),
        propToSrc: UML!Property (
            isComposite <- false,
            lower <- 0,
            upper <- 1,
            type <- mp.myMetaInstance
        ),
        propToTrg: UML!Property (
            isComposite <- mp.isAutoDel,
            lower <- 0,
            upper <- (if mp.kind=#Ref then 1 else -1 endif),
            name <- mp.name,
            type <- mp.metaType
        )
}
```

**Listing 6.2:** *Excerpt from the exemplary reference building model in XMI representation conforming to the VSD metamodel.*

```
<types xsi:type="VSD:MetaInstance" name="Shed" baseClass="//@types.4">
  <metaProperties name="volume" metaType="//@types.1"/>
  <metaProperties name="door" isAutoDel="true" metaType="//@types.9"
    kind="Ref"/>
</types>
```

**Listing 6.3:** *Excerpt from the exemplary reference building model in XMI representation conforming to the UML metamodel – derived by applying the transformation from Listing 6.1 on the input from Listing 6.2.*

```
<types xsi:type="UML:Class" name="Shed" general="//@types.10">
  <ownedAttribute name="door" isComposite="true" type="//@types.4"
    upper="1" association="//@types.12"/>
  <ownedAttribute name="volume" type="//@types.7" upper="1"/>
</types>
<types xsi:type="UML:Association" name="(Shed::door-->Door)"
  memberEnd="//@types.4/@ownedAttribute.1 //@types.3/@ownedAttribute.0"
  endType="//@types.3 //@types.4"/>
```

`VSDMetaInstance2UMLClass`. The assocation's member ends are an ordered `Sequence` of the UML properties `propToSrc` and `propToTrg`. In this case, operator `resolveTemp` is not needed as the properties are created within the same rule. The properties shall only be member ends but not owned ends of the association. Instead, rule `VSDMetaInstance2UMLClass` makes them owned attributes of their respective class. UML property `propToSrc` represents the reverse direction of VSD metaproperty `mp` by pointing at `mp.myMetaInstance`. Thus, this UML property can never be composite (i.e., never own its target) and is restricted to one or none target element. UML property `propToTrg` is composite if the metaproperty has the `isAutoDel` flag set. Its type is the metaproperty's target type and its multiplicity is 1 for kind `#Ref` (ATL notation for Ecore enumeration values) and $-1$, i.e., unlimited, for `#RefList`. Finally, its name is the metaproperty's name. Note that the property for the reverse direction as well as the association itself are not assigned any name thus staying anonymous as VSD does not have an immediate equivalent for an UML association.

Altogether, on schema level, the `VSD2UML` module transforms metainstances to UML classes, value-typed metaproperties to UML properties, and reference metaproperties to UML properties as well as stand-alone UML associations. Additionally, core instances of metaclass `MetaTypeValAtomicBasic` like `QString` etc. are explicitly transformed to their UML `PrimitiveType` counterpart and enumerations are transformed to enumerations. VSD container data types are not mapped to any immediate counterpart in UML. Instead, VSD metaproperties using them are mapped to UML properties with unlimited multiplicity.

On instance level, VSD instances are transformed to UML objects (`InstanceSpecifications` with classifier `Class`), and VSD value-properties to UML slots with value specifications. Furthermore, VSD reference-properties are transformed to UML links (i.e., `InstanceSpecifications` with a classifier of metatype `Association`) as well as corresponding UML slots. Other than UML properties (schema level), UML slots (instance level) are not shared between a link and the connected objects. Thus, for each VSD property (instance level) with reference-kind metaproperty (schema level), four slots are created: For the source object to point at the target object, for the target object to point at the source object, and for the link to point at the source and at the target object.

Most of the rules for the module `UML2VSD` can be derived by reversing their corresponding counterparts in `VSD2UML`. Special care has to be taken so that the modules are inverse to each other. That is, transforming a UML model to a VSD model with `UML2VSD` and transforming the result back from VSD to UML using `VSD2UML` should lead to the same initial UML model (round-trip). The same should apply to the reverse order. Otherwise, using the UML as a pivot metamodel leads to ambiguities when an element does not adhere its identity under such chained transformations. For example, an object must remain the identical object. Obviously, as the UML is a full-fledged General Purpose Modeling Language, its modeling concepts usually excel those of a database metamodel like VSD's. As mentioned above, for the methods presented in Chapter 5, a simplified excerpt of the UML metamodel suffices. The diversity of allowed UML models may additionally be restricted when the approach is to be used with a database that does not completely support them. In this case, VSD does not provide a native counterpart concept for UML associations. Thus, an inverse to `VSDMetaPropertyRef2UMLAssociation` of module `VSD2UML` in Listing 6.1 can only exist for equally restricted UML models. Hence, `UML2VSD` can only unambiguously transform such binary UML associations with no self-owned member ends (both must be owned attributes of the corresponding classes) that have a main direction identifiable by a named UML property to the target class and are otherwise anonymous. Altogether, the pair of model transformations is a bijective mapping between the simplified VSD metamodel and a restricted subset of the UML's language unit classes.

To summarize, on schema level `UML2VSD` transforms UML classes to VSD metainstances, UML properties to VSD metaproperties, core `PrimitiveTypes` like `String` to their VSD counterpart `MetaTypeValAtomicBasic`, and enumerations to enumerations. Associations are only indirectly mapped to reference-kind metaproperties. On instance level, UML objects are mapped to VSD instances, and UML slots and their value specifications are mapped to VSD properties with variants. Like associations, links are only mapped indirectly by setting corresponding member objects.

Using the presented transformations and the reference UML building model given in Subsection 6.2.1, all model elements are successfully transformed from UML to VSD and back to UML. In the absence of a concrete syntax for the VSD metamodel, the corresponding VSD building model is shown in a tree-like representation in Figure 6.7. Altogether, Requirement 4 (UML as pivot metamodel) can be seen as fulfilled for VSD when respecting the mentioned restrictions (in particular for UML associations). Consequently, Requirement 2 (model transformations) is implicitly also fulfilled by the transformations from and to UML.

### 6.3.3 VSD Runtime System

After verifying VSD's fulfillment of the metamodel-based requirements, the runtime system requirements are verified. For Requirement 5, a reflection interface must be provided. VSD offers such an interface by design. The metadata elements modeled in its metamodel are not only conceptually present but also exist as reified (see Subsection 4.2.1) elements in the runtime system. Thus, when using VSD, not only instances and properties are directly accessible during runtime. Also metainstances and metaproperties are so-called "first-class citizens" of VSD, i.e., not only a concept but also accessible from the runtime system. Any instance in VSD can be queried for its metainstance, which itself is technically speaking an object of the underlying programming language C++. A metainstance can be queried for its name, its base metainstance, its metaproperties or the aforementioned metamethods. A new instance can be instantiated given its metainstance, its properties can be set given its metaproperties, and its operations can be executed given only its metamethods. Besides querying and using the metadata of instances, it can also be created during runtime. For this, new metainstances are created and provided with a name and a base metainstance. Metaproperties are created equally and attached to the new metainstance. Thus, Requirement 5 can be seen as fulfilled by VSD's runtime system.

Requirement 6 (identification of instances) is fulfilled by an ID (Identifier) managed for each instance existing in the runtime database. Instances can be queried for their ID and they can also be retrieved from the runtime system by this ID. This can be seen as an implementation of OIDs (Object Identifiers) as presented in Subsection 3.1.3.

Finally, Requirement 7 (notifications) has to be verified. As mentioned above, VSD is an active database. This includes a notification mechanism for changes to the data. Components can subscribe to such notifications on different levels of detail: on single-instance level, on metainstance level, or on database level. Changes include instance insertion or removal, value property updates, as well as insertions in and removals from reference properties. Hence, this requirement is fulfilled as well.

**Figure 6.7:** *VSD model corresponding to the exemplary reference UML building model from Figures 6.3–6.4. The upper part comprises elements for schema description, the lower part for instance data description.*

## 6.4 ExtDB: SupportGIS Java (SGJ)

SGJ is an object-oriented abstraction layer for standard relational database systems or other storage back-ends. Its main purpose and field of application is managing geodata for GISs (Geo Information Systems). Supported back-ends include relational DBMSs (Database Management Systems) like PostgreSQL [129], Oracle [21], MySQL [14], a (transient) in-memory approach, or a WFS (Web Feature Service). Thus, in combination with an RDBMS (Relational Database Management System) back-end it can be seen as an implementation of the ORM (Object-Relational Mapping) approach.

One of the basic principles of SGJ is its adherence to international standards. OGC (Open Geospatial Consortium) standards like GML (Geography Markup Language [26]) are of particular interest. Application schemata in GML-compliant XSD (XML Schema Definition)-notation can be adopted. Subsequently, GML instance documents can be imported and exported. Thus, data exchange as well as management are both as-is standard compliant – without transformations to a another format. This flexibility is achieved by using a generic base schema within the back-end. This base schema is used to flexibly store a description of the respective application schema in terms of management table entries and generic data tables (in case of a relational back-end).

In particular, the combination of flexibly definable, object-oriented schemata with standard relational back-ends motivate SGJ's usage within a reference implementation of the presented approach for database synchronization. To adopt the approach for SGJ as an ExtDB implementation, the requirements from Chapter 4 have to be verified. This is done in the following subsections.

### 6.4.1 SGJ Metamodel

An Ecore-based metamodel of SGJ is given in Figures 6.8–6.9. The first diagram depicts those metaclasses describing schema components. The object-oriented SGJ uses a metaclass `Class` with metaattribute name. A class can have different types, modeled by the `ClassType` metaenumeration. It can `default` to a normal class, be `abstract`, or an `enum`. However, due to its origin from GML- and thus XML-based data models, a class can also be of type `choice`. This special type allows a corresponding object to only have one of its attributes set at a time – in the style of an XML choice type. Finally, a class can have one or no base class. An SGJ class can own `Attributes`, which can be multiple, and have a name and a type. The type, in turn, is modeled as a metaenumeration including `bool`, `double`, `long`, `string` and `class` types. In the case of a class-type attribute, a reference to the `Class` metaclass is used to model the target type. Using a `class`-type attribute is one possibility to model references between objects in SGJ. Another independent approach is the so-called metaclass `Relation`. In SGJ, the term is used differently than in relational databases. A relation is a concept on schema level similar to (unidirectional) UML binary associations. It describes a named connection between two classes. Furthermore, relations always come in pairs, i.e., one relation describing the reverse direction of the other. The metareference `backRelation` models this relationship. Thus, a single relation is always directed from `source` to `target` class. If the utilized schema definition itself omits the back relation it is automatically added. Below, this is called an *anonymous* back relation. Furthermore, a relation can allow multiple instances (i.e., objects) of its target class using metaattribute `isMultiple`. It can also model ownership of the target objects by the source object using `isComposite`.

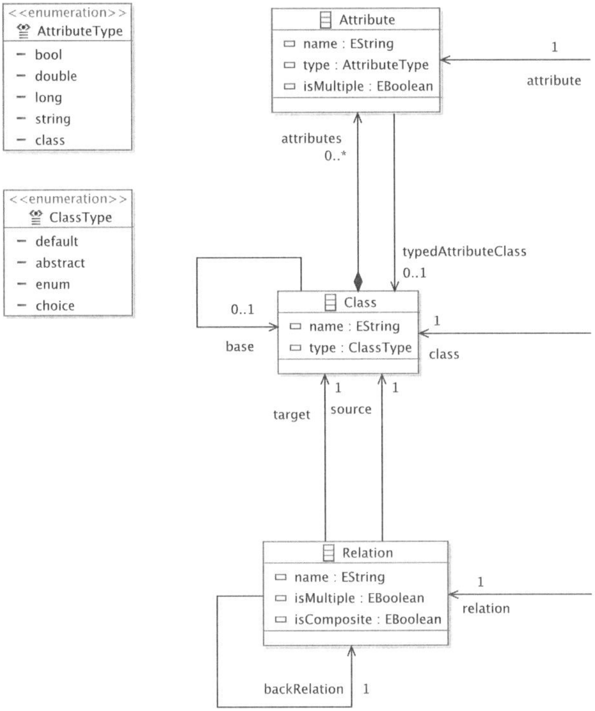


**Figure 6.8:** *A metamodel of SGJ – Metaclasses for schema description.*

On the instance part of the SGJ metamodel, the metaclass `Object` is used to model ontological instances of `Class`. An object can hold a `Value` for each of its attributes. A value may be `isDefault` if it was not explicitly set. If a single value is present, one of the corresponding types is used: `ValueLong`, `ValueBoolean`, `ValueDouble`, `ValueString`, or - `ValueObject` for class-type attributes. These metaclasses are always used for single-valued attributes, but also for multiple-valued attributes in case they only hold one value. Multiple values are modeled using `ValueMultiple`. Finally, an ontological instance of `Relation` is

`RelationInstance`. A relation instance connects a single source object with a single target object and thus resembles a directed UML link. Note that for each back relation, a separate back relation instance exists. For multiple relations, multiple relation instances may exist for the same source object.

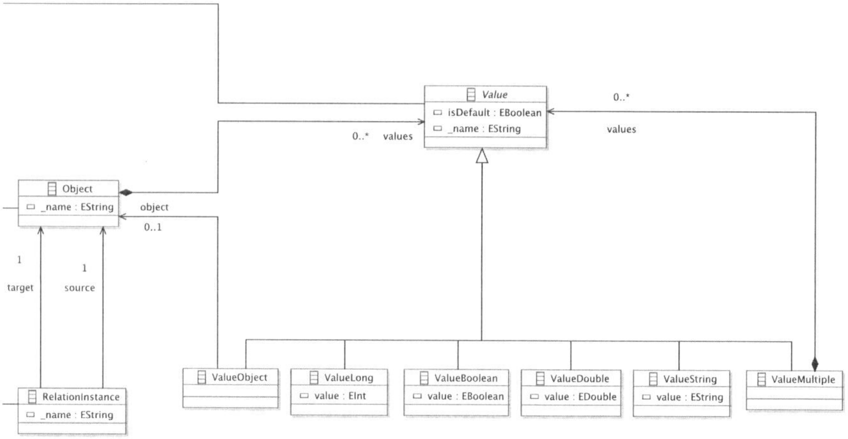


**Figure 6.9:** *A metamodel of SGJ – Metaclasses for instance data description.*

### 6.4.2 Model Transformation SGJ–UML

The ATL module `SGJ2UML` transforms a model given in the SGJ metamodel into the (simplified) UML metamodel presented in Figure 3.12–3.13. On initialization of the transformation, UML primitive types are created and mapped to the literals of the `AttributeType` enumeration. Furthermore, all pairs of non-anonymous SGJ relations and their anonymous back relation counterpart are determined (for later transformation to UML associations). To comply with the restrictions for directed associations mentioned above, only directed SGJ relations with an anonymous back direction shall be allowed. After initialization, SGJ classes are transformed into UML classes. SGJ attributes are transformed to UML properties either with a primitive type or with the target UML class for class-typed attributes. Note that this kind of modeling references is currently not supported by `UML2VSD`. The initially collected pairs of counterpart SGJ relations are mapped to UML associations with member end properties that are also owned attributes of their corresponding source and target classes.

On instance level, SGJ objects are transformed into UML instance specifications with class-type classifier. For each single value of an SGJ object, a UML slot and a corresponding value specification of the appropriate type is created. For instances of `ValueMultiple`, a single UML slot with a value specification for each member SGJ value is created. Like SGJ relations, pairs of relation instances are transformed into UML links with a slot and an instance value for source and target. Likewise, slots with instance values are created for the member objects representing the owned attributes of source and target class. Thus, just as with `VSD2UML`, a total of four slots are created for each pair of relation instances.

The reverse module `UML2SGJ` operates similarly. Again, care has to be taken so that rules are inverse to each other. On schema level, UML classes are transformed into SGJ classes, properties into attributes (only value-typed for now), and associations into pairs of counterpart relations. On instance level, UML objects are mapped to SGJ objects. All associated slots with primitive type are transformed into SGJ values (with separate rules for single and multi-valued slots). Slots with instance value are ignored here as only the corresponding links have to be considered. Finally, UML links are transformed to pairs of SGJ relation instances. A result for transforming the reference UML building model from Figures 6.3–6.4 to the SGJ metamodel is shown in Figure 6.10.

By giving a metamodel including metaclasses for ontological instantiation and by complementing model transformations from and to the UML metamodel, SGJ fulfills Requirements 1, 3 and 4 as well as implicitly Requirement 2.

### 6.4.3 SGJ Runtime System

SGJ must also be checked towards the runtime system requirements. The first is Requirement 5 (reflection). Similar to VSD, SGJ supports reflection by reifing instances of schema-describing metaclasses like `SGJClass` or `SGJAttribute`. Accessing an object (instance of `S-GJObject`) through the SGJ API (Application Programming Interface), its class (`SGJClass`) can be retrieved. In turn, attributes (`SGJAttribute`) and relations (`SGJRelation`) can be retrieved from this class. They can be used to query the object's value for an attribute or to retrieve associated objects. Given a class, new objects can be instantiated (ontologically) and attribute values and relations can be set. Finally, new schema components (i.e., new classes, attributes, and relations) can be created during runtime. Altogether, this suffices to fulfill Requirement 5.

Like VSD, SGJ fulfills Requirement 6 (identifiable instance data) by implementing the concept of OIDs.

Finally, Requirement 7 (notifications) is fulfilled by a notification subsystem. It allows to register for changes on instance (object, relation instance) and even on schema (class, relation) level. In the context of this work, only the former are used. Object notifications inform about object insertions, removals, and changes to attribute values. Relation instance notifications work similarly: Insertions and removals of relation instances between a pair of objects are notified. Note that changes to the central data storage caused by any client are

**Figure 6.10:** *SGJ model corresponding to the reference UML building model from Figures 6.3–6.4. The upper part comprises elements for schema description, the lower part for instance data description.*

notified to all registered clients. This is a difference to VSD (and perhaps any implementation of SimDB), which is only changed locally by components of the simulation system itself. Thus, to locally (i.e., at one simulation client) distinguish between the changes actively synchronized from VSD to SGJ and those coming from other SGJ clients, a client ID is attached to every notification allowing to differentiate in between.

## 6.5 VSD–SGJ Reference Implementation

The first reference implementation of the presented approach consists of the simulation system VEROSIM and its simulation database VSD as well as the object-oriented data management component SupportGIS Java. The reference implementation is quite sophisticated and has been used for different types of applications (see Chapter 7).

### 6.5.1 Java API in C++

A special feature of the VSD–SGJ reference implementation is that a C++-based simulation system (VEROSIM and VSD) has to be connected to a Java-based system (SupportGIS Java). Again, for performance reasons, the Java API of SGJ should directly be used by the simulation system. In general, this can be realized using the JNI (Java Native Interface [130]). However, this only allows for a very basic C-style access to Java objects, methods and the like. Therefore, in the scope of the reference implementation, a generic C++ wrapper framework yielding object-oriented C++ wrapper classes for Java classes was developed. Wrappers were created for necessary SGJ API classes (wrapper code creation for the framework was also automated). The C++ wrapper classes allow for an almost identical usage of the Java-based API within C++ with only some management commands for the JVM (Java Virtual Machine).

## 6.6 ExtDB: XML and XSD

As presented in Chapter 3, XML and the XSD Language are widespread means for data modeling. This suggests an adoption of the presented approach for XML data and schemata ([131]).

The challenge, however, is to map XML-represented data and XSD-represented schemata to an object-oriented representation like UML, i.e., to transform the metamodel of XML and XSD to (and from) the UML metamodel. Such a mapping corresponds to the concept of XML data binding [132, 133]. In a process called unmarshalling or deserialization, an XML document's content is mapped to corresponding objects. To provide the necessary object-oriented structures, appropriate classes and attributes have to be derived, typically from the corresponding XSD. Here, compared to generic XML access methods like DOM (Document

Object Model) or SAX (Simple API for XML), XML data can intuitively be handled in terms of objects. Different tools for XML data binding exist, like JAXB (Java Architecture for XML Binding [134]) for Java or Codesynthesis XSD [135] for C++. However, the mapping from XSD to OO (Object-Oriented or Object-Orientation) is not as straightforward as it may seem. [132] even states "XML Schemas are designed to model XML documents, not data, and data is better modeled in an object schema or a design language such as UML."

This impedance mismatch can be depicted with the example of XSD complex types and elements and their ambiguous mapping to the object-oriented class concept. Figure 6.11 gives a simplified XSD metamodel excerpt. On schema level (left), an element has a complex type. The latter defines inheritance and contents. Both can independently be either abstract or not. On XML document level, ontological instances of elements (`ElementInstance`) are used. Listing 6.4 shows an exemplary XSD defining a complex type and a corresponding element, Listing 6.5 a conforming instance document. An XSD element definition can be mapped to a class. However, an element is partly also defined by its complex type. The mapping of a complex type itself is ambiguous. For example, it can be mapped to a separate base class. This class should be abstract as XML data can only be instantiated for element definitions. In the example listing, `aComplexType` would become a class with a string property `val`. This class is an abstract base class of a concrete class `anElement`. From the instance XML document, an object of class `anElement` with property value "Hello World" would be created. However, this way, the "abstract" property of the complex type definition gets irrelevant. Another alternative is to map a pair of complex type and element definition to a single class. This may be ambiguous if the same complex type is reused for different element definitions. Besides the mapping of complex types, other XSD aspects add to the impedance mismatch, like the differentiation between child elements and XML attributes, or element and attribute groups. The examples are taken from a detailed survey in [132].

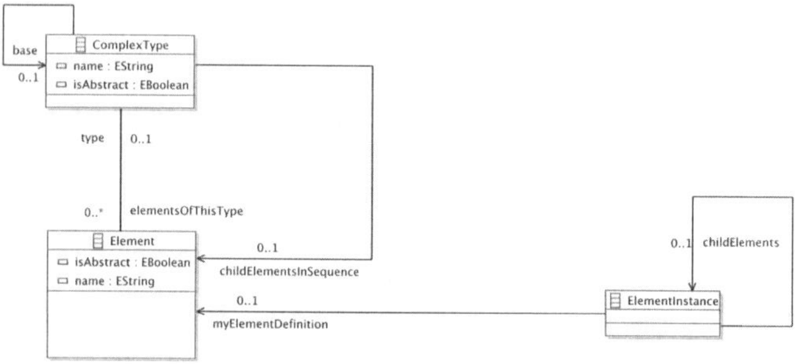


**Figure 6.11:** *Simplified XSD metamodel excerpt: Relationship between XSD complex type and element.*

**Listing 6.4:** *Example of XSD element and complex type.*

```
<xs:element name="anElement" type="aComplexType"/>
<xs:complexType name="aComplexType">
  <xs:complexContent>
    <xs:sequence>
      <xs:element name="val" type="xs:string"/>
    </xs:sequence>
  </xs:complexContent>
</xs:complexType>
```

**Listing 6.5:** *Example of an XML document conforming to the XSD in Listing 6.4.*

```
<anElement>
  <val>Hello World</val>
</anElement>
```

As a conclusion, a *generic* mapping (i.e., model transformation) between XSD and UML seems unsuitable. Instead, in practical data models, XML is typically used with a limited set of modeling primitives, well-defined modeling rules, and additional semantics. This can be seen in different standardized data models in various fields of application like industrial automation (AutomationML (Automation Modeling Language [6])), geography information systems (GML), or 3D data (X3D (Extensible 3D [39])).

Thus, to use XML as a generic exchange format for object-oriented data, rules restricting the diversity of XSD and defining semantics for certain modeling constructs have to be defined. This concept is followed by another reference implementation realizing a file-based variation of the approach presented in this work. Here, the focus is on standardized data exchange and integration of loosely coupled systems rather than on a centralized platform like a database. Nevertheless, a subset of the presented methods can be applied. The following subsection describes the modeling concepts developed for this approach.

### 6.6.1 XML Modeling in an Object-Oriented Context

As previously stated, in general, the concepts of XML and object-orientation do not match one-to-one. However, in this context the aim is not to map arbitrary XML documents with each and every possible XML modeling technique to an object-oriented representation and vice versa (round-trip). Instead, a common schema definition is agreed on, where modeling techniques can be limited and corresponding semantics be defined. Such conventions comprise restriction to certain XSD constructs, coding conventions, usage of a non-application specific base schema, and an agreement on semantics in an object-oriented context. For this purpose, approaches from the GML specification can be adopted. In annexes E and F, it defines mappings between UML and XSD constructs for GML schema definitions. In a generalized form, these mappings are the conceptual basis for the following XSD modeling conventions.

One convention is to always define pairs of XSD elements and corresponding complex types. In an object-oriented context, such a pair can be mapped to a single class. The example in Listing 6.6 would be mapped to a class `SomeClass` derived from a class `SomeBaseClass` and with class attributes `someClassAttribute` as well as `someOtherClassAttribute`. While the element part of the definition allows to use instances in XML documents, the type part (with the standardized `Type` suffix to the name) is used to define content and inheritance. Although there are different approaches for mapping such XSD pairs to object-oriented structures (see [132]), this approach is well-suited when schema definitions can be restricted to the aforementioned pairing.

**Listing 6.6:** *Class definition in XSD.*

```
<xs:element name="SomeClass" type="SomeClassType"
  substitutionGroup="SomeBaseClass"/>
<xs:complexType name="SomeClassType">
  <xs:complexContent>
    <xs:extension base="SomeBaseClassType">
      <xs:sequence>
        <xs:element name="someClassAttribute" type="xs:string"/>
        <xs:element name="someOtherClassAttribute" type="xs:double"/>
      </xs:sequence>
    </xs:extension>
  </xs:complexContent>
</xs:complexType>
```

An exemplary instance conforming to this schema fragment could look like Listing 6.7. Note that a child element `someBaseClassAttribute` is assumed to be derived from `SomeBaseClassType`.

**Listing 6.7:** *Example for instance of class.*

```
<SomeClass>
  <someBaseClassAttribute>a value</someBaseClassAttribute>
  <someClassAttribute>another value</someClassAttribute>
  <someOtherClassAttribute>12.3</someOtherClassAttribute>
</SomeClass>
```

Another convention is to only use XML child elements as class attributes, like the `someClassAttribute` and `someOtherClassAttribute` definitions above. Note that these attributes are not XML attributes but XML child elements. The rationale for this approach is that object-orientated metamodels usually cannot reflect and distinguish these two concepts. Therefore, XML attributes are rather used for special properties of class attributes or things like ids, ID-based references or units of physical quantities. Examples for this usage are shown below.

In a mechanism for typed reference properties, one can differentiate between references with or without transitive deletion characteristics. The former corresponds to UML composite aggregations while the latter to UML shared aggregations or "normal" UML associations. Other than UML, relations are typically modeled without independent association types but rather using references from one object to another. Also adopted from GML, two modeling techniques for such references are used. Listing 6.8 shows an example for a composite-like reference. The aim here is to model a `Composite` class referencing its `Part` instances using a named property called `parts`. This is realized by defining a special type for referencing a part called `PartCompositionType` (with standardized name suffix `CompositionType`). This type holds a reference to a `Part` element.

**Listing 6.8:** *Composite reference definition.*

```
<xs:element name="Composite" type="CompositeType"/>
<xs:complexType name="CompositeType">
  <xs:complexContent>
    <xs:sequence>
      <xs:element name="parts" type="PartCompositionType"
        minOccurs="0" maxOccurs="unbounded"/>
    </xs:sequence>
  </xs:complexContent>
</xs:complexType>
<xs:element name="Part" type="PartType"/>
<xs:complexType name="PartType"/>
<xs:complexType name="PartCompositionType">
  <xs:sequence>
    <xs:element ref="Part"/>
  </xs:sequence>
</xs:complexType>
```

In an instance document, the list of part instances is defined inline, each encapsulated by a parts tag (see Listing 6.9). In particular, this shows the difference to directly using `PartType` as the type for the parts element, which would lead to the contents of `PartType` being inserted within the parts tag (instead of instances of `Part`). Furthermore, type safety within the parts tag can be checked with standard XML validation because of the employed XSD `ref` definition.

As a part is usually only referenced by one composite at a time, the proposed composite reference mechanism only allows inline definition of target elements. In contrast, for shared

**Listing 6.9:** *Composite reference example.*

```
<Composite>
  <parts>
    <Part/>
  </parts>
  <parts>
    <Part/>
  </parts>
  <parts>
    <Part/>
  </parts>
</Composite>
```

aggregations or simple cross references, targets may be referenced from several properties. Thus, an ID-based mechanism is necessary. Adopted from GML, a reference type can be defined that uses XLink (XML Linking Language [136]) to refer to the target of the reference. This approach is generic and can thus be defined as part of a base schema. As shown in Listing 6.10, the generic `ReferenceType` itself only holds an attribute group containing a simple xlink and an optional remote schema for the target. The xlink can be used to reference a target using a URI (Uniform Resource Identifier). In this context, this is realized as an XPointer (XML Pointer Language [137]) expression to address another element, usually in the same document. Therefore, elements need an identifier, which is realized as an XML attribute of a common base type like `SuperBaseType` within the base schema. Using the XML type ID, the identifier is forced to be unique within the document.

**Listing 6.10:** *Generic non-composite reference type definition.*

```
<xs:complexType name="ReferenceType">
  <xs:sequence/>
  <xs:attributeGroup ref="AssociationAttributeGroup"/>
</xs:complexType>
<xs:attributeGroup name="AssociationAttributeGroup">
  <xs:attributeGroup ref="xlink:simpleLink"/>
  <xs:attribute ref="remoteSchema" use="optional"/>
</xs:attributeGroup>
<xs:complexType name="SuperBaseType">
  <xs:complexContent>
    <xs:sequence/>
    <xs:attribute name="id" type="xs:ID" use="optional"/>
  <xs:complexContent>
</xs:complexType>
```

Application schemata can include this base schema to define types that reference each other. In Listing 6.11, a source type references a target type. Particularly, the target type has to be derived from the super base type defining the ID attribute. The source type contains a child element `target` of type `ReferenceType`. It holds an XML annotation-appinfo-construct to restrict the allowed target elements of the reference. Due to the capabilities of XML, this type restriction cannot be explicitly modeled. Thus, it can only be checked within an application but not using XML validation mechanisms.

**Listing 6.11:** *Usage of reference type in an application schema.*

```
<xs:element name="Source" type="SourceType"/>
<xs:complexType name="SourceType">
  <xs:complexContent>
    <xs:sequence>
      <xs:element name="target" type="base:ReferenceType" minOccurs="0">
        <xs:annotation>
          <xs:appinfo>
            <targetElement>Target</targetElement>
          </xs:appinfo>
        </xs:annotation>
      </xs:element>
    </xs:sequence>
  </xs:complexContent>
</xs:complexType>
<xs:element name="Target" type="TargetType" substitutionGroup="base:SuperBase"/>
<xs:complexType name="TargetType">
  <xs:complexContent>
    <xs:extension base="base:SuperBaseType"/>
  </xs:complexContent>
</xs:complexType>
```

Listing 6.12 shows an exemplary fragment from an XML instance document using the previously defined reference mechanism without transitive deletion characteristics. An instance of the source type uses its `target` child element to reference an instance of the target type with a simple xlink.

**Listing 6.12:** *Example for instance of reference type.*

```
<Source>
  <target xlink:href="#id1"/>
</Source>
<!-- ... -->
<Target id="id1"/>
```

### 6.6.2 XML Metamodel

The previously described, restricted XSD modeling approach can as well be formalized using a metamodel. Figure 6.12 shows the metaclasses for schema description. The central metaclass is the `GlobalElementDefinition`. An example would be `SomeClass` from Listing 6.6. Each global element definition has an associated complex type (`ComplexType-4GlobalElement`). Inheritance is modeled with the base type, together with the global element definition's substitution group. The complex type also models the contents of the global element definition using property element definitions. In the aforementioned example, `SomeClassType` is modeled as a linguistic instance of `ComplexType4GlobalElement` and has two property element definitions `someClassAttribute` and `someOtherClassAttribute`. Their types are both simple types. In contrast, Listing 6.8 shows a property element definition `parts` with a composition type `PartCompositionType`. Each global element definition can own such a type for referencing instances of itself by composition. Furthermore, the target element for non-composite references (see Listing 6.11) is modeled as a metareference from property element definition to global element definition.

Figure 6.13 shows the instance part of the metamodel. The ontological instance of a global element definition is modeled as a `GlobalElementInstance`. It can have several -`PropertyElementInstances` – defined by property element definitions – representing the global element's contents. Each such property can either have a single target element for a non-composite reference, a single child element for a composite reference, or a single simple value. Property definitions with a `maxOccurs` larger than one have one property element instance per occurrence.

### 6.6.3 Model Transformation XML–UML

The restricted XSD metamodel is mapped to and from the (simplified) UML metamodel using two ATL model transformations. They formalize the mapping described in Subsection 6.6.1.

For each UML class, the transformation from UML to XSD creates a global element definition, an associated complex type, and a composition type. UML properties are mapped to property element definitions. UML primitive types (string, integer, ...) are mapped to XSD simple types. Thus, the type of a UML property is either mapped to the corresponding XSD simple type for primitive typed properties, to the appropriate XSD composition type for composite UML properties, or to the generic reference type for non-composite references. In the latter case, the target element is set adequately. Similar to the transformation from UML to VSD, associations are omitted and only non-owned member ends are allowed. On instance level, UML instance specifications representing objects are mapped to global element instances. UML slots and value specifications are transformed to XSD property element instances with either an appropriate `Value` specialization in case of simple types or an

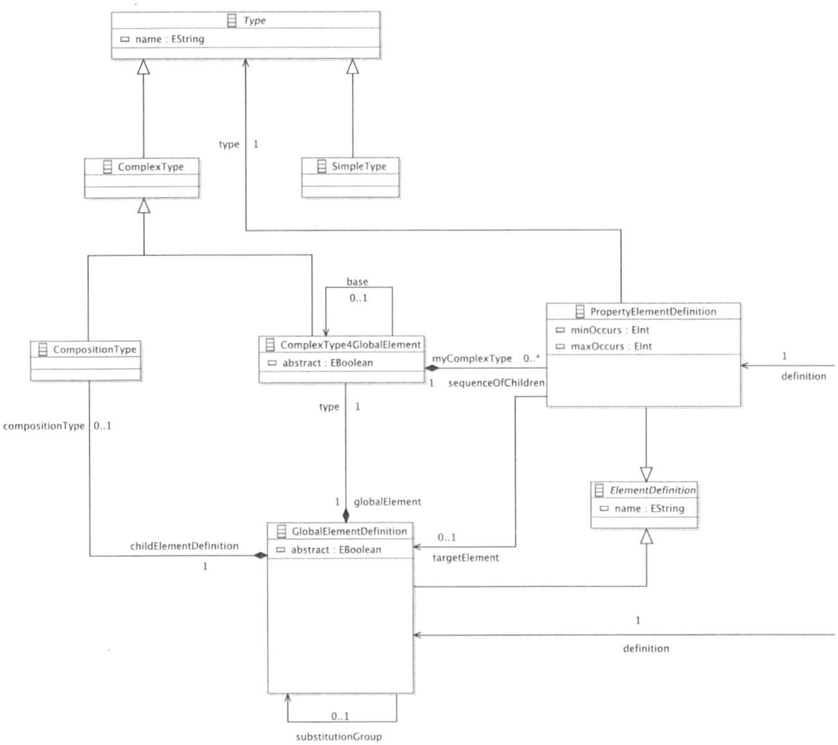


**Figure 6.12:** *A metamodel describing the utilized restricted XSD language – Left part: metaclasses for schema description, continued in Figure 6.13.*

appropriate child or target reference. Here, the different modeling of multiplicity has to be matched: In UML, there is one slot per property possibly holding several value specifications. In XSD, there is one property element instance per value, child or target.

The result for testing the transformation on the reference UML building model from Figures 6.3–6.4 is shown in Figure 6.14.

The back transformation from XSD to UML is mostly straightforward. Each global element definition and its complex type is mapped to a UML class. XSD property element definitions are mapped to UML properties. Like with the transformation from VSD to UML, UML associations are created from XSD reference properties (composite or non-composite) adding an additional property for back references at each UML class. Simple types are mapped to UML primitive types. On instance level, global elements are mapped to UML objects (instance specifications with class-typed classifier). Their corresponding property element instances (and possibly available values) are transformed to UML slots and value

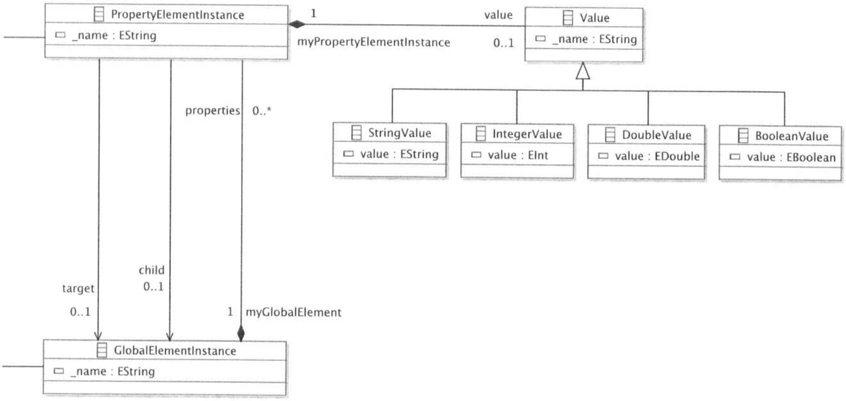


**Figure 6.13:** *A metamodel describing the utilized restricted XSD language – Right part: metaclasses for instance data description, continuation of Figure 6.12.*

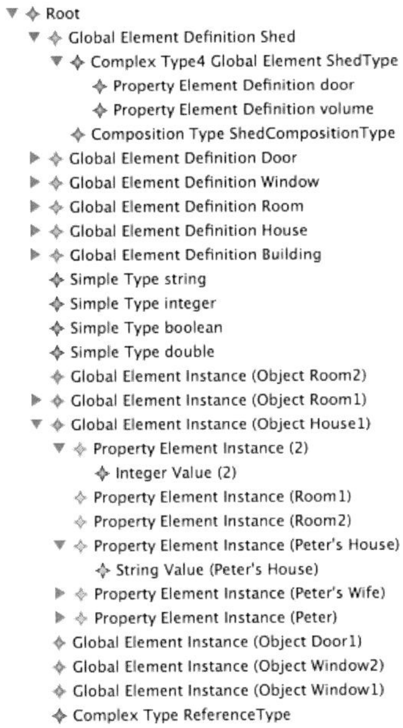


**Figure 6.14:** *XSD model corresponding to the reference UML building model from Figures 6.3–6.4. The upper part comprises elements for schema description, the lower part for instance data description.*

specifications. Again, multiplicity has to be treated specially. UML links (instance specifications with association-typed classifier) are created from non-simple-valued property element instances.

Given this and the previous subsection, the metamodel requirements are fulfilled for the XML-based approach. As mentioned above, runtime system requirements cannot be completely fulfilled using a simple file-based approach. Only Requirement 6 (identification of instances) is met using the ids, e.g., presented in Listing 6.12. Requirement 5 (reflection) is fulfilled to some degree by accessing the XSD file. However, Requirement 7 (notifications) is not fulfilled. To cope with these restrictions, an appropriate XML database might be considered.

### 6.6.4 Advanced Modeling Techniques

Besides the aforementioned basic modeling rules, some more advanced techniques were also integrated into the approach.

A variation of the previously introduced document-internal references are document-external references. In the context of Semantic World Models, such references can be used as an include mechanism for sub models from a catalog XML file. References are usually defined similarly to compositions because sub models are interpreted as being instantiated as a part of a composite. Therefore, an extended variation of Listing 6.8 is given in Listing 6.13. In this example, a workcell can have a robot. This robot can either be defined inline within the workcell as before or it can be referenced within another document using the association attribute group. An example catalog and an example document are given in Listing 6.14 and Listing 6.15.

**Listing 6.13:** *Extended composition reference definition for sub models in an application schema.*

```
<xs:element name="Workcell" type="WorkcellType"/>
<xs:complexType name="WorkcellType">
  <xs:complexContent>
    <xs:sequence>
      <xs:element name="robot" type="RobotCompositionType" minOccurs="0"/>
    </xs:sequence>
  </xs:complexContent>
</xs:complexType>
<xs:element name="Robot" type="RobotType" substitutionGroup="base:SuperBase"/>
<xs:complexType name="RobotType">
  <xs:complexContent>
    <xs:extension base="base:SuperBaseType"/>
  </xs:complexContent>
</xs:complexType>
<xs:complexType name="RobotCompositionType">
  <xs:sequence minOccurs="0">
    <xs:element ref="Robot"/>
  </xs:sequence>
  <xs:attributeGroup ref="AssociationAttributeGroup"/>
</xs:complexType>
```

**Listing 6.14:** *Example catalog.*

```
<Catalog>
  <predefinedRobots>
    <Robot id="id1"/>
    <Robot id="id2"/>
    <Robot id="id3"/>
    <Robot id="id4"/>
  </predefinedRobots>
</Catalog>
```

**Listing 6.15:** *Example for a document fragment referencing a sub model in a catalog.*

```
<Workcell>
  <robot xlink:href="catalog.xml#id1"/>
</Workcell>
```

Another more advanced modeling technique, similarly used in GML, is to define physical quantities with units. Within the base schema, special derived simple types are defined that combine a floating point value with a unit enumeration (Listing 6.16). In an application schema (Listing 6.17), such simple types may be used. In a conforming XML document (Listing 6.18), instances of the child element can be combined with a unit attribute value. The document will only be valid with one of the predefined unit values. Such unit information can subsequently be mapped into object-oriented structures (as far as they support this feature).

**Listing 6.16:** *Exemplary physical quantity definition within the base schema.*

```
<xs:simpleType name="length">
  <xs:complexContent>
    <xs:extension base="xs:double">
      <xs:attribute name="unit">
        <xs:simpleType>
          <xs:restriction base="xs:string">
            <xs:enumeration value="m"/>
            <xs:enumeration value="km"/>
            <xs:enumeration value="cm"/>
            <!-- ... -->
          </xs:restriction>
        </xs:simpleType>
      </xs:attribute>
    </xs:extension>
  </xs:complexContent>
</xs:simpleType>
```

## 6.7 VSD–XML Reference Implementation

In contrast to databases, the XML-based reference implementation uses files for schema (XSD) and instance data (XML) handling. The implementation is based on the simulation system VEROSIM and its simulation database VSD as introduced above. The pair of XSD and XML file represent the external database (ExtDB). The implementation represents an XML data binding approach. Figure 6.15 gives an overview.

**Listing 6.17:** *Exemplary application schema fragment using defined physical quantity.*

```
<xs:element name="Factory" type="FactoryType"/>
<xs:complexType name="FactoryType">
  <xs:complexContent>
    <xs:sequence>
      <xs:element name="height" type="base:length"/>
    </xs:sequence>
  </xs:complexContent>
</xs:complexType>
```

**Listing 6.18:** *Exemplary instance document fragment using a physical quantity.*

```
<Factory>
  <height unit="m">25</height>
</Factory>
```

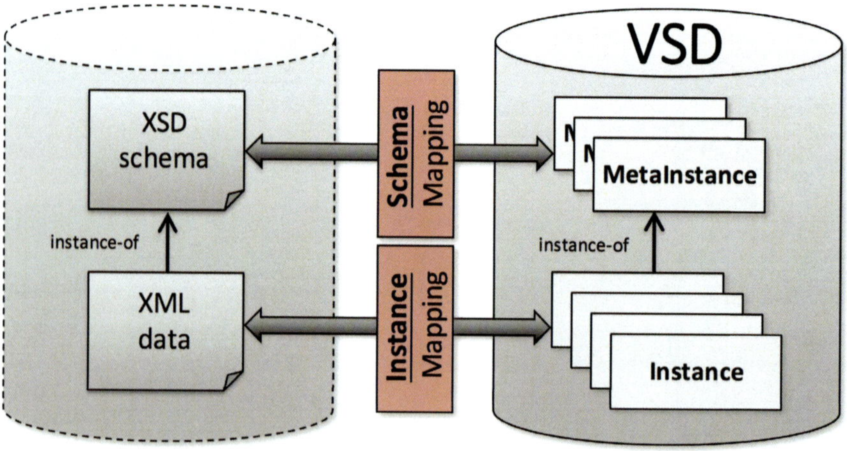


**Figure 6.15:** *Basic idea of the VSD–XML reference implementation: While schema sync is realized via the XSD file, data sync is based on the corresponding XML data file.*

Methods for schema synchronization can be implemented straightforwardly. The XSD file defining the data schema is used to synchronize the schema to the VSD. The aforementioned pairs of XML elements and complex type definitions are either mapped to existing VSD metainstances (schema sync by matching) or new metainstances are created (schema sync by transfer). Accordingly, XML child element definitions are synchronized to VSD metaproperties. These can either be value or reference metaproperties. For value metaproperties, the XML type is translated to the corresponding VSD metatype. For example, an `xs:integer` type is mapped to an `int` within VSD. Composite references are identified by the `CompositionType` suffix. The corresponding target type can be derived from the encapsulated XML ref element. Non-composite references are identified by the usage of -`ReferenceType`. Here, the target type is derived from the `targetElement` notation in the XML-annotation-appinfo structure. The special types for physical quantities with units are mapped to value metaproperties with units. VSD supports unit definition on schema level. Thus, the base SI (International System of Units) unit is used (e.g., meter for the physical quantity "length").

Due to limited query and non-existent notification capabilities, a plain XML document does not seem to be adequate for concurrent data exchange or huge amounts of data. Therefore, the methods presented in Chapter 5, especially in Section 5.2, are limited to loading (i.e., unmarshalling) and saving (i.e., marshalling) of complete XML instance documents. For each XML element, loading retrieves the corresponding metainstance from the schema mapping. Accordingly, for child elements, corresponding metaproperties are retrieved. The metainstance is ontologically instantiated, value metaproperties are replicated, and the value of the ID attribute is retrieved if available. Standard composite references are defined inline and are replicated recursively. For non-composite references, the xlink information is evaluated. When the corresponding target element is already loaded (determined by the ID attribute value), the reference is also resolved within VSD. Otherwise, it is kept for a downstream secondary pass that resolves all remaining non-composite references.

In case of a composite reference with an external xlink target element, the corresponding external file is opened, the referenced element is searched, the subtree rooted at this element is loaded, and the result is attached to the composite reference. The original XML file location and element ID are stored, so the external reference can be restored when marshaling (saving) the data back to file. For physical quantities, the unit specified in the instance document is compared to the unit of the metaproperty defined on schema level. If they differ, the value is converted accordingly.

Saving the contents of the VSD to an XML document also works recursively, beginning at the root instance. Each instance's metainstance is retrieved and using the schema mapping an appropriate XML element is created. For each metaproperty, XML child elements are added, which either contain simple values, further child elements representing target instances for composite references, xlink attribute values for internal non-composite references, or xlinks to external sub model elements. For the latter, the additionally stored information mentioned above is used. For physical quantities, the current normalized value with the base SI unit is written.

Except for units, this approach allows for a lossless round-trip of XML documents with an application schema conforming to the aforementioned XML modeling conventions. That is, an XML document can be loaded into VSD and saved back to an identical XML document.

Complementing this interface, an XSD generator has also been realized. It can be used to create an XSD file (compatible with the presented approach) from existing metainstances during runtime of VEROSIM.

# Chapter 7

# Applications

This chapter gives an overview of the various eRobotics applications already realized based on the presented data management architecture and its reference implementations shown in the previous chapter. They range from as different fields of applications as environment, industry, and space applications (see Figures 1.1–1.3). Nevertheless, they all benefit from the flexibility provided by the approach. Another commonality is the usage of Semantic World Models as introduced in Chapter 1.

## 7.1 Environment

This section presents applications concerning the environment, i.e., natural resources like forests or urban environments like cities and buildings.

### 7.1.1 Forest Inventory, Management and Simulation

In the field of forestry, the approach allows for new types of forest inventory, management and simulation applications. Most of the works where realized in the context of the research project Virtual Forest [138, 139, 140]. One of the core ideas of this project is to provide a consistent, shared data model and a common data management in the Virtual Forest database (Figure 7.1). Provided to all stakeholders in this field, it facilitates the exploitation of know-how and synergies. Furthermore, it supports the transfer of industrial automation techniques to the forest industry. Based on this architecture, various applications are realized (Figure 7.2).

An important application in this context is forest inventory (Figure 7.2d), the acquisition and management of environmental data in forestry. In the Virtual Forest, this is realized using a semi-automatic approach. Based on remote sensing and other data, algorithms for tree species classification, single tree delineation and attribution, and forest stand delineation and attribution are used to automatically process huge amounts of data (Figure 7.2b). The results of these Semantic World Modeling processes are stored in the common Virtual Forest

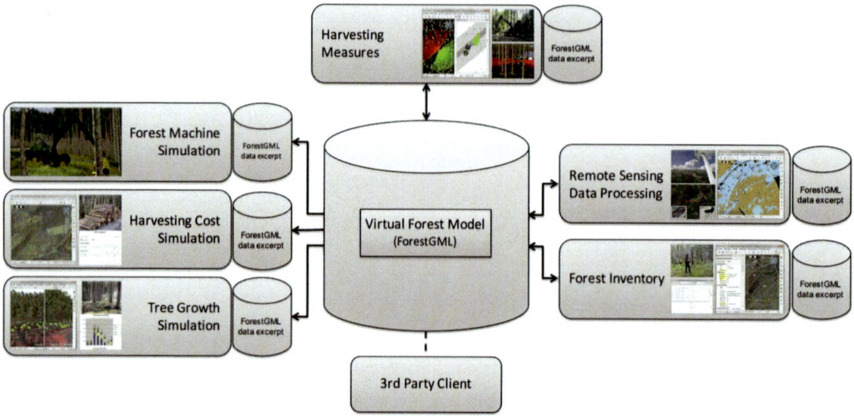


**Figure 7.1:** *Architecture of a Virtual Forest scenario.*

model. Expert users can then use them for quality inspection and data refinement. To improve their work, another important aspect are convenient user interfaces to algorithms and supportive tools.

The inventory tools have been used and tested in actual measures. In this context, they were evaluated for their real-world applicability – implicitly evaluating the presented approach utilized by these tools as well. Users attested the tools a very good performance. Currently, the inventory tool is being adopted by two state forestry administrations in Germany.

Based on inventory data, other applications in the forestry context can be driven. There are simulation applications for decision support to predict harvesting costs (Figure 7.2c) or forest growth (Figure 7.2e). Driver assistance (Figure 7.2a) or 3D simulations (Figure 7.2f) can be used to support and to train the usage of harvesters and forwarders in real world environments. Techniques for the automated feedback from harvesting allows for a perpetual inventory. Here, results from felling measures are transferred back into the central model to keep it up-to-date. User-friendly query interfaces and reporting tools can help to evaluate and interpret the shared forest model. All in all, several applications for processing remote sensing data, semi-automatic inventory, simple forest information, forest planning, and wood production planning, and navigation have been developed. Furthermore, web technologies like portals and services make the model available to even more users.

Concerning the use of Semantic World Modeling, the combination of geometry data and corresponding descriptive attributes is another important advantage. Conventional data modeling in geographic applications often separates geometric from non-geometric data. Data is mostly stored in different relational databases and entity pairs are built using key references. However, this separation always holds the danger of divergence. An integrated

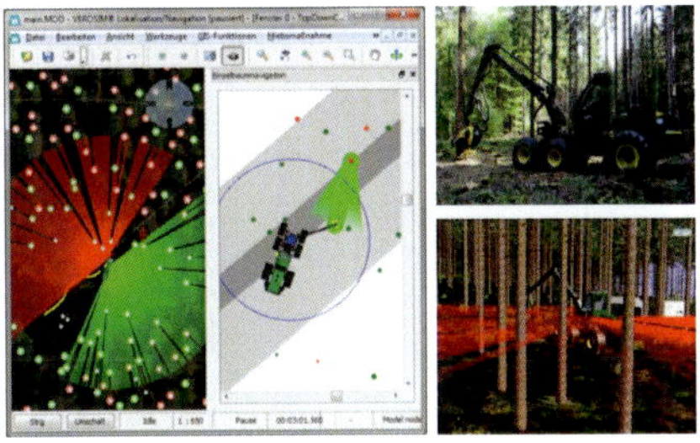

(a) *Harvesting measures assistance.*

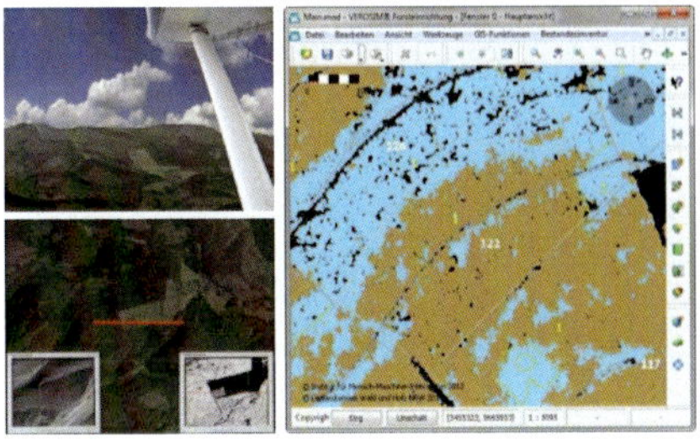

(b) *Remote sensing data processing.*

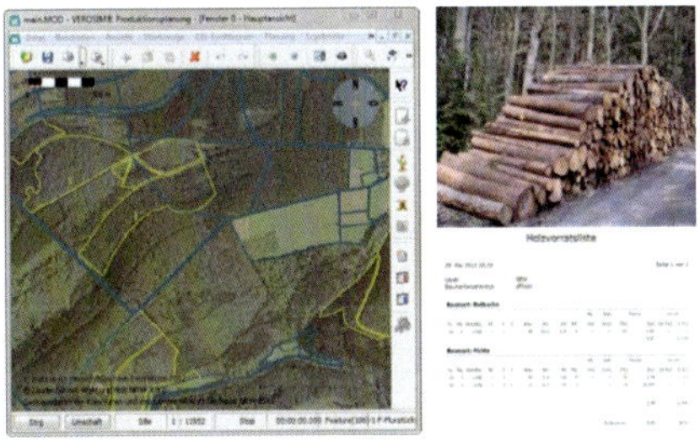

(c) *Harvesting cost simulation.*

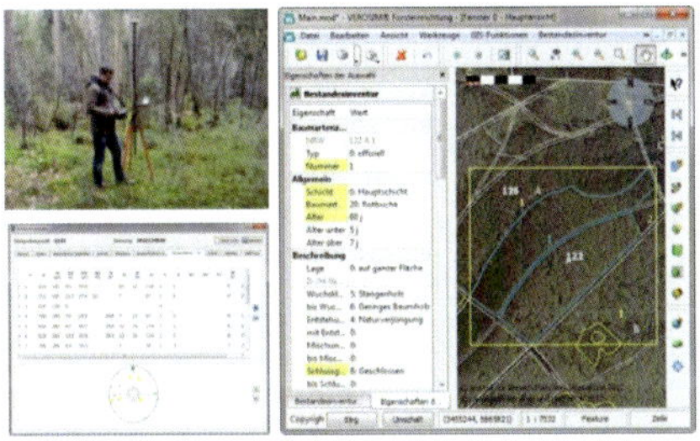

(d) *Forest inventory.*

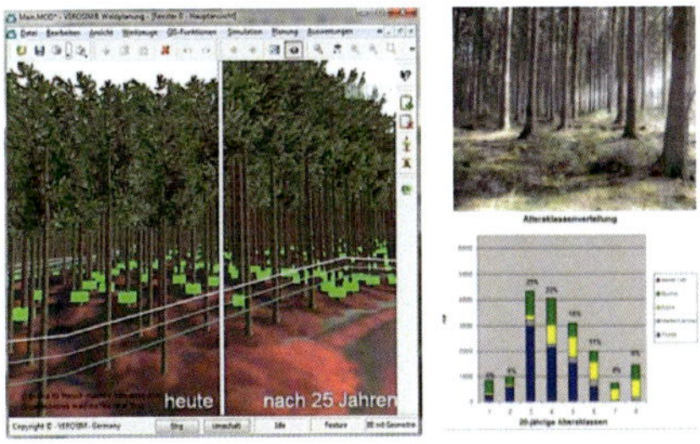


(e) *Tree growth simulation.*

(f) *Forest machine simulation.*

**Figure 7.2:** *Various forestry applications realized using the presented approach.*

object-oriented model describing inventory objects with geometric and descriptive attributes at the same time avoids this problem.

The data models employed for the Virtual Forest are all based on GML (Geography Markup Language [26]). A specialized base schema called ForestGML was developed to provide core data constructs to facilitate the Virtual Forest's usage in different areas, states, or administrations. Furthermore, GML as a base schema allows a standardized exchange of data using the corresponding standard web services like WFS (Web Feature Service) or WMS (Web Map Service). This guarantees interoperability between different clients connected to the Virtual Forest database.

To integrate and realize the central database and all the applications, the Virtual Forest needs an $n$D GIS (Geo Information System). It integrates 3D geo data into object-oriented Semantic World Models and combines them with additional time dimensions in terms of a temporal database and simulation techniques. While the temporal database is used to preserve and access historic versions, different simulation techniques are provided for prediction of future scenarios.

The three time dimensions presented in Section 5.4 perfectly fit the requirements of the Virtual Forest. Transaction time is used to model the technical change history. It allows to determine when forestal data was changed, thus, documenting work processes. The second time dimension is valid time. In particular for individual tree objects, it is used to directly model the actual age. Thus, planting a tree is modeled as a new tree object inserted with the corresponding valid time. Any change to its properties is equally updated, e.g., a height measured at a certain point in time. Effectivity time is used to model the point in time when new values shall become the official representation of the forest. Updating huge forest datasets using fieldwork or automated processes (as developed in the Virtual Forest project) can take a longer period. By using an effectivity time well after this period (e.g., next New Year's Day), no intermediate results are visible to other users evaluating the currently effective data.

The $n$D-GIS is realized using the simulation system VEROSIM (Virtual Environments and Robotic Simulation [127]), the geo database SGJ (SupportGIS Java [123]) and the presented reference implementation for database synchronization. Thus, the latter is a core component of the whole Virtual Forest infrastructure enabling the effective and efficient integration of its fundamental subsystems (Figure 7.1). It propagates the common ForestGML language and makes the data available throughout the distributed system, provides persistence and means for communication, enables temporal data management, and supports the decoupling of the subsystems. Regarding the huge amounts of inventory and other data, the presented streaming approaches are very helpful, as well. Typically, inventory data is structured hierarchically to reflect, e.g., administrative units and contains spatial data. Thus, hierarchical and spatial streaming are used within expert tools to navigate through the data based on its structure or its location. Spatial streaming is also used for 3D simulation, e.g., to drive a harvester through a large forest without loading the whole data set in one chunk. Streaming for data processing is also applied – in particular for deriving, refining, or updating the large amounts of inventory data. Another advantage is the collaboration feature, so multiple users at a central database work with consistent states. For field work, necessary data sets are made portable using a WFS-based check-out/-in mechanism to a secondary database, which in turn serves as a local ExtDB.

In summary, the main benefits of using the presented approach for the Virtual Forest applications are

- a flexible access to the central Virtual Forest database with its ForestGML schema series customized to different users,
- support for temporal data management yielding an $n$D GIS,
- efficient simulation and data processing of huge geo data sets using streaming techniques,
- decoupling of algorithms from the external Virtual Forest database implementation,
- collaboration via the central database,
- support for Semantic World Modeling fusing geo data with descriptive attributes, and
- transparent interface to standard DBMS (Database Management System).

*The project Virtual Forest is co-financed by the European Union and the federal state of North Rhine-Westphalia, European Regional Development Fund (ERDF). Europe – Investing in our future.*

### 7.1.2 City and Urban (Distributed) 3D Simulation

Another application in the field of geo information systems are city simulations. Nowadays, a 3D city model exists for many cities in Germany like Düsseldorf (Figures 7.3 and 7.4), Recklinghausen (Figure 7.7), Frankfurt/Main (Figure 7.5, left), Stuttgart (Figure 7.5, middle), or Mönchengladbach (Figure 7.5, right). Typically, these are maintained by urban authorities, e.g., by land-registry. A widespread data model is the CityGML [24, 25] standard, which is also based on GML. However, a problem is to access, display, and use these huge data sets efficiently. Most tools can either access data in the original, highly semantic CityGML format, but cannot efficiently display its 3D content or even do 3D simulation. Others can only efficiently use derived and optimized geometric representations, e.g., in VRML (Virtual Reality Modeling Language [9]), which lack the semantic richness and need to be created by offline conversion. Using the presented reference implementation, however, city data can be accessed in its original highly semantic schema making it available to a real-time capable 3D simulation system at the same time (Figure 7.6).

3D simulation scenarios include driving cars (with realistic physical correct behavior) or flying a helicopter through different city models (Figure 7.3). At the same time, the associated descriptive data can be accessed as the connection between geometry and object

**Figure 7.3:** *Bringing large city models to life by combining database and simulation technology (data: Düsseldorf).*

is never broken (Figure 7.4). As the proposed approach has read and write support, city data can even be updated from within the simulation system. A modeling specialty of CityGML are so-called implicit geometry representations referencing detail models. Here, functional data synchronization is the key to supplement such data with the corresponding details. This was used for street furniture like street lights or benches or vegetation like trees (Figure 7.7). For that purpose, the implicit representation contains references to external model files (e.g., in VRML format), which are subsequently loaded into the simulation system. For vegetation, it may also just denote a tree type. Additionally, pose and size information are given, which are applied to the supplement.

In another urban scenario, the presented methods have been used as the basis for a new approach to distributed 3D simulation using a central database (Figure 7.8) [141]. An important precondition is that the shared Semantic World Model within ExtDB not only contains static model data like buildings, street furniture or vegetation. It also has to contain dynamic objects like a car or helicopter. A locally running simulation changes these dynamic objects (e.g., the cars position) within SimDB. Using the mechanisms described in Section 5.2, these changes are synchronized to ExtDB, hence communicating the new state of the local copy to the shared Semantic World Model. The database's notification service actively notifies any subscribed simulation client. Each client adopts the changes by synchronizing their own local replicate copies accordingly. All in all, this realizes a database-driven distributed 3D simulation.

In training scenarios using 3D simulation techniques – like driving or flying a virtual vessel or operating a virtual model of a machine – there is an interest in recording a simulation run. Recorded data can be used for replay, analysis, debriefing, and archival. This may be realized using external tools that log all interactions between the participants of the distributed simulation. Here, additional tools are needed to replay these logs. In the presented approach, however, all changes are centrally routed through the shared model within ExtDB. Thus, as

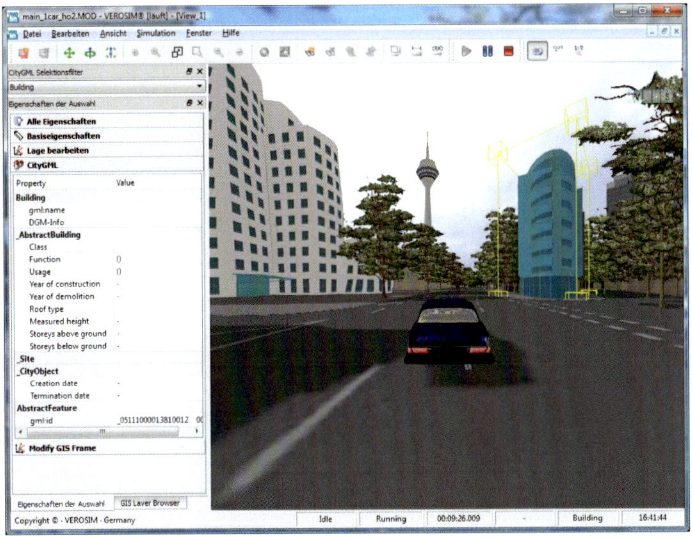


**Figure 7.4:** *Accessing object data from within virtual scenes (data: Düsseldorf).*

**Figure 7.5:** *Other CityGML-based city models accessed using the presented approach. From left to right: Frankfurt/Main, Stuttgart, Mönchengladbach (data: accordingly).*

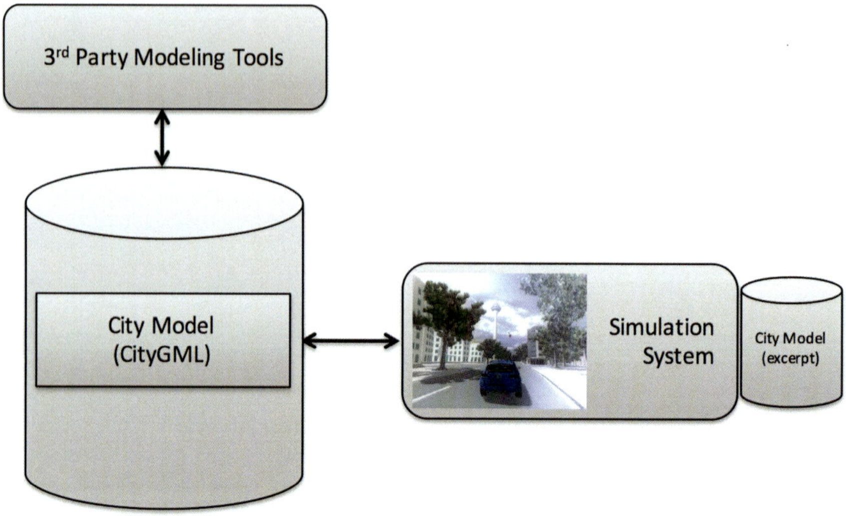


**Figure 7.6:** *Architecture of the basic 3D city simulation application.*

all intermediate states of the simulation are made persistent in the shared model, a simulation run can easily be captured by using a temporal database for ExtDB. The recorded time-stamped values not only represent a queryable 4D archive of the scenario. A simulation client can also be used in an off-line viewing mode to replay a simulation run step by step, allowing analysis and debriefing. A transaction time database was chosen for this scenario.

Using these two core concepts, a database-driven distributed 3D city simulation application has been realized. The scenario consists of a heterogeneous shared model with a generic Arab village in CityGML format as static model data and SEDRIS-based car and helicopter models as dynamic model data (Figure 7.9). Data is loaded from a central SGJ database into two attached VEROSIM simulation clients. Here, simulation specific data is reconstructed using functional data synchronization. In particular, this includes relative transformations, which are synchronized bidirectionally to distribute movements of the dynamic objects. Dynamic parameters of the Semantic World Model like physical characteristics of a car's drive were also encoded within the SEDRIS schema and reconstructed as supplementing structures in SimDB. These active components of the simulation are specially treated to configure responsibilities. That is, the car shall only be actively simulated by one simulation client and only passively retraced within the other. The same applies to the helicopter vice versa. An ID (Identifier)-based approach is used to configure these active and passive components per client. After replicating the data, the simulation is started in each client. Movements in one client are resynchronized to the central database and distributed to the respective other client. At the end of the simulation, the aforementioned usage of a temporal database

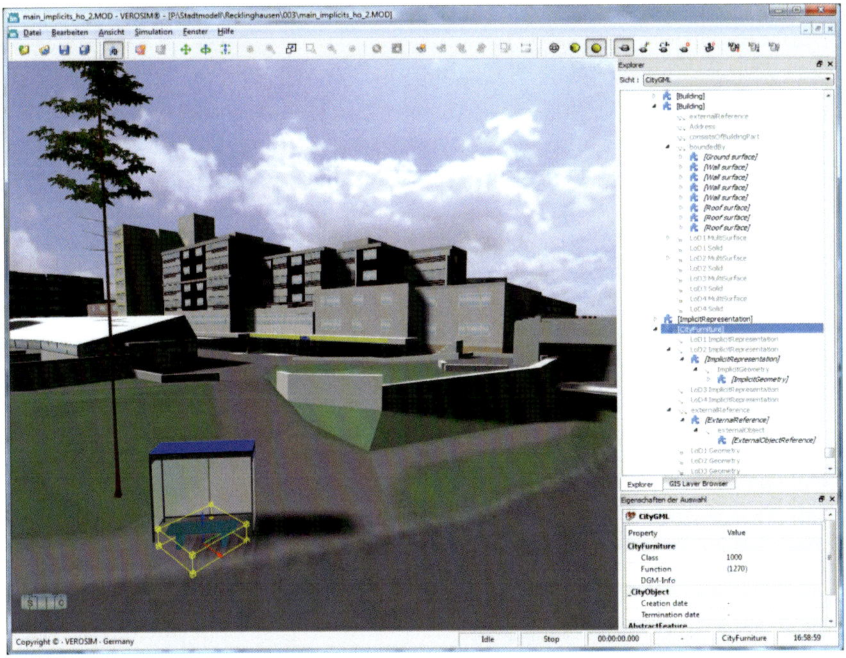


**Figure 7.7:** *Adding details to a city model using functional data synchronization (data: district of Recklinghausen).*

allows an off-line replay of the simulation run. For that purpose, temporal snapshots are incrementally replicated to one of the simulation clients' SimDB.

To measure the performance of this distributed simulation, two personal computers (PC1, PC2) were set up and connected via a Gigabit Ethernet switch. PC1 ran the central database and one VEROSIM client, PC2 the second VEROSIM client. On one machine, the car was configured to automatically drive in a circle while at the same time, on the other machine, the helicopter was configured to turn itself around an axis. On each machine, both movements were visualized – one locally simulated and one transmitted. Thus, both clients need to permanently read from and write to the central database to resynchronize their data. Two passes with an alternating assignment of configuration (helicopter, car) to machine (PC1, PC2) ensured comparability. Table 7.1 shows the associated measurements for reading and writing (example: when the helicopter is simulated locally on PC1 the system needs 0.65ms/op to read a new value (for the car) from the central database).

As writing values triggers versioning and notifications it is slower than reading values (factor $3-3.5$). The results for PC2 are slower because PC1 locally runs the central database (factor 2), which could be improved using other network hardware. To obtain another reference, pure writing performance to the database using its API (Application Programming

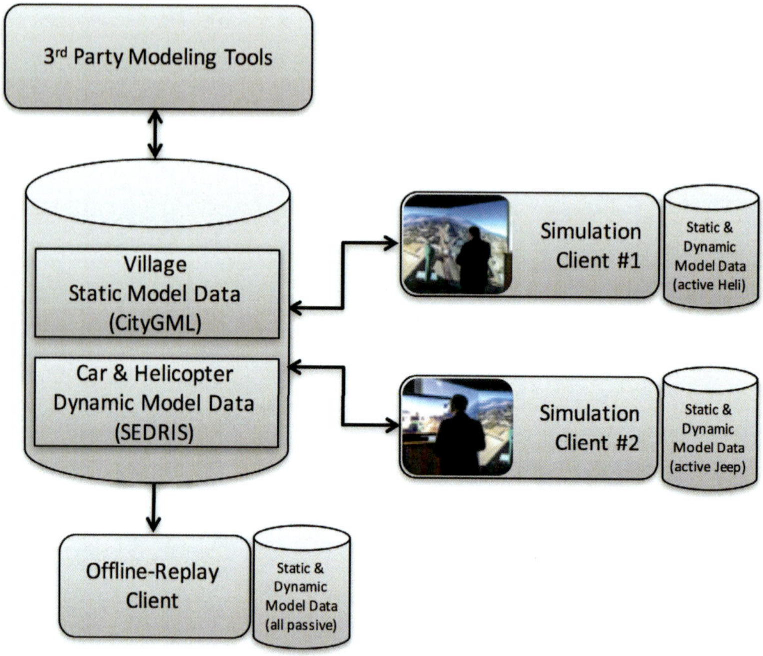


**Figure 7.8:** *Architecture of the database-driven distributed 3D city simulation application.*

**Figure 7.9:** *Database-driven distributed 3D simulation scenario.*

**Table 7.1:** *Performance in milliseconds per read (left) and (write) operation.*

| **read** | helicopter | car |
|---|---|---|
| PC1 | 0.65ms/op | 0.72ms/op |
| PC2 | 1.28ms/op | 1.32ms/op |

| **write** | helicopter | car |
|---|---|---|
| PC1 | 2.30ms/op | 2.26ms/op |
| PC2 | 4.70ms/op | 4.60ms/op |

Interface) without VEROSIM was also measured. When constantly writing new values to a local database, about 2.00ms/op (including versioning and notifications) are reached. Thus, compared to 2.30ms/op and 2.26ms/op, the simulation system's overhead seems to be within tolerance.

Thus, the main benefits when applying the presented approach in the context of city models are

- a flexible support for different schemata like CityGML or SEDRIS,
- an efficient access to the original semantically modeled data without offline conversions,
- the streaming of large city models,
- managing static as well as dynamic model data in the same database,
- an integrated distributed 3D simulation mechanism,
- an integrated simulation logging using temporal databases,
- translating semantics to enable simulation using functional data sync, and
- in general: bringing (distributed) 3D simulation to city models.

### 7.1.3 Virtual Testbeds for Building Information Modeling

In BIM (Building Information Modeling) [142], highly detailed building models are used by architects, civil engineers, owners and other stakeholders in the design, planning, construction and operation of buildings. While the field is similar to city models, the necessary level of detail is much higher. The VTB (Virtual Testbed) approach is ideally suited to integrate these Semantic World Models either as environment models for the simulation of complex technical systems operating within buildings or as the system under development itself considering modern buildings and their high degree of automation.

Current software solutions in this context are mainly construction tools allowing for BIM data generation, rendering and inspection. For further usages, the data is exported to formats like VRML to allow for its further use, e.g., in VR (Virtual Reality) environments or for specialized simulations. However, in this unidirectional process, the originally rich semantics of BIM data is lost. For example, in a VR scenario, only the geometric building model can be examined and neither all model details can be accessed nor can in situ changes be returned.

A far more flexible concept for exchanging and interacting with BIM data is based on the data management concepts for eRobotics presented in this thesis (Figure 7.10).

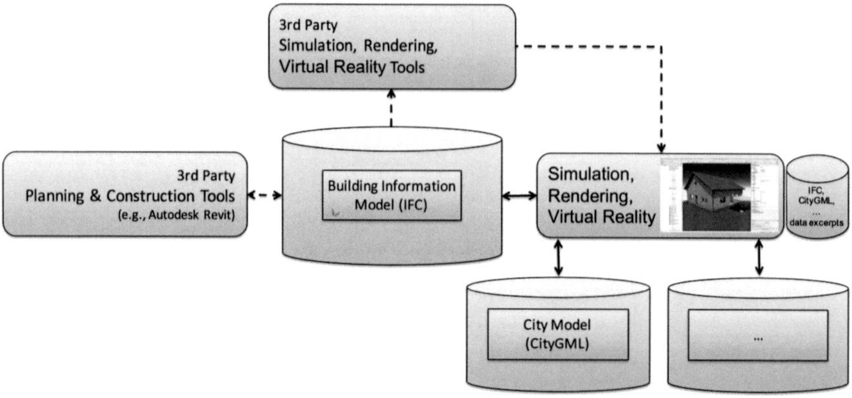


**Figure 7.10:** *Structure of the presented data management approach applied to BIM data, integrated with other data sources like city models.*

A prerequisite is to use a common language for data exchange that preserves semantics. A widespread, standardized and neutral data exchange format in BIM is IFC (Industrial Foundation Classes [5]), which is based on STEP (Standard for the Exchange of Product model data). Additionally, an XML (Extensible Markup Language)-based representation exists. The idea is to use IFC as a pivot format to bidirectionally exchange building data between third party planning and construction tools and a multi-purpose 3D simulation system used for simulation, rendering and VR. Using the synchronization approach, IFC schema and data can be synchronized to the simulation database making it natively available to the simulation system. Using functional data synchronization, relevant parts of the IFC data are translated on-the-fly to structures known by the simulation system. In particular, this is needed for geometric data that has to be translated from CSG (Constructive Solid Geometry) or implicit geometries often used in architectural tools to the boundary representations common in 3D simulation. Additional data can be synchronized from other sources – in particular, city models as shown in Section 7.1.2 – and thus integrated within the simulation database. Moreover, third party tools for simulation, rendering and VR can be supplied with data by unidirectionally exporting the IFC data. In turn, their results might be integrated into the simulation system and its database, as well.

Results from a first implementation of an IFC interface for VEROSIM and VSD (Versatile Simulation Database) are shown in Figure 7.11.

Altogether, the main advantages of using the presented data management approach for eRobotics applications in connection with the highly detailed BIM data are

- access to the full semantics of the original BIM data,
- a flexible translation of IFC semantics using functional data synchronization,
- read and write access to the native IFC data,

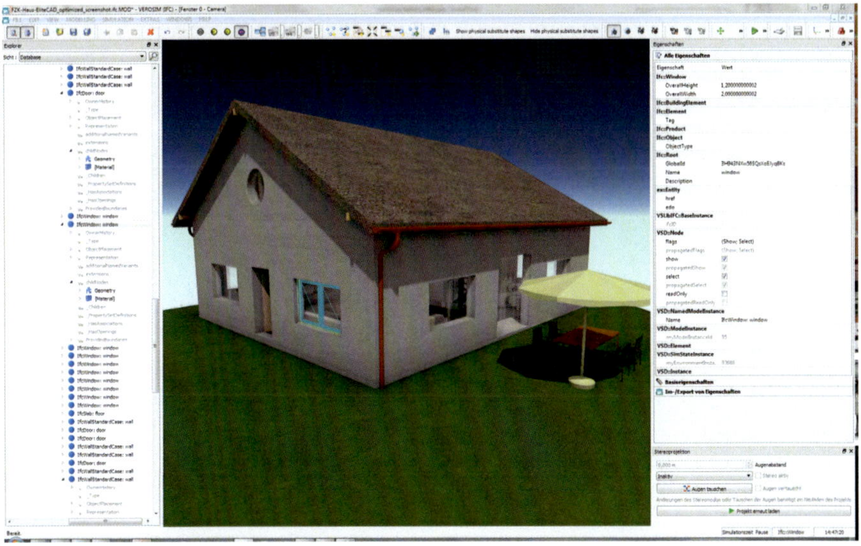

**Figure 7.11:** *Results from an IFC interface for VEROSIM and VSD based on the concepts presented in this work (from [142]).*

- with the avoidance of offline conversions, and
- the integration of different Semantic World Models within the simulation database.

## 7.2 Industry

In the industrial field, the presented approach has been used for different application scenarios: An interface for two standard data formats from the field of eRobotics (X3D (Extensible 3D [39]) and AutomationML (Automation Modeling Language [6])), a concept to support scalable automation technology, and a data management approach for industrial robots.

### 7.2.1 X3D

X3D is the XML-based successor of VRML [39]. It allows to model 3D scenes with different geometry representations, transformations, lights, materials, and textures. Furthermore, it provides various extensions, e.g., for animation, multimedia, user interaction, or scripting. An X3D document (or model) contains a scene graph describing the structure of the scene. X3D's object model (Figure 7.12) comprises complex objects called nodes and their properties called fields describing a node's current state. A field either holds simple property values (which can also be used for event interchange) or contains other nodes. The latter is the basis for building up scene graph hierarchies. Using the special DEF and USE statements, nodes can be given unique names (DEF) by which they can be referenced (without copying) from other nodes (USE) allowing a node to have more than one parent. X3D object types are structured by inheritance in an interface hierarchy where only leaf classes are non-abstract. Besides an XML encoding, X3D also supports binary and VRML97 encodings. The XML encoding is defined by an XSD (XML Schema Definition).

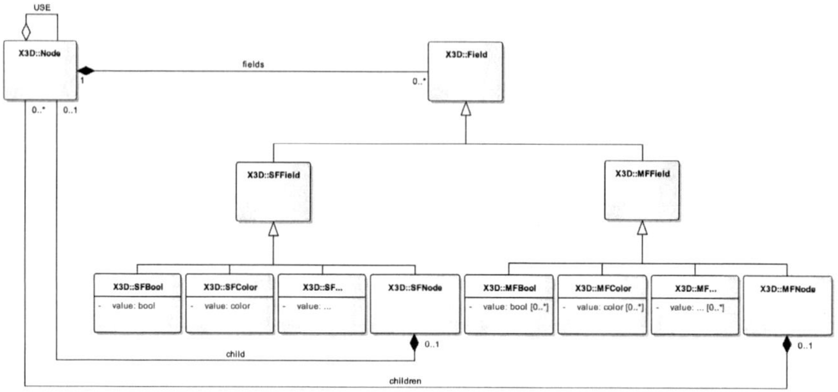


**Figure 7.12:** *Simplified X3D object model.*

In eRobotics, 3D models are of particular interest. Hence, corresponding file formats for data interchange must be supported. Usually, this is realized by hard-coded interfaces or by integrating an existing third-party API. In contrast, using the flexible XML data binding concepts presented in this thesis, the simulation system is automatically adapted to "speak the language" represented by the XSD and to load corresponding X3D data. Subsequently, functional data synchronization can be applied to translate semantics where necessary, e.g., for geometry or material representations (from X3D to the simulation system's native format). For that purpose, first of all, an analysis of the X3D XML schema and its mapping to object-oriented structures is necessary. Based on these results, a reference implementation was realized using VEROSIM and VSD [143]. Its basic structure is shown in Figure 7.13.

Following the analysis of the X3D format, abstract X3D node types are represented by global abstract XSD complex types. In turn, concrete X3D node types are represented by global XSD element definitions with an embedded, anonymous complex type to realize the content model and inheritance. Inheritance is modeled using XSD complex type's extension mechanism. X3D fields representing simple (i.e., non-node) values are represented by XML attributes with special XSD simple types derived by restriction from build-in basic types (e.g., SFBool derived from xs:boolean). X3D fields that contain other nodes are modeled as XSD child elements referencing the corresponding node's global element definition. XSD groups and attribute groups are used to model recurring content models and reference them from

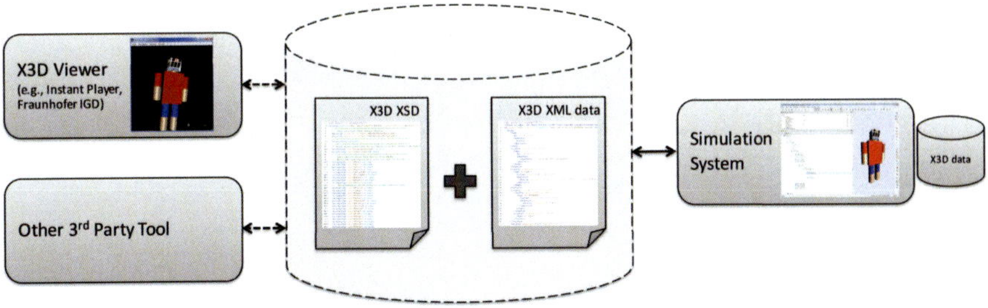


**Figure 7.13:** *Structure of the X3D data binding solution.*

respective complex type content models (mostly sequences). Finally, the aforementioned DEF/USE statements are modeled using XSD ID/IDREF attributes, which are members of every base complex type and thus of every type and global element. This allows each and every complex child element to become a reference to another existing element of the same type, which was declared somewhere else using a DEF statement.

These modeling concepts are then mapped to the VSD meta system as follows:

- Abstract XSD complex types are mapped to also abstract VSD-`MetaInstances` with the same name.
- XSD element definitions combined with their anonymous complex type are likewise mapped to a single (non-abstract) VSD-`MetaInstance` with the same name as the global element.
- Inheritance between XSD complex types is mapped to inheritance between VSD-`Meta-Instances`.
- References to XSD groups and attribute groups are dissolved into the respective referring type definition. Multiplicities are expanded to the individual group member elements or attributes. Likewise, XSD sequence, XSD choice and XSD all content models are dissolved.
- XSD simple types are mapped to appropriate VSD-`MetaTypeVals` for derived simple value types with the same names.
- XSD attributes with these simple types are mapped to VSD value Meta-Properties with the same names and the corresponding VSD-`MetaTypeVals`.
- XSD child element definitions referencing global element definitions are mapped to VSD reference `MetaProperties` with the same name and transitive deletion characteristics (like a UML (Unified Modeling Language [8]) composition) with the VSD--`MetaInstance` corresponding to the global element definition as its Meta-Type.
- To support DEF/USE semantics, for each of these child elements a second VSD reference `MetaProperty` with a name variation (e.g., suffix "USE"), but *without* transitive deletion characteristics (like a UML shared aggregation) is created.

Using these mappings, the X3D schema and corresponding data can be loaded into VSD. Based thereupon, a functional data synchronization approach translates geometry representations, transformations, materials, and texture definitions. An example is given in Figure 7.14.

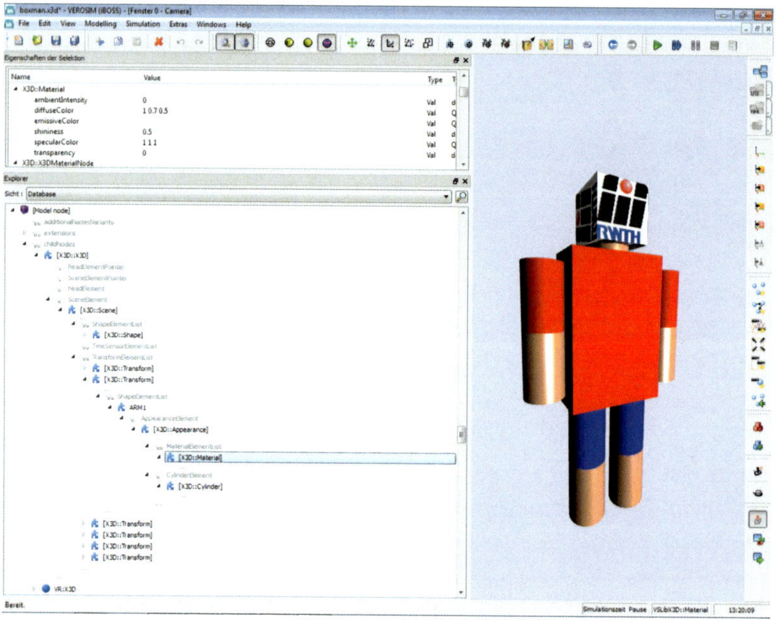


**Figure 7.14:** *Simple exemplary X3D document loaded in VEROSIM (data: Schwellenbach & MMI).*

The X3D reference implementation is based upon the concepts described in Chapter 6. The mappings between the X3D and VSD structures presented above could be generalized in terms of an X3D metamodel and model transformations to and from the UML metamodel (Figure 7.15).

The main benefits for using the presented approach in the context of X3D are

- the decoupling of internal simulation system components from XML data binding technology or a proprietary X3D API,
- the automatic adaption to different versions of the X3D standard,
- no offline conversion of original data,
- translating semantics to enable simulation using functional data sync, and
- in general: a flexible access to data modeled in X3D.

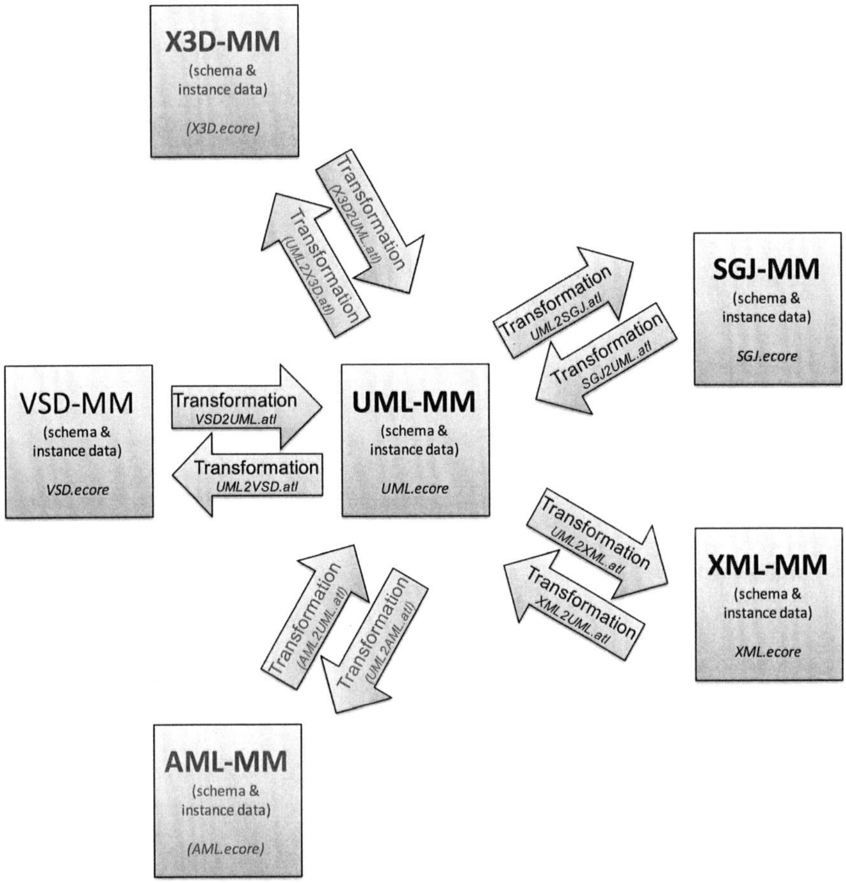


**Figure 7.15:** *The reference implementations for the X3D and AutomationML (see next section) applications can be integrated into the concepts from Chapter 6.*

### 7.2.2 AutomationML

AutomationML is an XML-based language for modeling and interchanging engineering data for automation technology [6, 144]. It combines the existing languages CAEX (Computer Aided Engineering Exchange [6, 145]), COLLADA (Collaborative Design Activity [6]), and PLCopen XML. CAEX is the main language used to model object structures and to integrate the other languages. It provides various concepts of object-oriented modeling. The so-called `InstanceHierarchy` models a facility's structure composed of objects, their properties, interfaces, and relations to other objects. The `InterfaceClassLib` describes interfaces from CAEX objects to other CAEX objects or external documents. The `SystemUnitClassLib` contains class definitions for CAEX objects including inheritance. Finally, the `RoleClass-Lib` defines roles, i.e., classes that model an abstract behavior, e.g., a Robot. Roles can be used as placeholders for actual implementations. Besides CAEX, COLLADA is used to model a facility's geometric data and kinematics, and PLCopen XML to model its logic, i.e., its behavior.

Apparently, for eRobotics applications, it is beneficial to be able to access engineering data in such a standardized exchange format. For example, to perform simulations on a modeled production facility. As in the previous subsection on X3D, in contrast to laboriously hard-coding AutomationML structures into the system or to integrate a proprietary API, the methods presented in this dissertation offer a more adaptive, i.e., a more flexible approach by automatically configuring the simulation system to the given schema on startup. Thus, preceded by the necessary analysis of the general data modeling concepts within the CAEX XSD, a VEROSIM-/VSD-based XML data binding solution was realized [146] based on the approach presented in this thesis. Its basic structure is shown in Figure 7.16.

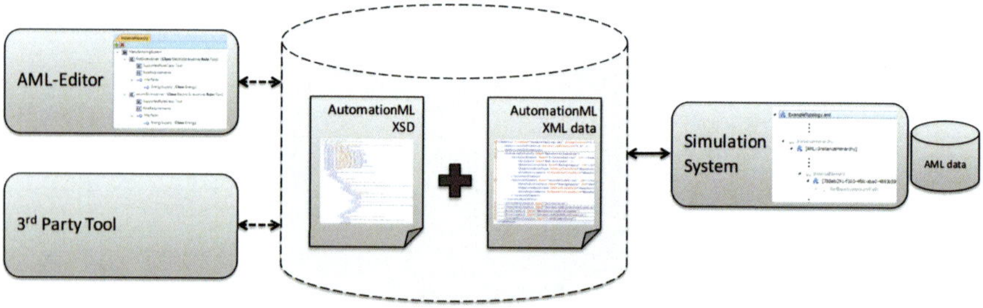


**Figure 7.16:** *Structure of the AutomationML data binding solution (with images from [146]).*

In general, CAEX uses a single global element definition `CAEXFile` with an anonymous complex type as an entry point to every document (Figure 7.17). Alongside, some basic global XSD complex types are defined. Within `CAEXFile`'s complex type, local elements with anonymous or named complex types are interleaved in a "russian-doll" design. Besides, local elements as well as attributes with simple types are used to model non-complex properties. There are no abstract element or type definitions in the CAEX XML Schema Definition.

```
<?xml version="1.0" encoding="UTF-8"?>
<!-- CAEX - Computer Aided Engineering Data-Exchange-Metamodel -->
<!-- Version 2.15, 16.05.2007 -->
<xs:schema xmlns:xs="http://www.w3.org/2001/XMLSchema" elementFormDefault="qualified" attributeFormDefault="unqualified">
    <xs:simpleType name="ChangeMode"> ... </xs:simpleType>
    <xs:group name="Header"> ... </xs:group>
    <xs:complexType name="CAEXBasicObject"> ... </xs:complexType>
    <xs:complexType name="CAEXObject"> ... </xs:complexType>
    <xs:complexType name="InterfaceClassType"> ... </xs:complexType>
    <xs:complexType name="InterfaceFamilyType"> ... </xs:complexType>
    <xs:complexType name="RoleClassType"> ... </xs:complexType>
    <xs:complexType name="RoleFamilyType"> ... </xs:complexType>
    <xs:complexType name="SystemUnitClassType"> ... </xs:complexType>
    <xs:complexType name="SystemUnitFamilyType"> ... </xs:complexType>
    <xs:complexType name="InternalElementType"> ... </xs:complexType>
    <xs:complexType name="AttributeType"> ... </xs:complexType>
    <xs:complexType name="AttributeValueRequirementType"> ... </xs:complexType>
    <xs:complexType name="MappingType"> ... </xs:complexType>
    <xs:element name="CAEXFile">
        <xs:annotation>
            <xs:documentation>Root-element of the CAEX schema. </xs:documentation>
        </xs:annotation>
        <xs:complexType>
            <xs:complexContent>
                <xs:extension base="CAEXBasicObject">
                    <xs:sequence>
                        <xs:element name="ExternalReference" minOccurs="0" maxOccurs="unbounded">
                            <xs:annotation>
                                <xs:documentation>Container element for the alias definition of external CAEX files.</xs:documentation>
                            </xs:annotation>
                            <xs:complexType>
                                <xs:complexContent>
                                    <xs:extension base="CAEXBasicObject">
                                        <xs:attribute name="Path" type="xs:string" use="required">
                                            <xs:annotation>
                                                <xs:documentation>Describes the path of the external CAEX file. Absolute and relative path
                                            </xs:annotation>
                                        </xs:attribute>
                                        <xs:attribute name="Alias" type="xs:string" use="required">
                                            <xs:annotation>
                                                <xs:documentation>Describes the alias name of an external CAEX file to enable referencing
                                            </xs:annotation>
                                        </xs:attribute>
                                    </xs:extension>
                                </xs:complexContent>
                            </xs:complexType>
                        </xs:element>
                        <xs:element name="InstanceHierarchy" minOccurs="0" maxOccurs="unbounded">
                            <xs:annotation>
                                <xs:documentation>Root element for a system hierarchy of object instances.</xs:documentation>
                            </xs:annotation>
                            <xs:complexType>
                                <xs:complexContent>
                                    <xs:extension base="CAEXObject">
                                        <xs:sequence>
                                            <xs:element name="InternalElement" type="InternalElementType" minOccurs="0" maxOccurs="unbound
                                                <xs:annotation>
                                                    <xs:documentation>Shall be used in order to define nested objects inside of a SystemUn
```

**Figure 7.17:** *Excerpt of the CAEX XSD file (from [146]).*

Accordingly, in the data binding solution, global complex types as well as global element definitions are both mapped to VSD-`MetaInstances` with the same name and corresponding inheritance (for the complex types). Local element and attribute definitions with simple types are mapped to VSD value `MetaProperties`. Local element definitions with complex type are mapped to VSD-`MetaProperty` references (with transitive deletion characteristics). In case of an anonymous complex type, an additional VSD-`MetaInstance` with the local element's name is created.

Furthermore, AutomationML offers a string-based mechanism for cross referencing between certain elements. These XML string attributes may either contain path statements or global identifiers for the target objects. Similar to the special treatment for the DEF/USE attributes in X3D (see Subsection 7.2.1), additional VSD-`MetaProperty` references (*without* transitive deletion characteristics) are created for those CAEX base types defining these attributes.

Using these mappings, the CAEX schema is synchronized to VSD and corresponding instance documents can subsequently be unmarshalled (loaded) into the simulation system. Figure 7.18 gives an example of an AutomationML sample file's object structure loaded into VEROSIM. Using appropriate semantic mappings, functional data synchronization can be used to interpret, e.g., those parts needed to run a simulation.

As with X3D, the AutomationML reference implementation is based upon the concepts from Chapter 6 and the mappings between AutomationML and VSD could as well be generalized in terms of an AutomationML metamodel and model transformations to and from the UML metamodel (Figure 7.15).

Furthermore, as mentioned above, AutomationML provides its own metadata concept. For example, a `SystemUnitClass` is used to describe an `InternalElement`'s class. This metadata, however, is modeled on instance document level making `SystemUnitClass` itself more of a *meta*class within the XSD. Mapping such metadata from an instance document to the object-oriented structures of a target system (like VSD) would be an interesting enhancement of the presented XML data binding approach.

The main benefits for using the presented approach in the context of AutomationML are

- the decoupling of internal simulation system components from XML data binding technology or a proprietary AutomationML API,
- the automatic adaption to different versions of the AutomationML standard,
- no offline conversion of original data,
- translating semantics to enable simulation using functional data sync, and
- in general: a flexible access to data modeled in AutomationML.

### 7.2.3 Scalable Automation in Production Technology

To bring scalable automation technology to assembly lines for individualized products, a modular system architecture provides the necessary flexibility for their distributed control but also for their distributed simulation as analyzed in the research project SCALAB [147, 148]. Its flexibility is based on an architecture with an active communication hub using agents, all controlled by a central supervisor. The general concept of this modular control system architecture (MCSA) is shown in Figure 7.19

Data management requirements in the MCSA are complex. Its information backbone must provide means for the communication between agents, planners and the central supervisor. It must also provide a persistence layer to securely manage and store all the objects involved in the system. Thus, the approach presented in this thesis builds an excellent basis for

**Figure 7.18:** *Example for an AutomationML document loaded into the simulation system VEROSIM (from [146]).*

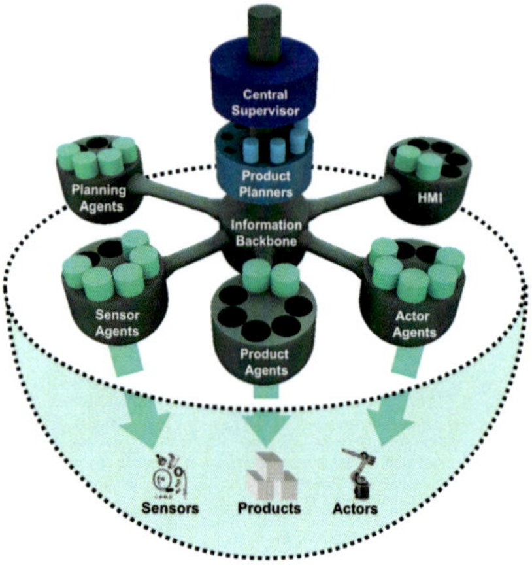


**Figure 7.19:** *General concept of the modular control system architecture (MCSA).*

this core component of the MCSA. The central database not only provides the necessary persistence, storage for large scenarios and features such as temporal data management, version control, access control, complex queries, and transactional integrity. It also defines a "common language" (schema synchronization) and constitutes a communication hub (data synchronization) for all subsystems. On the other hand, local simulation databases provide the necessary real-time capabilities and access speed to allow for simulation and control tasks.

Figure 7.20 shows an example for schema synchronization in the MCSA context. Classes (for product planner, robot and sensor agent) with attributes and relations from an object-oriented central database are mapped to metainstances and metaproperties in the simulation database. An example for data synchronization with a communication sequence is shown in Figure 7.21. A (physical) laser scanner connected to instance #1 of the simulation system provides data via a sensor agent. It is replicated to the central database where it is stored and propagated to instance #2. This instance also has a replicate copy of a robot agent to control a connected (physical) robot using the sensor data.

Thus, the main benefits when realizing the MCSA with the presented approach for database synchronization are

- a central communication hub for the information backbone
- with an active driving of distributed simulations or control scenarios,
- a persistence layer for the shared (simulation) model,
- cached access to parts of the shared model relevant to a client, and
- a common schema for the participating systems.

*The research project SCALAB is supported by* .

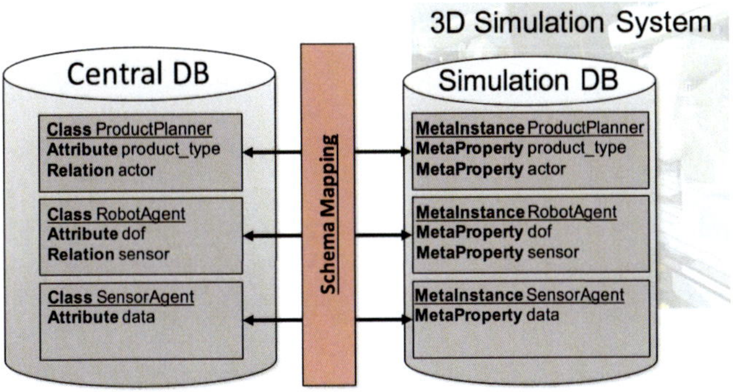


**Figure 7.20:** *An example for schema synchronization in the MCSA context.*

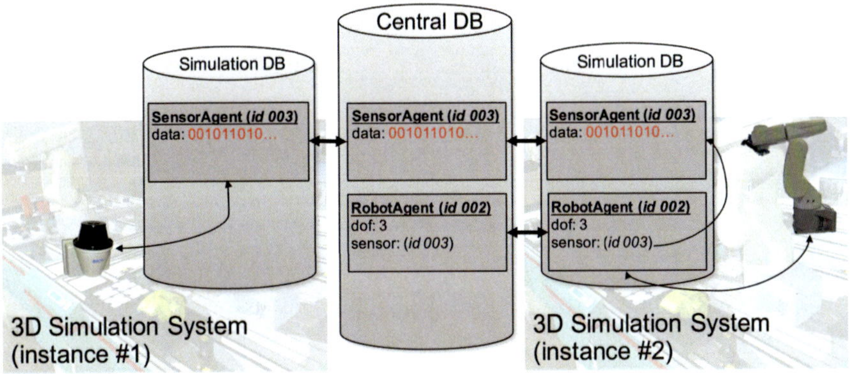


**Figure 7.21:** *An example for data synchronization with a communication sequence in the MCSA context.*

### 7.2.4 Industrial Robotics

Database technology is also ideally suited to manage Semantic World Models of industrial robots. In contrast to a file-based approach, models can flexibly be stored and managed in a decomposed form in a model repository, i.e., in terms of objects, their properties and relationships. For that purpose, a native format of the simulation system like VSDML (VSD Modeling Language) (see Subsection 7.3.3) or a standardized schema like AutomationML can be used. This allows to make changes persistent and support multiple versions on object and property level rather than on whole-file level.

Based on the concepts presented in this thesis, two more database interfaces for VSD have been developed and used to manage Semantic World Models of industrial robots. The first uses the graph database Neo4j [149, 150] to flexibly manage models. Figure 7.22 shows an example of an industrial robot modeled in VSDML. A graph reproduces a Semantic World Model's hierarchical structure with interdependencies especially well making Neo4j ideally suited for managing them.

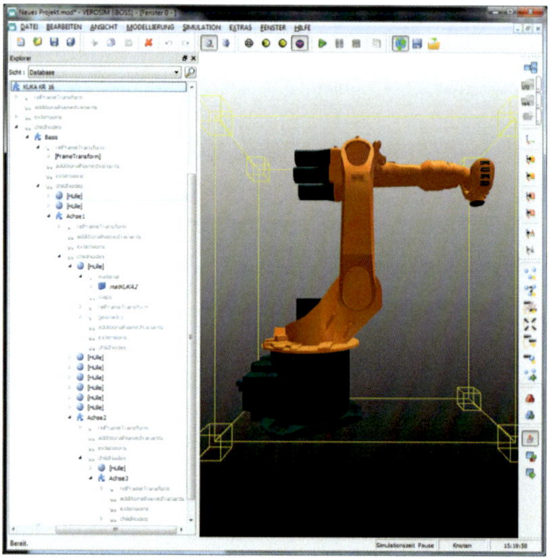

**Figure 7.22:** *A simulation model of an industrial robot loaded from a Neo4j graph database into VSD.*

The second interface prototype realizes a native ORM (Object-Relational Mapping) approach for VSD [151]. The advantage over a separate third party mapping solution like SGJ is the immediate mapping between VSD instances and tuples in a relational database.

The overall structure of the presented approach applied for the management of industrial robots is shown in Figure 7.23. Altogether, main benefits are

- flexible data management for robot simulation models,

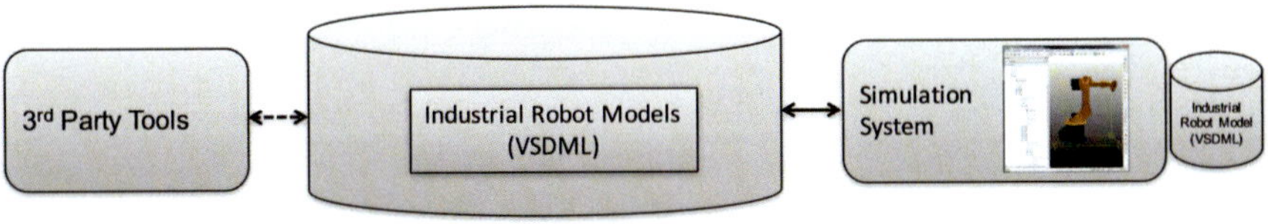


**Figure 7.23:** *Structure of the presented data management approach used as an industrial robot model repository.*

- support for native or standardized schemata,
- persistence for changes to the managed models,
- versioning on object and property level, and
- transparent interface to different DBMS.

## 7.3 Space

As a third area of application, the presented approach is used in different scenarios in the space context.

### 7.3.1 Virtual Space Robotics Testbed

As introduced in Chapter 1, VTBs follow a holistic approach to 3D simulation [152, 153]. In contrast, conventional 3D simulation applications, typically, use very specialized techniques and only focus on certain details. VTBs, however, incorporate a diversity of problem aspects and their interactions into a single application that integrates all relevant objects and parameters, their environment, and documentation. They are used in a much broader scope from design to testing, production and training. The Virtual Space Robotics Testbed's (VSRT) (Figure 7.24) purpose is to support the development of future space missions. It integrates the aspects of planetary landing missions, self-localization and exploration. For that purpose, it combines simulation algorithms, methods for system analysis, Virtual Reality techniques, and data processing. Furthermore, simulated and physical hardware components are seamlessly integrated and interchangeable.

To realize a VTB's high degree of integration and to support the various kinds of data interchange within, a Semantic World Model is used to represent (or define) the overall system (see Subsection 7.3.3). For that purpose, an efficient data management is vital. The approach presented in this thesis constitutes the ideal basis for that purpose by providing core benefits like a persistence back-end with a common language for all components, an integrated communication as well as logging and versioning infrastructure, support for distributed data processing, or the general enabling of Semantic World Modeling.

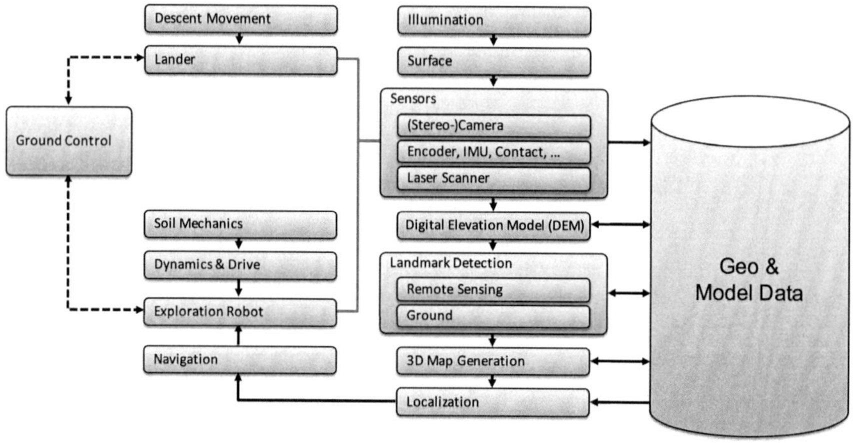


**Figure 7.24:** *Structure of the Virtual Space Robotics Testbed (VSRT) (adopted from [154]).*

As mentioned above, one aspect of the VSRT is the study of planetary landing missions. Such studies are conducted using the VSRT in the context of the research project FastMap [155, 156]. Its major goal is the automatic generation of navigation maps from images taken during the descent phase of a landing mission. To calibrate the VSRT – in particular for camera and lighting – a physical planetary landing mockup (Figure 7.25, right) is used. It consists of scaled realistic surface models and two robot arms carrying a light source and a camera. The flexibility of the VTB even allows for its usage as a control system of this facility. The VTB contains a model of a planetary descent scenario (Figure 7.26) and additionally a virtual model of the physical mockup (Figure 7.25, left). All three scenarios (physical mockup, virtual mission and virtual mockup) are driven by the very same software components.

Figure 7.27 shows the integration of the planetary landing mission components (FastMap) together with self-localization (research project SELOK) and crater exploration (research project Virtual Crater) using the presented approach for database synchronization within the VSRT.

A central active database is used to manage the shared model comprising mission specific data, sensor data, a DEM (Digital Elevation Model), i.e., a 3D model of the planet's ground, detected landmarks, and the resulting navigation map. Its main purpose is to make the model persistent and to actively drive the distributed data processing approach by communicating changes between the clients. The state of the distributed overall map derivation process is reflected by a central `mission` object holding a phase indicator, which is replicated to the local databases of all FastMap components. In each phase, a different client is responsible for finishing the phase (by incrementing it). To drive the distributed approach,

**Figure 7.25:** *FastMap virtual (left) and physical (right) mockup [155, 156].*

**Figure 7.26:** *FastMap virtual mission [155, 156].*

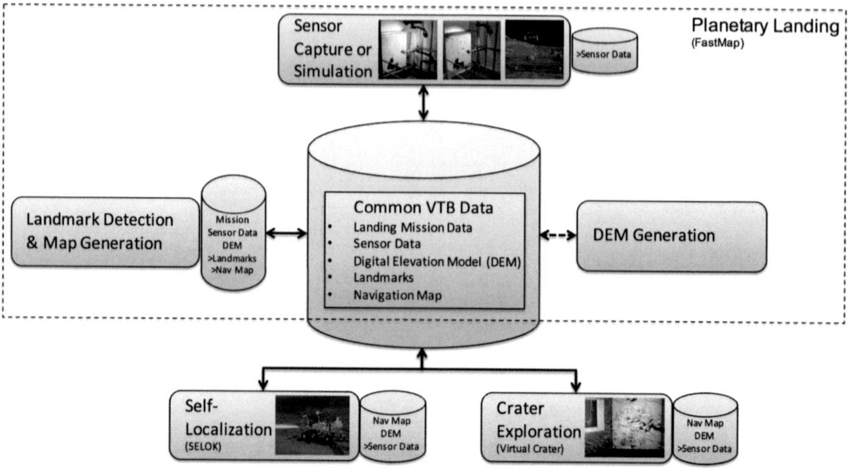


**Figure 7.27:** *Integration of the planetary landing mission components together with self-localization and crater exploration using the presented approach.*

phase changes and all other data modifications including the insertion of new objects are actively synchronized to the central database and from there to all other clients.

In the first phase, a client processes sensor data, which can either stem from the physical mockup's camera or from one of the virtual scenarios. For each of these captured images, an object with the image's data is replicated to the central database using data synchronization. When all images are captured, the phase is incremented. However, following a pipelining approach, as soon as the first image objects are stored in the database, the second client is notified and fetches these objects (directly accessing the central database). It uses image processing algorithms to reconstruct a DEM. Subsequently, DEM fragment objects holding the rasterized elevation data are stored in the central database. When all captured images are processed, the phase is once again incremented. This phase change triggers the third client. Based on the images and the DEM, it applies different detection algorithms to create a map of landmarks like craters, rocks, or mountain tops. These landmarks are also synced in objects of the corresponding classes of the common application schema, which is initially distributed to all clients using schema synchronization. To end the distributed data processing, the detector client increments the phase of the mission for a last time.

Subsequently, the completed map is used as a basis for self-localization and navigation of mobile robots during the exploration of the planetary surface (Figure 7.28) [157, 158]. This is the subject of the research project SELOK. Here, mobile robots use sensors like stereo cameras or laser scanners to capture their surroundings. Within this data, landmarks like the aforementioned rocks or craters are detected. These so-called local landmarks are then matched against the global landmarks from the navigation map synchronized from the central active database using the presented approach yielding a self-localization of the robot.

**Figure 7.28:** *The SELOK scenario: A mobile robot navigates by finding landmarks stored in a global map.*

Finally, the third research project Virtual Crater is concerned with the development of a VTB for mobile robots with planetary exploration missions [159]. The testbed allows for a cost-efficient and realistic simulation of mobile robots in a virtual lunar environment. Here, they can be developed, programmed, tested, and optimized. Furthermore, the project comprises a physical testbed to compare and verify simulation results with reality. The results of Virtual Crater can be complemented by the navigation map and the digital elevation model from FastMap also synchronized from the central active database using the presented approach.

Altogether, the main benefits when using the presented approach for the Virtual Space Robotics Testbed are

- the efficient management of a shared Semantic World Model,
- persistence for changes to this model,
- a "common language" for the participating systems,
- the active driving of distributed data processing processes,
- providing a central communication hub for collaboration,

- enabling Semantic World Modeling,
- supporting the flexible adaption to evolving schemata, and
- in general: the active integration of different systems.

*Supported by the German Aerospace Center (DLR) with funds of the German Federal Ministry of Economics and Technology (BMWi), support codes 50 RA 1034 (FastMap), 50 RA 0911 (SELOK) und 50 RA 0913 (Virtual Crater).*

### 7.3.2 Satellite Data Management

The research project iBOSS [160] aims at bringing modular concepts to satellites to support flexible On-Orbit Servicing. In the second phase of the project, previous concepts and developments are integrated into a VTB. The 3D simulation system VEROSIM is used to simulate the actual servicing while other project partners provide tools for computer aided satellite design (semiautomatic building block selection based on a user's satellite requirements) or automated model generation and parameterization (parameter optimization for a given satellite configuration). Thus, the XML-based reference implementation of the presented approach (see Section 6.6) is a convenient choice to support the collaboration between the (loosely coupled) partners (Figure 7.29). It offers the advantage of standardized object-oriented data exchange with a well-defined common data format. While the format itself is extensible to satisfy application specific requirements, the synchronization approach flexibly adapts to schema changes (schema evolution) without the need to rebuild applications.

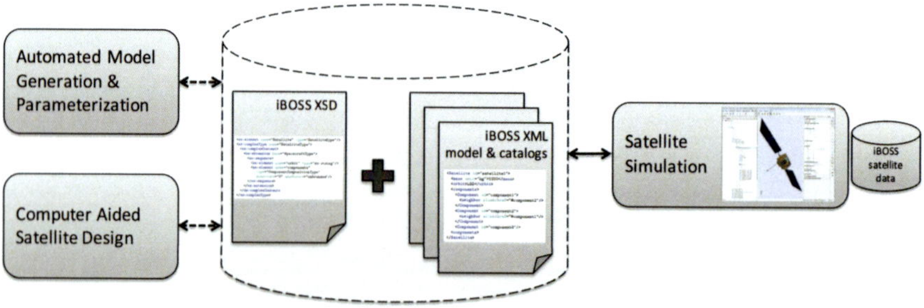


**Figure 7.29:** *Structure of the XML-based iBOSS scenario (data: [160]).*

To support integration, a common data modeling language for modular satellites was defined using an XSD file [161]. This schema is used to create valid XML documents for data exchange between project partners. To modularize construction, the iBOSS application schema defines an abstract satellite building block. It has common properties like position, orientation, and its interfaces. An interface is another type that can be used to logically connect blocks. Therefore, an interface element has non-composite reference to its neighbor interface it is connected to. Using the building block base type, specialized blocks like a thruster block or a payload block are derived.

A catalog XML file is used to offer a predefined choice of building blocks and components. Upon a closer view, these building blocks can be identified to also have some individual properties for each usage. In contrast to parameters of a building block, such state variables shall not be stored in a catalog. Listing 7.1 shows an example of a battery with one state variable (charge) and two parameters (capacity, voltage).

**Listing 7.1:** *Building block with state variable and parameters.*

```
<Battery>
  <charge unit="Ah">1000</charge>
  <capacity unit="Ah">2000</capacity>
  <voltage unit="V">10</voltage>
</Battery>
```

To match this requirement with the XML modeling techniques for object-oriented systems presented in Section 6.6, a partitioning of building block types is a worthwhile approach. Listing 7.2 shows an adapted example. While the battery itself only stores the state variable charge, it is extended by a reference to a battery definition. This definition type holds the parameters for defining a battery with particular characteristics. Finally, the definition can be externalized into a catalog file (Listing 7.3).

**Listing 7.2:** *Building block with separated state variable.*

```
<Battery>
  <charge unit="Ah">1000</charge>
  <definition>
    <BatteryDef>
      <capacity unit="Ah">2000</capacity>
      <voltage unit="V">10</voltage>
    </BatteryDef>
  </definition>
</Battery>
```

**Listing 7.3:** *Building block using catalog reference.*

```
<Battery>
  <charge unit="Ah">1000</charge>
  <definition xlink:href="catalog.xml#id1"/>
</Battery>
```

Altogether, the presented approach supports the complete iBOSS application schema and conforming data. On system startup, given the corresponding XSD file, VEROSIM is automatically configured to speak this common language of the project partners. Subsequently, iBOSS-compliant XML files can be loaded and used in the simulation system (Figure 7.30). Additionally, methods of functional data synchronization map special data types to their native VSD representations, e.g., iBOSS positions and orientations to frames (poses).

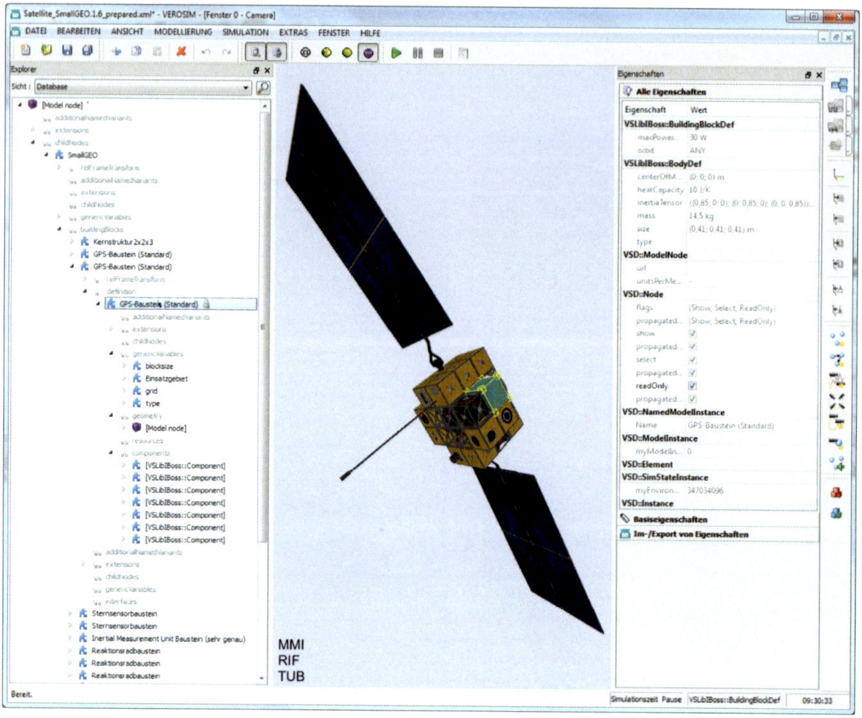


**Figure 7.30:** *An iBOSS satellite model loaded from an XML file (data: [160])*

This file-based (XML/XSD) approach can be seen as a pre-stage to a database-driven solution (Figure 7.31) better suiting the VTB integration intentions.

Figure 7.32 shows an exemplary result from a partially database-driven solution. Here, only the developed iBOSS schema is imported into a central database. From there, it is replicated (schema transfer) to connected VEROSIM clients' VSD simulation databases. Subsequently, data synchronization can be used to replicate corresponding data, as well. Finally, different functional data synchronization components are used to load the referenced geometric sub models from file and to apply the encoded pose (position and orientation) information for alignment. Likewise, object names are functionally synchronized (from GML description to VSD name property).

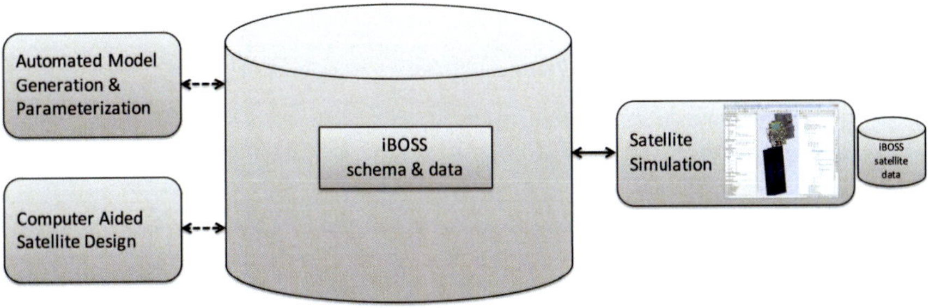


**Figure 7.31:** *Structure of the database-driven iBOSS scenario (data: [160]).*

A third integration stage completely managing the model using database technology is shown in the next section.

The main benefits when using the presented approach in the context of satellite data management are

- enabling the simulation system to speak a common modeling language,
- the flexible adaption to changes in an evolving modeling language,
- support for a neutral object-oriented modeling language,
- integrating semantics translation (functional data sync), and
- in general: the integration of different systems.

Using the database-driven solution adds even more benefits like

- persistence within a central data repository,
- live collaboration between project partners,
- more flexible access to large models (e.g., using streaming), and
- additional services like temporal data management and versioning.

*Supported by the German Aerospace Center (DLR) with funds of the German Federal Ministry of Economics and Technology (BMWi), support code 50 RA 1203 (iBOSS-2).*

### 7.3.3 Space Project Data Management

Another field of application for the presented database synchronization approach is data management for space projects in general. The previous subsections already showed corresponding applications. The research project INVIRTES [153], however, aims at providing an integrated approach for the development of such complex space related mechatronic systems like satellites or rovers. For that purpose, VTBs are used as a basis to integrate all relevant data – similar to a "space PDM (Product Data Management) system." Besides data, methods – primarily simulation methods – are also part of such a VTB.

In the context of INVIRTES, a so-called "system model" integrates all relevant aspects including system specification, structure and geometry, state and configuration, internal and

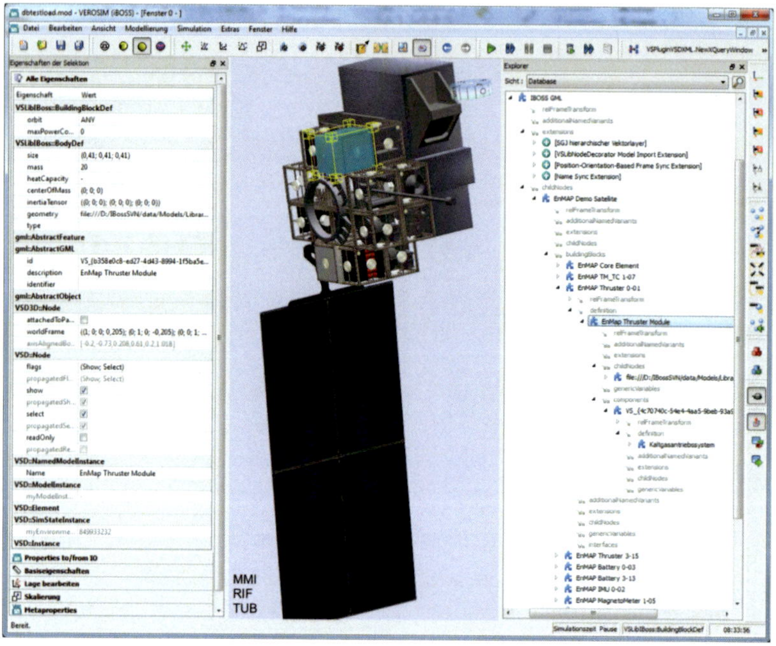


**Figure 7.32:** *Partially database-driven data management for the iBOSS scenario (data: [160])*

external interfaces, or programs of control components. As this model represents the central entity within a space project in INVIRTES, the corresponding data management component – following [162] – is called a CWM (Central World Model). It shall provide the methods of an active, $n$D temporal, real-time capable and object-oriented database.

Thus, the presented approach for database synchronization builds the ideal basis to integrate the simulation system VEROSIM and its VSD in-memory database with the utilized SGJ, where the latter realizes the CWM.

The aforementioned system model can be more coarsely divided into system specification and detail model where the latter is a representation of the former. While the system specification is based on the CONSENS language [163] (based on SysML (Systems Modeling Language [7])), the detail model uses the VSD's native modeling concepts as an ideal basis for an experimentable model. For that purpose, the relevant schema structures are abstracted (and extracted) as a modeling language: The VSDML. Figure 7.33 depicts the approach. The implementation of VSD's reflective API (VSD-Meta) as well as basic classes only used for data management (VSD-Core) are separated from classes used for actual data modeling like VSD-Base for basic graph-based data modeling, VSD-3D for 3D modeling, or VSD-IO for input/output networks.

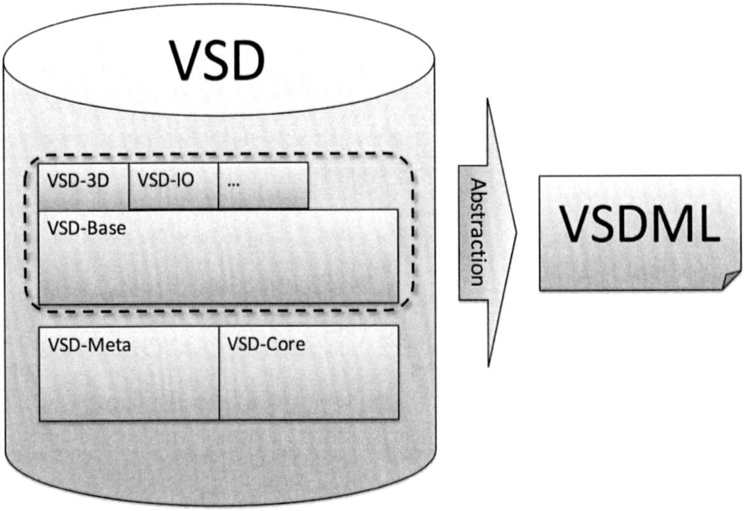


**Figure 7.33:** *Abstraction of VSDML from the VSD database.*

For a standardized representation and simplified integration with the SysML-based CONSENS system specification, VSDML is represented using the Ecore meta-metamodel and its XMI (XML Metadata Interchange [108])-based representation. Viewing VSD's schema as a modeling language makes it a metamodel on its own. In this context, VSD's metamodel as previously presented in Subsubsection 6.3.1 (or rather its implementation VSD-Meta) becomes the corresponding meta-metamodel. Thus, abstracting the structures from the in-memory database to the Ecore-based modeling language corresponds to a meta-metamodel exchange from VSD-Meta to Ecore (Figure 7.34).

The overall data management architecture of the INVIRTES scenario that uses the presented approach is illustrated in Figure 7.35.

Using VSDML, a third integration stage of the scenario from the previous section has been realized which now manages the satellite in its entirety within the central database. In particular, it also stores the data of the aforementioned geometric sub models modeled in basic VSDML structures (in particular, using VSD-Base and VSD-3D constructs). The database also does without the GML base schema. Figures 7.36–7.37 show the contents of the central database and the model loaded into the simulation system. Using this approach, full database functionality is available for the satellite and any other VSDML-based scenario providing all the benefits of the presented approach for database synchronization.

Benefits when using the presented approach in the context of the INVIRTES project are

- flexibly enabling the simulation system to access the system model,
- with a flexible adaption to evolving schemata,

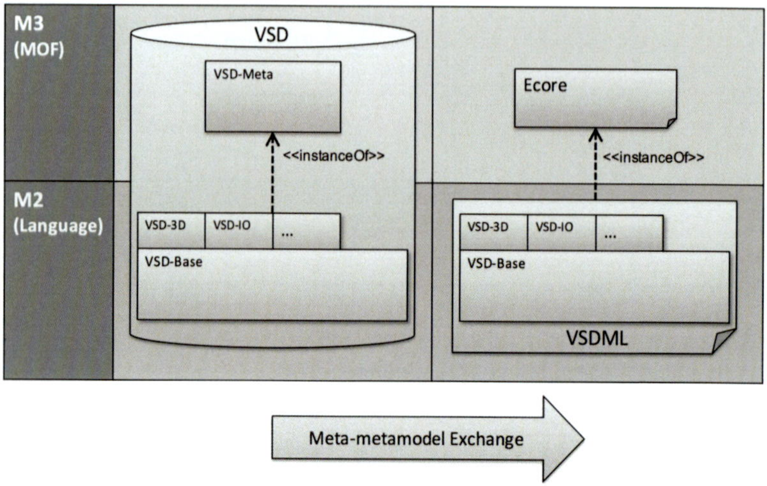


**Figure 7.34:** *Abstracting VSDML from VSD corresponds to an exchange of the meta-metamodel.*

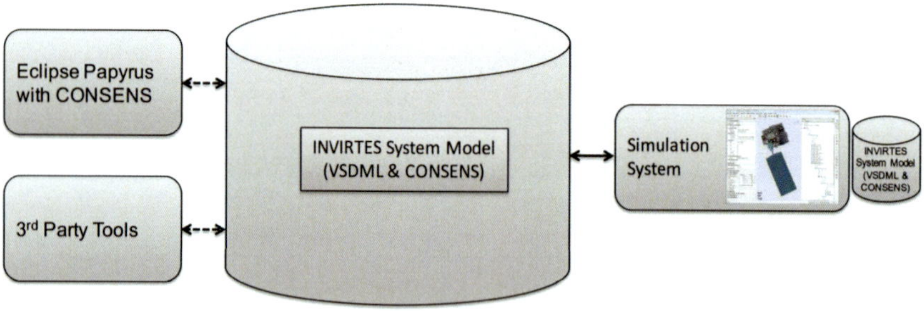


**Figure 7.35:** *Data management architecture of the INVIRTES scenario (data: [160]).*

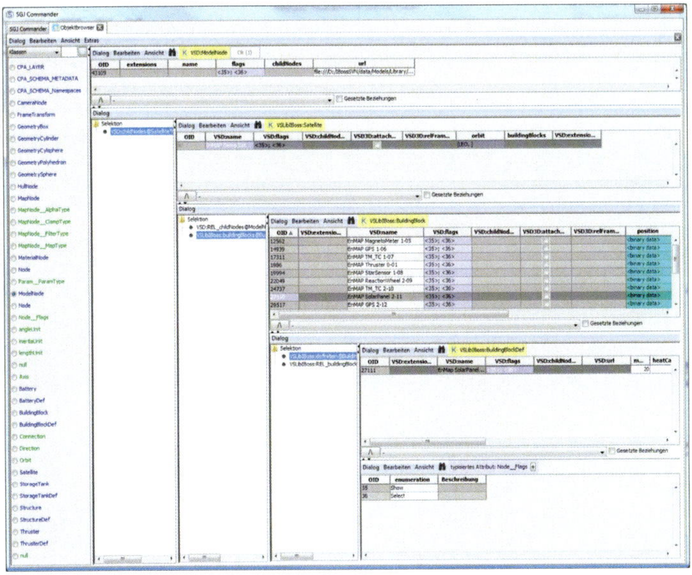

**Figure 7.36:** *VSDML-based satellite scenario completely managed within database (contents of central database) (data: [160])*

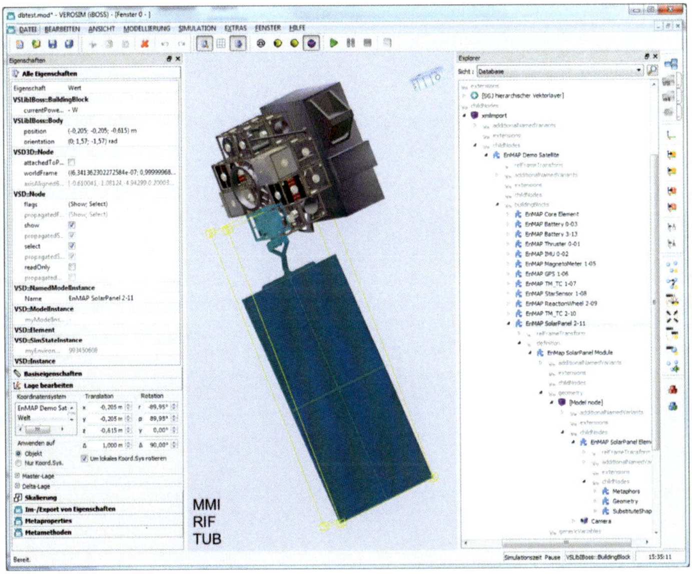


**Figure 7.37:** *VSDML-based satellite scenario completely managed within database (loaded into simulation system) (data: [160])*

- no offline conversion of the original data,
- providing persistence for the system model,
- active driving of the communication between the connected systems,
- providing a common schema (i.e., language) for the distributed system,
- supporting temporal data management,
- with integrated simulation logging,
- and a versioning scheme for modeling processes,
- enabling distributed data processing,
- enabling Semantic World Modeling,
- supporting Semantic World Models with static and dynamic parts, and
- decoupling the simulation system from the central database.

*Supported by the German Aerospace Center (DLR) with funds of the German Federal Ministry of Economics and Technology (BMWi), support code 50 RA 1306 (INVIRTES).*

# Chapter 8

# Summary

The development and the whole lifecycle of robotic and mechatronic systems is characterized by a high degree of complexity. The eRobotics approach aims at making this complexity manageable by combining the usage of electronic media, modern 3D simulation techniques and robotic concepts. A core technology of eRobotics are Virtual Testbeds, a holistic approach to 3D simulation that considers the integrated system under development within its operational environment. Based on VTB (Virtual Testbed) technology, Simulation-based X approaches are used to optimize the properties of a system under development itself (X=Optimization), as a mental model of the system in operation to optimize decision-making (X=Reasoning), or for system control itself reusing the developments from the VTB (X=Control). The basis for any eRobotics application is a Semantic World Model – a comprehensive 3D model of the system and its environment offering closeness to reality and a self-describing meaning whose complex hierarchical structures advise an object-oriented modeling.

This thesis presents a universal data management approach for eRobotics applications that uses databases to efficiently manage these models offering many advantages over flat model files (multiuser support, distributed processes, huge models, consistent schema, ...). The basic idea of this flexible approach is to combine the advantages of an active in-memory simulation database (SimDB) with an external database (ExtDB), which provides persistence, versioning and a communication infrastructure. An important technical contribution of this work is the new approach to synchronize these two databases on schema, data, semantics as well as on version level.

Initially, to provide a sound theoretical basis, system requirements for database candidates are investigated. For that purpose, a new MDE (Model-Driven Engineering)-based concept to ensure the general compatibility of two databases is developed using the databases' metamodels and model transformations. Additionally, the UML (Unified Modeling Language [8]) metamodel is used as a pivot to enforce an object-oriented modeling, provide a neutral specification language and reduce the number of required transformations. This is an important foundation for the universal applicability of the approach on arbitrary databases. In particular, it simplifies the problem of predominant relational databases on the one side and the advantages of an object-oriented modeling for Semantic World Models on the other side.

Based on these system requirements, a neutral and thorough specification of database synchronization methods is given using UML metaclasses. In schema synchronization, the Semantic World Model's schema within ExtDB is mapped to each connected SimDB, creating schema structures on the fly as required and yielding a schema mapping. This enables the distributed system to be flexibly adapted to arbitrary application schemata supporting eRobotics applications from various fields.

In data synchronization, based on the schema mapping, data is replicated on-demand from ExtDB to each synchronized SimDB. This allows to load the Semantic World Model in its native representation into the simulation database without the need for (offline) conversions to a simplified exchange format like VRML (Virtual Reality Modeling Language [9]) preserving the rich semantics of the original data. Furthermore, data can be loaded and also unloaded, allowing eRobotics applications to access even huge models like cities or forests piece by piece. ExtDB's query interface allows to query the necessary model parts – usually unfeasible when using flat files. To resynchronize replicated data, a novel distributed concurrency control approach using database change notifications is developed that avoids locks, which are inappropriate for live 3D simulations. Altogether, this realizes a communication infrastructure for eRobotics applications based on a distributed Semantic World Model.

Functional data synchronization allows an eRobotics application to interpret the semantics or function of a Semantic World Model's unknown parts where necessary. For that purpose, replicated model data within SimDB is translated on-the-fly to equivalent structures recognized by the simulation system.

Temporal data management is realized using a temporal database for ExtDB allowing to manage Semantic World Models in multiple, time-dependent versions and to select reference times for snapshot replication to SimDB. This integrated temporal data management is ideally suited for model versioning as well as simulation logging and replay in eRobotics applications. Furthermore, it avoids separate file versioning or simulation logging infrastructures.

Furthermore, a novel $n$D temporal data management approach is developed. It supports multiple time dimensions (exceeding the standard bitemporal case), allows retroactive updates to "slide in between" along the valid time dimension, and lets the order of updates only have influence on the resulting transaction timestamps. As an example, it is used in eRobotics-based forestry applications to decouple transaction and valid time from the official effectivity of a datum.

This thesis also identifies appropriate database choices that are subsequently used for two reference implementations. For SimDB, the simulation database VSD (Versatile Simulation Database) of the simulation system VEROSIM (Virtual Environments and Robotic Simulation [127]) is chosen, in particular, for its proven suitability for eRobotics applications. For

ExtDB, the object-oriented database management layer SGJ (SupportGIS Java [123]) as well as a modeling approach using XML (Extensible Markup Language) and XSD (XML Schema Definition) files are selected. The former for its flexible object-oriented management of data in standard relational databases, the latter for a simple data exchange between decoupled development teams. All databases are thoroughly examined towards the system requirements by specifying Ecore-based database metamodels and ATL (ATL Transformation Language [103, 104]) model transformations to and from the UML metamodel.

Due to the universality of the presented data management approach and based on the reference implementations, various eRobotics applications from such different fields as environment, industry and space are already realized today. Amongst others, they comprise applications for forest inventory, management and simulation, a database-driven distributed 3D city simulation system, flexible interfaces for standard industrial formats like AutomationML (Automation Modeling Language [6]), a Virtual Space Robotics Testbed, or a MBE (Model-Based Engineering)- and VTB-based development environment for space projects. As diverse these eRobotics applications may be – they all benefit from the presented new data management approach.

Chapter 1 defines five main demands for data management in eRobotics applications. Existing database-based approaches in similar fields with a 3D context each only account for some of these aspects. In contrast, the presented novel approach completely meets these demands

1. by *supporting an object-oriented data modeling* already in the formal system requirements using model transformations to and from the UML,
2. by featuring an inherent *distributed architecture* with ExtDB as a communication hub specifying a DDB (Distributed Database) and, furthermore, allowing the combination with other distribution mechanisms like database check-out/-in for different sites or a direct simulation state distribution for projection screens [164],
3. by making the concept of an active *in-memory database* SimDB an integral part of its specification,
4. by *being schema-adaptive* using schema synchronization to flexibly adapt to arbitrary schemata and using functional data synchronization for selective semantics translation,
5. by *supporting Simulation-based X* by integrating temporal data management for comparative analyses in Simulation-based Optimization and Reasoning and being adequately universal for reuse in live operation for Simulation-based Reasoning and Control.

Altogether, the work at hand presents a comprehensive data management solution for modern eRobotics applications and is the only one to fulfill all the identified requirements by proposing a flexible distributed database synchronization approach with a thorough theoretical basis and by demonstrating its practical feasibility and usefulness in various applications.

# Acronyms

| | |
|---|---|
| ACID | atomicity, consistency, isolation and durability. |
| ADT | Abstract Data Type. |
| AI | Artificial Intelligence. |
| API | Application Programming Interface. |
| AR | Augmented Reality. |
| ATL | ATL Transformation Language [103, 104]. |
| AutomationML | Automation Modeling Language [6]. |
| | |
| BIM | Building Information Modeling. |
| | |
| CA$x$ | Computer-Aided $x$. |
| CAD | Computer-Aided Design. |
| CAE | Computer-Aided Engineering. |
| CAEX | Computer Aided Engineering Exchange [6, 145]. |
| CAM | Computer-Aided Manufacturing. |
| CASE | Computer-Aided Software Engineering. |
| CIM | Computation-Independent Model. |
| COBOL | Common Business-Oriented Language. |
| COLLADA | Collaborative Design Activity [6]. |
| CORBA | Common Object Request Broker Architecture. |
| CSG | Constructive Solid Geometry. |
| CWM | Central World Model. |
| | |
| DAO | Data Access Object. |
| DB | Database. |
| DBMS | Database Management System. |
| DBS | Database System. |

| | |
|---|---|
| DDB | Distributed Database. |
| DDBMS | Distributed Database Management System. |
| DDBS | Distributed Database System. |
| DDL | Database Definition Language. |
| DEM | Digital Elevation Model. |
| DES | Discrete Event Simulation. |
| DML | Data Manipulation Language. |
| DOM | Document Object Model. |
| DSL | Domain-Specific Language. |
| DTD | Document Type Definition. |
| ECA | Event Condition Action. |
| EDM | Engineering Data Management. |
| EMF | Eclipse Modeling Framework [109]. |
| ER | Entity-Relationship. |
| GIS | Geo Information System. |
| GML | Geography Markup Language [26]. |
| GPL | General-Purpose Language. |
| HTML | HyperText Markup Language. |
| HTTP | Hypertext Transfer Protocol. |
| ID | Identifier. |
| IEEE | Institute of Electrical and Electronics Engineers. |
| IFC | Industrial Foundation Classes [5]. |
| IGES | Initial Graphics Exchange Specification. |
| ISO | International Organization for Standardization. |
| IT | Information Technology. |
| JAXB | Java Architecture for XML Binding [134]. |
| JNI | Java Native Interface [130]. |
| JT | Jupiter Tesselation. |
| JVM | Java Virtual Machine. |
| LOD | Level of Detail. |

| | |
|---|---|
| MARTE | Modeling and Analysis of Real Time and Embedded systems [100]. |
| MBE | Model-Based Engineering. |
| MDA | Model-Driven Architecture. |
| MDD | Model-Driven Development. |
| MDE | Model-Driven Engineering. |
| MDI | Model-Driven Interoperability. |
| MDPE | Model-Driven Product Engineering. |
| MDSE | Model-Driven Software Engineering. |
| MOF | Meta-Object Facility [99]. |
| NURBS | Non-Uniform Rational B-Splines. |
| NVE | Networked Virtual Environment. |
| OCL | Object Constraint Language [101]. |
| ODB | Object Database. |
| ODL | Object Definition Language. |
| ODMG | Object Data Management Group. |
| ODMS | Object Data Management System. |
| OGC | Open Geospatial Consortium. |
| OID | Object Identifier. |
| OM | Object Model. |
| OMG | Object Management Group. |
| OO | Object-Oriented or Object-Orientation. |
| OODB | Object-Oriented Database. |
| OODBMS | Object-Oriented Database Management System. |
| OODBS | Object-Oriented Database System. |
| OODM | Object-Oriented Data Model. |
| OQL | Object Query Language. |
| ORB | Object Request Broker. |
| ORDB | Object-Relational Database. |
| ORDBMS | Object-Relational Database Management System. |
| ORM | Object-Relational Mapping. |
| P2P | Peer-to-Peer. |
| PDF | Portable Document Format. |
| PDM | Product Data Management. |

| | |
|---|---|
| PHP | PHP: Hypertext Preprocessor [15]. |
| PIM | Platform-Independent Model. |
| PK | Primary Key. |
| PLM | Product Lifecycle Management. |
| PSM | Platform-Specific Model. |
| QVT | MOF (Meta-Object Facility [99]) Query/-View/Transformation [105, 98, 106, 107]. |
| RDB | Relational Database. |
| RDBMS | Relational Database Management System. |
| SAX | Simple API (Application Programming Interface) for XML. |
| SDE | Spatial Database Engine [20]. |
| SDM | Simulation Data Management. |
| SGJ | SupportGIS Java [123]. |
| SHP | Esri Shapefile. |
| SI | International System of Units. |
| SLM | Simulation Lifecycle Management. |
| SOA | Service-Oriented Architecture. |
| SQL | Structured Query Language. |
| STEP | Standard for the Exchange of Product model data. |
| SVG | Scalable Vector Graphics. |
| SVN | Apache Subversion. |
| SysML | Systems Modeling Language [7]. |
| TIFF | Tagged Image File Format. |
| UDT | User Defined Type. |
| UML | Unified Modeling Language [8]. |
| URI | Uniform Resource Identifier. |
| VDAFS | Federation of the Automobile Industry, Surface Interface. |
| VE | Virtual Environment. |
| VEROSIM | Virtual Environments and Robotic Simulation [127]. |

| | |
|---|---|
| VR | Virtual Reality. |
| VRML | Virtual Reality Modeling Language [9]. |
| VSD | Versatile Simulation Database. |
| VSDML | VSD Modeling Language. |
| VTB | Virtual Testbed. |
| | |
| W3DS | Web 3D Service. |
| WFS | Web Feature Service. |
| WMS | Web Map Service. |
| WTK | WorldToolKit. |
| | |
| X3D | Extensible 3D [39]. |
| XLink | XML Linking Language [136]. |
| XMI | XML Metadata Interchange [108]. |
| XML | Extensible Markup Language. |
| XPath | XML Path Language. |
| XPointer | XML Pointer Language [137]. |
| XSD | XML Schema Definition. |
| XSLT | Extensible Stylesheet Language Transformation [18]. |

# Bibliography


[1] J. Rossmann, M. Schluse, M. Rast, and L. Atorf, "eRobotics Combining Electronic Media and Simulation Technology to Develop (Not Only) Robotics Applications," in *E-Systems for the 21st Century: Concept, Developments, and Applications*, S. Kadry and A. El Hami, Eds. Apple Academic Press, 2015.

[2] Verein Deutscher Ingenieure (VDI), "VDI 3633 - Simulation of systems in materials handling, logistics and production - Fundamentals," Düsseldorf, 2013.

[3] R. Rosen, G. Von Wichert, G. Lo, and K. D. Bettenhausen, "About the importance of autonomy and digital twins for the future of manufacturing," in *IFAC Proceedings Volumes (IFAC-PapersOnline)*, vol. 48, no. 3, 2015, pp. 567–572.

[4] R. Elmasri and S. B. Navathe, *Database Systems: Models, Languages, Design, And Application Programming*, 6th ed. Prentice Hall International, 2010.

[5] buildingSMART International, "Industry Foundation Classes (IFC)." [Online]. Available: http://www.buildingsmart-tech.org/specifications/ifc-releases/summary [Accessed: 2016-05-18]

[6] AutomationML e.V., "AutomationML." [Online]. Available: https://www.automationml.org [Accessed: 2016-05-18]

[7] SysML Open Source Specification Project, "SysML Specification." [Online]. Available: http://www.sysml.org/sysml-specifications/ [Accessed: 2016-05-18]

[8] Object Management Group (OMG), "Unified Modeling Language (UML)." [Online]. Available: http://www.uml.org [Accessed: 2016-05-18]

[9] Web3D Consortium, "VRML97 Specification." [Online]. Available: http://www.web3d.org/documents/specifications/14772/V2.0/index.html [Accessed: 2016-05-18]

[10] R. T. Azuma, "A survey of augmented reality," *Presence*, vol. 6, no. 4, pp. 355–385, 1997.

[11] S. Julier, Y. Baillot, M. Lanzagorta, D. Brown, and L. Rosenblum, "Bars: Battlefield augmented reality system," in *NATO Symposium on Information Processing Techniques for Military Systems*, 2000, pp. 9–11.

[12] B. Damer, D. Rasmussen, M. Neilson, P. Newman, R. Norkus, W. Clancey, M. Sierhuis, R. Van Hoof, M. Shirley, and T. Cochrane, "Data-Driven Virtual Environment Assembly and Operation," in *Virtual Ironbird Workshop*, 2004, p. 1.

[13] M. Sierhuis, W. J. Clancey, and R. J. V. Hoof, "Brahms: a multi-agent modelling environment for simulating work processes and practices," *International Journal of Simulation and Process Modelling*, vol. 3, no. 3, pp. 134–152, 2007.

[14] Oracle, "MySQL." [Online]. Available: http://www.mysql.com [Accessed: 2016-05-18]

[15] Zend Technologies Inc., "An overview on PHP," 2007. [Online]. Available: http://static.zend.com/topics/overview_on_php.pdf [Accessed: 2016-05-18]

[16] D. Schmalstieg, G. Schall, D. Wagner, I. Barakonyi, G. Reitmayr, J. Newman, and F. Ledermann, "Managing complex augmented reality models," *IEEE Computer Graphics and Applications*, vol. 27, no. 4, pp. 48–57, 2007.

[17] D. Wagner and D. Schmalstieg, "Muddleware for Prototyping Mixed Reality Multiuser Games," in *2007 IEEE Virtual Reality Conference*. IEEE, 2007, pp. 235–238.

[18] The World Wide Web Consortium (W3C), "XSL Transformations (XSLT)." [Online]. Available: http://www.w3.org/TR/xslt [Accessed: 2016-05-18]

[19] G. Van Maren, R. Germs, and F. Jansen, "Integrating 3D-GIS and Virtual Reality Design and implementation of the Karma VI system," in *Proceedings of the Spatial Information Research Centre's 10th Colloquium. University of Otago, New Zealand*, 1998, pp. 16–19.

[20] ESRI, "ArcSDE Technology." [Online]. Available: http://www.esri.com/software/arcgis/arcsde [Accessed: 2016-05-18]

[21] Oracle, "Oracle Database." [Online]. Available: http://www.oracle.com/us/products/database/index.html [Accessed: 2016-05-18]

[22] C. Borgatti, M. Felicori, M. Mauri, L. Calori, A. Guidazzoli, S. Pescarin, T. Diamanti, M. Liguori, and L. Valentini, "Databases and virtual environments: a good match for communicating complex cultural sites," in *ACM SIGGRAPH 2004 Educators program*. ACM, 2004, p. 30.

[23] J. Haist and V. Coors, "The W3DS-Interface of Cityserver3D," in *European Spatial Data Research (EuroSDR) u.a.: Next Generation 3D City Models. Workshop Papers : Participant's Edition*, Kolbe and Gröger, Eds., Bonn, 2005, pp. 63–67.

[24] OGC CityGML Standards Working Group, "CityGML," 2014. [Online]. Available: http://www.citygml.org [Accessed: 2016-05-18]

[25] T. H. Kolbe, G. Gröger, and L. Plümer, "CityGML: Interoperable access to 3D city models," in *Geo-information for Disaster Management*, 2005, pp. 883–899.

[26] Open Geospatial Consortium (OGC), "Geography Markup Language (GML)." [Online]. Available: http://www.opengeospatial.org/standards/gml [Accessed: 2016-05-18]

[27] J. Haist, R. Schnuck, and T. Reitz, "Usage of persistence framework technologies for 3D geodata servers," in *AGILE 2006, 9th AGILE Conference on Geographical Information Science. Shaping the future of Geographic Information Science in Europe*, 2006, pp. 43 – 50.

[28] Red Hat, "Hibernate." [Online]. Available: http://www.hibernate.org/ [Accessed: 2016-05-18]

[29] H. Takemura, Y. Kitamura, J. Ohya, and F. Kishino, "Distributed Processing Architecture for Virtual Space Teleconferencing," in *Proc. of ICAT*, vol. 93, 1993, pp. 27–32.

[30] Y. Masunaga and C. Watanabe, "Design and implementation of a multi-modal user interface of the Virtual World Database system (VWDB)," in *Proceedings Seventh International Conference on Database Systems for Advanced Applications. DASFAA 2001.* IEEE Comput. Soc, 2001, pp. 294–301.

[31] Y. Masunaga, C. Watanabe, A. Osugi, and K. Satoh, "A New Database Technology for Cyberspace Applications," in *Nontraditional Database Systems*, Y. Kambayashi, M. Kitsuregawa, A. Makinouchi, S. Uemura, K. Tanaka, and Y. Masunaga, Eds. London: Taylor & Francis, 2002, ch. 1, pp. 1–14.

[32] C. Watanabe and Y. Masunaga, "VWDB2: A Network Virtual Reality System with a Database Function for a Shared Work Environment," in *Information Systems and Databases*, K. Tanaka, Ed., Tokyo, Japan, 2002, pp. 190–196.

[33] Oracle, "Java3D." [Online]. Available: http://java3d.java.net/ [Accessed: 2016-05-18]

[34] H. Eriksson, "The multicast backbone," *Communications of the ACM*, 1994.

[35] T. Manoharan, H. Taylor, and P. Gardiner, "A collaborative analysis tool for visualisation and interaction with spatial data," in *Proceedings of the seventh international conference on 3D Web technology.* ACM, 2002, pp. 75–83.

[36] G. Reitmayr, S. Carroll, A. Reitemeyer, and M. G. Wagner, "DeepMatrix - An open technology based virtual environment system," *The Visual Computer*, vol. 15, no. 7-8, pp. 395–412, nov 1999.

[37] K. Kaku, H. Minami, T. Tomii, and H. Nasu, "Proposal of Virtual Space Browser Enables Retrieval and Action with Semantics which is Shared by Multi Users," in *21st International Conference on Data Engineering Workshops (ICDEW'05)*. IEEE, apr 2005, pp. 1259–1259.

[38] T. R. Gruber, "A translation approach to portable ontology specifications," *Knowledge Acquisition*, vol. 5, no. 2, pp. 199–220, 1993.

[39] Web3D Consortium, "Extensible 3D (X3D)." [Online]. Available: http://www.web3d.org/x3d/specifications/ [Accessed: 2016-05-18]

[40] M. Kamiura, H. Oisol, K. Tajima, and K. Tanaka, "Spatial views and LOD-based access control in VRML-object databases," in *Worldwide Computing and Its Applications*, ser. Lecture Notes in Computer Science, T. Masuda, Y. Masunaga, and M. Tsukamoto, Eds. Springer Berlin / Heidelberg, 1997, vol. 1274, pp. 210–225.

[41] E. V. Schweber, "SQL3D - Escape from VRML Island," 1998. [Online]. Available: http://www.infomaniacs.com/SQL3D/SQL3D-Escape-From-VRML-Island.htm [Accessed: 2016-05-18]

[42] T. Connolly and C. Begg, *Database systems: a practical approach to design, implementation, and management*, 5th ed. Pearson Education (US), 2009.

[43] Object Management Group (OMG), "Common Object Request Broker Architecture (CORBA)." [Online]. Available: http://www.omg.org/corba/ [Accessed: 2016-05-18]

[44] A. Vakaloudis and B. Theodoulidis, "Spatiotemporal Database Connection to VRML," in *Proceedings of the 9th UK Electronic Imaging & the Visual Arts Conference, EVA '98*, Cambridge, 1998.

[45] K. Walczak, "Dynamic Database Modeling of 3D Multimedia Content," in *Interactive 3D Multimedia Content*, W. Cellary and K. Walczak, Eds. London: Springer London, 2012, ch. 4, pp. 55–102.

[46] K. Walczak and W. Cellary, "Building database applications of virtual reality with X-VRML," in *Proceeding of the seventh international conference on 3D Web technology - Web3D '02*. New York, New York, USA: ACM Press, feb 2002, pp. 111–120.

[47] U. Sendler, *Das PLM-Kompendium: Referenzbuch des Produkt-Lebenszyklus-Managements*. Berlin: Springer, 2009.

[48] Verein Deutscher Ingenieure (VDI), "VDI 2219 - Information technology in product development Introduction and economics of EDM/PDM Systems (Issue German/English)," Düsseldorf, 2002.

[49] M. Abramovici and D. Gerhard, "A Flexible Web-Based PDM Approach to Support Virtual Engineering Cooperation," in *Proceedings of the 33rd Hawaii International Conference on System Sciences*, 2000.

[50] A. Katzenbach, "Informationstechnik und Wissensverarbeitung in der Produktentwicklung," 2014.

[51] International Organization for Standardization (ISO), "ISO 10303: Industrial automation systems and integration - Product data representation and exchange (STEP)."

[52] ——, "ISO 14306: Industrial automation systems and integration - JT file format specification for 3D visualization."

[53] Siemens PLM Software, "Teamcenter." [Online]. Available: http://www.plm.automation.siemens.com/en_us/products/teamcenter/ [Accessed: 2016-05-18]

[54] PTC, "Windchill." [Online]. Available: http://www.ptc.com/product/windchill [Accessed: 2016-05-18]

[55] Dassault Systèmes, "ENOVIA V6." [Online]. Available: http://www.3ds.com/products-services/enovia/products/enovia-v6/ [Accessed: 2016-05-18]

[56] ——, "ENOVIA V6 Technical Advantages Whitepaper," 2008. [Online]. Available: http://www.3ds.com/fileadmin/PRODUCTS/ENOVIA/PDF/WHITE-PAPERS/PCSWhitepaper-0807_final_July_29.pdf [Accessed: 2016-05-18]

[57] CIMdata, "Teamcenter "unified" "Siemens PLM Software's Next Generation PLM Platform" White Paper," 2010. [Online]. Available: http://www.plm.automation.siemens.com/en_us/Images/21848_tcm1023-100227.pdf [Accessed: 2016-05-18]

[58] Siemens PLM Software, "Teamcenter 10.1 - Getting Started with Teamcenter," 2013. [Online]. Available: http://m.plm.automation.siemens.com/en_us/Images/Teamcenter-start-guide_tcm1224-149467.pdf [Accessed: 2016-05-18]

[59] PLM Dojo, "What are Classes and Business Objects? Attributes and Properties?" [Online]. Available: http://plmdojo.com/classes-business-objects-attributes-properties/ [Accessed: 2016-05-18]

[60] Siemens PLM Software, "Teamcenter's Service-Oriented Architecture White Paper," 2010. [Online]. Available: http://www.plm.automation.siemens.com/en_us/products/teamcenter/library.shtml [Accessed: 2016-05-18]

[61] K. M. Waldenmeyer and N. W. Hartman, "Multiple CAD Formats in a Single Product Data Management System: A Case Study," *Journal of Industrial Technology*, vol. 25, no. 3, pp. 1–7, 2009.

[62] CIMdata, "Simulation Lifecycle Management "More than data management for simulation"," pp. 1–16, 2011.

[63] Siemens PLM Software, "Simulation process management - Managing simulation tools, data, process and workflow in a common, open PLM environment," 2011.

[64] H. Richards-Rissetto, F. Remondino, G. Agugiaro, J. Von Schwerin, J. Robertsson, and G. Girardi, "Kinect and 3D GIS in archaeology," in *Proceedings of the 2012 18th International Conference on Virtual Systems and Multimedia, VSMM 2012: Virtual Systems in the Information Society*, 2012, pp. 331–337.

[65] M. Forte and G. Kurillo, "Cyberarchaeology: Experimenting with teleimmersive archaeology," in *2010 16th International Conference on Virtual Systems and Multimedia, VSMM 2010*, 2010, pp. 155–162.

[66] A. Guarnieri, F. Pirotti, and A. Vettore, "Cultural heritage interactive 3D models on the web: An approach using open source and free software," *Journal of Cultural Heritage*, vol. 11, no. 3, pp. 350–353, 2010.

[67] M. F. Shiratuddin and W. Thabet, "Utilizing a 3D game engine to develop a virtual design review system," *Journal of Information Technology in Construction (ITcon)*, vol. 16, no. Special Issue Use of Gaming Technology in Architecture, Engineering and Construction, pp. 39–68, 2011.

[68] S. Wang, Z. Mao, C. Zeng, H. Gong, S. Li, and B. Chen, "A new method of virtual reality based on Unity3D," in *2010 18th International Conference on Geoinformatics*, 2010, pp. 1–5.

[69] Y. Zhao, C. Yan, X. Zhou, Q. Zhu, S. Wang, and W. Guo, "The research and development of 3D urban geographic information system with Unity3D," in *Geoinformatics (GEOINFORMATICS), 2013 21st International Conference on*, 2013, pp. 1–4.

[70] D. Pacheco and S. Wierenga, "Spatializing experience: a framework for the geolocalization, visualization and exploration of historical data using VR/AR technologies," in *Proceedings of the 2014 Virtual Reality International Conference*, 2014.

[71] A. Martina and A. Bottino, "Using Virtual Environments as a Visual Interface for Accessing Cultural Database Contents," in *International Conference of Information Science and Computer Applications (ICISCA 2012)*, Bali, Indonesia, 2012, pp. 1–6.

[72] T. Guan, B. Ren, and D. Zhong, "The Method of Unity3D-Based 3D Dynamic Interactive Query of High Arch Dam Construction Information," *Applied Mechanics and Materials*, vol. 256-259, pp. 2918–2922, 2012.

[73] T. Scully, J. Doboš, T. Sturm, and Y. Jung, "3drepo. io: building the next generation Web3D repository with AngularJS and X3DOM," in *Proceedings of the 20th International Conference on 3D Web Technology*, 2015.

[74] Z. Wang, H. Cai, and F. Bu, "Nonlinear Revision Control for Web-Based 3D Scene Editor," in *Virtual Reality and Visualization (ICVRV), 2014 International Conference on*, 2014, pp. 73–80.

[75] J. Doboš and A. Steed, "Revision Control Framework for 3D Assets," in *Eurographics 2012 - Posters*, Cagliari, Sardinia, Italy, 2012, p. 3.

[76] J. Beetz, L. van Berlo, R. de Laat, and P. van den Helm, "bimserver.org - An Open Source IFC Model Server," in *Proceedings of the CIB W78 2010: 27th International Conference*, no. Weise 2006, Cairo, Egypt, 2010, pp. 16–18.

[77] H.-s. Kang and G. Lee, "Development of an object-relational IFC server," in *ICCEM/ICCPM*, 2009.

[78] S. Malaikrisanachalee and H. Vathananukij, "Integration of java-based BIM with spatial database," *International Journal of Civil Engineering*, vol. 9, no. 1, pp. 17–22, 2011.

[79] V. Tarandi, "The BIM Collaboration Hub: A model server based on IFC and PLCS for Virtual Enterprise Collaboration," in *Proceedings of the CIB W78-W102 2011: International Conference*, Sophia Antipolis, France, 2011, pp. 26–28.

[80] M. Nour, "Using Bounding Volumes for BIM based electronic code checking for Buildings in Egypt," *American Journal of Engineering Research (AJER)*, vol. 5, no. 4, pp. 91–98, 2016.

[81] B. Domínguez-Martín, "Methods to process low-level CAD plans and creative Building Information Models (BIM)," Doctoral Thesis, University of Jaén, 2014.

[82] S. Hoerster and K. Menzel, "BIM based classification of building performance data for advanced analysis," in *Proceedings of International Conference CISBAT 2015 Future Buildings and Districts Sustainability from Nano to Urban Scale*, 2015, pp. 993–998.

[83] H. Eisenmann, J. Fuchs, D. De Wilde, and V. Basso, "ESA Virtual Spacecraft Design," in *5th International Workshop on Systems and Concurrent Engineering for Space Applications*, 2012.

[84] M. Mahdjoub, D. Monticolo, S. Gomes, and J. Sagot, "A collaborative design for usability approach supported by virtual reality and a multi-agent system embedded in a PLM environment," *Computer-Aided Design*, vol. 42, no. 5, pp. 402–413, 2010.

[85] M. Roberts, N. Ducheneaut, and T. F. Smith, “The "3d Wiki": Blending virtual worlds and Web architecture for remote collaboration,” in *2010 IEEE International Conference on Multimedia and Expo, ICME 2010*, 2010, pp. 1166–1171.

[86] M. Fang, X. Yan, Y. Wenhui, and C. Sen, “The Storage and Management of Distributed Massive 3D Models based on G/S Mode,” in *Lecture Notes in Information Technology*, vol. 10, 2012.

[87] D. Iliescu, I. Ciocan, and I. Mateias, “Assisted management of product data: A PDM application proposal,” in *Proceedings of the 18th International Conference on System Theory, Control and Computing*, Sinaia, Romania, 2014.

[88] C. Shahabi, F. Banaei-Kashani, A. Khoshgozaran, L. Nocera, and S. X. S. Xing, “GeoDec: A Framework to Visualize and Query Geospatial Data for Decision-Making,” *IEEE Multimedia*, vol. 17, no. 3, pp. 14–23, 2010.

[89] M. Lobur, O. Matviykiv, A. Kernytskyy, and R. Dobosz, “Presentation of the heat simulation model with use of relational data model,” *2011 11th International Conference The Experience of Designing and Application of CAD Systems in Microelectronics CADSM*, pp. 228–229, 2011.

[90] A. Stadler, C. Nagel, G. König, and T. H. Kolbe, “Making interoperability persistent : A 3D geo database based on CityGML,” *3D Geo-Information Sciences*, pp. 175–192, 2009.

[91] U. Schöning, *Logik für Informatiker*, 3rd ed. Mannheim/Leipzig/Wien/Zürich: BI Wissenschaftsverlag, 1992.

[92] M. Atkinson, F. Bancilhon, D. DeWitt, K. Dittrich, D. Maier, and S. Zdonik, “The Object-Oriented Database System Manifesto,” in *1st International Conference on Deductive and Object-Oriented Databases*, Kyoto, 1989.

[93] Red Hat, “Hibernate - What is Object/Relational Mapping?” 2013. [Online]. Available: http://www.hibernate.org/about/orm.html [Accessed: 2016-05-18]

[94] R. G. G. Cattell and D. K. Barry, *The Object Data Standard: ODMG 3.0.* Morgan Kaufmann, 2000.

[95] International Organization for Standardization (ISO), “ISO/IEC 9075:2008 Information technology - Database languages - SQL,” 2008.

[96] M. Skulschus and M. Wiederstein, *XML Schema: Grundlagen, Praxis, Referenz.* Bonn: Galileo Press, 2004.

[97] E. Redmond, J. R. Wilson, and J. Carter, *Seven Databases in Seven Weeks: A Guide to Modern Databases and the NoSQL Movement*, ser. Oreilly and Associate Series. Pragmatic Bookshelf, 2012.

[98] M. Brambilla, J. Cabot, and M. Wimmer, *Model-Driven Software Engineering in Practice*, ser. Synthesis Lectures on Software Engineering. Morgan & Claypool Publishers, 2012.

[99] Object Management Group (OMG), "Meta Object Facility (MOF)." [Online]. Available: http://www.omg.org/mof/ [Accessed: 2016-05-18]

[100] ——, "UML Profile For MARTE: Modeling And Analysis Of Real-Time Embedded Systems." [Online]. Available: http://www.omg.org/spec/MARTE/ [Accessed: 2016-05-18]

[101] ——, "Object Constraint Language (OCL)." [Online]. Available: http://www.omg.org/spec/OCL/ [Accessed: 2016-05-18]

[102] J. Bézivin, "On the unification power of models," *Software and Systems Modeling*, vol. 4, no. 2, pp. 171–188, 2005.

[103] F. Jouault, F. Allilaire, J. Bézivin, and I. Kurtev, "ATL: A model transformation tool," *Science of Computer Programming*, vol. 72, no. 1-2, pp. 31–39, jun 2008.

[104] Obeo, "ATL Transformation Language." [Online]. Available: http://www.eclipse.org/atl/ [Accessed: 2016-05-18]

[105] Object Management Group (OMG), "MOF Query / View / Transformation (QVT)." [Online]. Available: http://www.omg.org/spec/QVT/ [Accessed: 2016-05-18]

[106] S. Nolte, *QVT - Relations Language*. Springer, 2009.

[107] ——, *QVT - Operational Mappings*, 1st ed. Springer, 2009.

[108] Object Management Group (OMG), "MOF 2 XMI Mapping (XMI)." [Online]. Available: http://www.omg.org/spec/XMI/ [Accessed: 2016-05-18]

[109] Eclipse Foundation, "Eclipse Modeling Framework Project (EMF)." [Online]. Available: http://www.eclipse.org/modeling/emf/?project=emf [Accessed: 2016-05-18]

[110] T. Myrach, *Temporale Datenbanken in betrieblichen Informationssystemen*, 1st ed. Wiesbaden: Teubner Verlag, 2005.

[111] C. S. Jensen and C. E. Dyreson, "The Consensus Glossary of Temporal Database Concepts," in *Temporal Databases – Research and Practice*, vol. 1399, 1998, pp. 357–405.

[112] J. Clifford and A. U. Tansel, "On an algebra for historical relational databases: two views," *ACM SIGMOD Record*, vol. 14, no. 4, pp. 247–265, may 1985.

[113] P. A. Bernstein and S. Melnik, "Model management 2.0: manipulating richer mappings," in *Proceedings of the 2007 ACM SIGMOD international conference on Management of data - SIGMOD '07*. New York, New York, USA: ACM Press, jun 2007, pp. 1–12.

[114] P. Atzeni, P. Cappellari, and P. Bernstein, "Model-Independent Schema and Data Translation," in *Advances in Database Technology - EDBT 2006*, ser. Lecture Notes in Computer Science, Y. Ioannidis, M. Scholl, J. Schmidt, F. Matthes, M. Hatzopoulos, K. Boehm, A. Kemper, T. Grust, and C. Boehm, Eds. Springer Berlin / Heidelberg, 2006, vol. 3896, pp. 368–385.

[115] P. Atzeni, L. Bellomarini, F. Bugiotti, and G. Gianforme, "A runtime approach to model-independent schema and data translation," in *Proceedings of the 12th International Conference on Extending Database Technology: Advances in Database Technology*, ser. EDBT '09. New York, NY, USA: ACM, 2009, pp. 275–286.

[116] A. Smith and P. McBrien, "A Generic Data Level Implementation of ModelGen," in *Sharing Data, Information and Knowledge*, ser. Lecture Notes in Computer Science, A. Gray, K. Jeffery, and J. Shao, Eds. Springer Berlin / Heidelberg, 2008, vol. 5071, pp. 63–74.

[117] P. Berdaguer, A. Cunha, H. Pacheco, and J. Visser, "Coupled Schema Transformation and Data Conversion for XML and SQL," in *Practical Aspects of Declarative Languages*, ser. Lecture Notes in Computer Science, M. Hanus, Ed. Springer Berlin / Heidelberg, 2007, vol. 4354, pp. 290–304.

[118] I. Kurtev and K. van den Berg, "MISTRAL: A Language for Model Transformations in the MOF Meta-modeling Architecture," in *Model Driven Architecture*, ser. Lecture Notes in Computer Science, U. Aßmann, M. Aksit, and A. Rensink, Eds. Springer Berlin / Heidelberg, 2005, vol. 3599, p. 901.

[119] C. Atkinson and T. Kuhne, "Model-Driven Development: A Metamodeling Foundation," *Software, IEEE*, vol. 20, no. 5, pp. 36–41, 2003.

[120] E. Seidewitz, "What models mean," *IEEE Software*, vol. 20, no. 5, pp. 26–32, sep 2003.

[121] M. Bräuer, "Design and Prototypical Implementation of a Pivot Model as Exchange Format for Models and Metamodels in a QVT/OCL Development Environment," 2007.

[122] P. Maes, "Concepts and experiments in computational reflection," *ACM Sigplan Notices*, vol. 22, no. 12, pp. 147–155, 1987.

[123] CPA Geo-Information, "CPA SupportGIS Java (SGJ)." [Online]. Available: http://www.supportgis.de [Accessed: 2016-05-18]

[124] D. Harel, "Statecharts: a visual formalism for complex systems," *Science of Computer Programming*, vol. 8, no. 3, pp. 231–274, jun 1987.

[125] SEDRIS Associates & Partners, "SEDRIS," 2013. [Online]. Available: http://www.sedris.org [Accessed: 2016-05-18]

[126] M. Hoppen, M. Schluse, J. Rossmann, and C. Averdung, "A new nD Temporal Geodata Management Approach using GML," in *GEOProcessing 2015 - The Seventh International Conference on Advanced Geographic Information Systems, Applications, and Services*, Rückemann and Doytsher, Eds. Lisbon, Portugal: IARIA (International Academy, Research, and Industry Association), 2015, pp. 110–116.

[127] J. Rossmann, M. Schluse, C. Schlette, and R. Waspe, "A New Approach to 3D Simulation Technology as Enabling Technology for eRobotics," in *1st International Simulation Tools Conference & EXPO 2013, SIMEX'2013*, J. F. M. Van Impe and F. Logist, Eds., Brussels, Belgium, 2013, pp. 39–46.

[128] Eclipse Foundation, "EMF UML2," 2013. [Online]. Available: http://www.eclipse.org/modeling/mdt/?project=uml2 [Accessed: 2016-05-18]

[129] The PostgreSQL Global Development Group, "PostgreSQL." [Online]. Available: http://www.postgresql.org [Accessed: 2016-05-18]

[130] Oracle, "Java Native Interface (JNI)." [Online]. Available: http://docs.oracle.com/javase/7/docs/technotes/guides/jni/index.html [Accessed: 2016-05-18]

[131] M. Schluse, M. Hoppen, and M. Rast, "XML data binding for VEROSIM," 2013, unpublished internal technical paper.

[132] R. Bourret, "Mapping W3C Schemas to Object Schemas to Relational Schemas," 2001. [Online]. Available: http://www.rpbourret.com/xml/SchemaMap.htm [Accessed: 2016-05-18]

[133] ——, "XML Data Binding Resources," 2011. [Online]. Available: http://www.rpbourret.com/xml/XMLDataBinding.htm [Accessed: 2016-05-18]

[134] Java Community Process, "JSR-000222 Java Architecture for XML Binding (JAXB) 2.2." [Online]. Available: http://jcp.org/aboutJava/communityprocess/mrel/jsr222/index2.html [Accessed: 2016-05-18]

[135] Code Synthesis Tools CC, "CodeSynthesis XSD," 2013. [Online]. Available: http://www.codesynthesis.com/products/xsd/ [Accessed: 2016-05-18]

[136] The World Wide Web Consortium (W3C), "XML Linking Language (XLink)." [Online]. Available: http://www.w3.org/TR/xlink/ [Accessed: 2016-05-18]

[137] ——, "XML Pointer Language (XPointer)." [Online]. Available: http://www.w3.org/TR/xptr/ [Accessed: 2016-05-18]

[138] J. Rossmann, M. Schluse, and A. Bücken, "The virtual forest - Space- and Robotics technology for the efficient and environmentally compatible growth-planing and mobilization of wood resources," *FORMEC 08 - 41. Internationales Symposium*, pp. 3 – 12, 2008.

[139] J. Rossmann, M. Schluse, R. Waspe, and R. Moshammer, "Simulation in the Woods: From Remote Sensing based Data Acquisition and Processing to Various Simulation Applications," in *Proceedings of the 2011 Winter Simulation Conference*, S. Jain, R. R. Creasey, J. Himmelspach, K. P. White, and M. Fu, Eds., 2011, pp. 984 – 996.

[140] J. Rossmann, M. Hoppen, and A. Bücken, "Semantic World Modelling and Data Management in a 4D Forest Simulation and Information System," *ISPRS - International Archives of the Photogrammetry, Remote Sensing and Spatial Information Sciences*, vol. XL-2/W2, pp. 65–72, 2013.

[141] M. Hoppen, M. Schluse, J. Rossmann, and B. Weitzig, "Database-Driven Distributed 3D Simulation," in *Proceedings of the 2012 Winter Simulation Conference*, 2012, pp. 1–12.

[142] J. Rossmann, M. Schluse, M. Hoppen, D. Losch, N. Hempe, and C. Schlette, "Virtual BIM Testbeds," in *2015 Developments in E-systems Engineering*, 2015.

[143] P. Schwellenbach, "X3D as an Interchange Format for Model Data in 3D Simulation," Aachen, 2014, unpublished bachelor thesis.

[144] R. Drath, Ed., *Datenaustausch in der Anlagenplanung mit AutomationML.* Berlin, Heidelberg: Springer Berlin Heidelberg, 2010.

[145] M. Fedai and R. Drath, "CAEX—a neutral data exchange format for engineering data," *ATP International Automation Technology*, vol. 1, p. 3, 2005.

[146] M. Konieczny, "Integration of AutomationML into a 3D simulation system using a flexible XML-Schema/XML-based interface," Aachen, 2014, unpublished seminar paper.

[147] J. Rossmann, M. Schluse, C. Schlette, and M. Hoppen, "A modular system architecture for the distributed simulation and control of assembly lines based on active databases," *Selected Topics in System Science and Simulation in Engineering*, pp. 244–252, oct 2010.

[148] C. Schlette and M. Hoppen, "Modular Control System Architecture," in *SCALAB Scalable Automation for Emerging Lab Production : Final Report of the MNT-ERA.net Research Project 'SCALAB'*, S. Haag, M., Härer, Ed., 2012, pp. 29–40.

[149] M. Hunger, *Neo4j 2.0 - Eine Graphdatenbank für alle [Neo4j 2.0 - A graph database for everyone]*, 1st ed. entwickler.press, 2014.

[150] M. Hoppen, J. Rossmann, and S. Hiester, "Managing 3D Simulation Models with the Graph Database Neo4j," in *DBKDA 2016,The 8th International Conference on Advances in Databases, Knowledge, and Data Applications*, Lisbon, Portugal, 2016, to be published.

[151] A.-M. Stapelbroek, M. Hoppen, and J. Rossmann, "Object-Relational Mapping in 3D Simulation," in *GraphSM 2016, The 3rd International Workshop on Large-scale Graph Storage and Management*, Lisbon, Portugal, 2016, to be published.

[152] M. Rast, *Domänenübergreifende Modellierung und Simulation als Grundlage für Virtuelle Testbeds.* Aachen: Apprimus Verlag, 2015.

[153] J. Rossmann, R. Dumitrescu, O. Stern, C. Averdung, M. Schluse, C. Bremer, F. Bluemel, M. Rast, M. Hoppen, and M. Hillebrand, "Architecture for Integrated Development of Complex Systems With Model-Based System Specification and Simulation," in *Proceedings of the ASME IDETC/CIE 2015*, Boston, 2015.

[154] O. Stern, "Robotergestützte Planetenexploration: Semantische Umweltmodellierung und VisualGPS," in *2. Nationale Konferenz zur Raumfahrt-Robotik*, Berlin, 2012.

[155] J. Rossmann, N. Wantia, M. Springer, O. Stern, H. Müller, and M. Ellsiepen, "Rapid Generation of 3d Navigation Maps for Extraterrestrial Landing and Exploration Missions : the Virtual Testbed Approach," in *Advanced Space Technologies for Robotics and Automation*, 2011, pp. 1–7.

[156] J. Rossmann, T. Steil, and M. Springer, "Validating the Camera and Light Simulation of a Virtual Space Robotics Testbed by Means of Physical Mockup Data," in *11th International Symposium on Artificial Intelligence, Robotics and Automation in Space (i-SAIRAS)*, 2012, pp. 1–6.

[157] J. Rossmann, C. Schlette, M. Emde, and B. Sondermann, "Discussion of a Self-Localization and Navigation Unit for Mobile Robots in Extraterrestrial Environments," *Artificial Intelligence*, pp. 46–53, 2010.

[158] J. Rossmann, B. Sondermann, and M. Emde, "Virtual Testbeds for Planetary Exploration: The Self-Localization Aspect," in *11th Symposium on Advanced Space Technologies in Robotics and Automation (ASTRA)*, 2011, pp. 1–8.

[159] Y.-H. Yoo, T. Jung, M. Langosz, M. Rast, J. Rossmann, and F. Kirchner, "Developing a Virtual Environment for Extraterrestrial Legged Robots with Focus on Lunar Crater Exploration," in *The 10th International Symposium on Artificial Intelligence, Robotics and Automation in Space (i-SAIRAS)*, 2010, pp. 206–213.

[160] J. Weise, K. Brieß, A. Adomeit, H.-G. Reimerdes, M. Göller, and R. Dillmann, "An Intelligent Building Blocks Concept for On-Orbit-Satellite Servcing," in *Proceedings of International Symposium on Artificial Intelligence, Robotics and Automation in Space (i-SAIRAS)*, 2012.

[161] M. Hoppen, M. Rast, M. Schluse, J. Rossmann, L. Pfotzer, and T. Meschede, "XML-based Modeling Languages and Data Binding for Collaborative Design in Multidisciplinary Teams," in *ECEC 2015 - 21st European Concurrent Engineering Conference*, S. Goncalves, Ed., Ghent, Belgium, 2015.

[162] E. Freund, M. Müller, and J. Rossmann, *Data storage and flow control in automation systems by means of an active database.* Vienna, Austria: Amsterdam: IOS Press; Tokyo: Ohmsha, 1999, pp. 235–240.

[163] J. Gausemeier, F. J. Rammig, and W. Schäfer, Eds., *Design Methodology for Intelligent Technical Systems - Develop Intelligent Technical Systems of the Future*, ser. Lecture Notes in Mechanical Engineering. Berlin, Heidelberg: Springer Berlin Heidelberg, 2014.

[164] M. Hoppen, R. Waspe, M. Rast, and J. Rossmann, "Distributed Information Processing and Rendering for 3D Simulation Applications," *International Journal of Computer Theory and Engineering (IJCTE)*, vol. 6, no. 3, pp. 247–253, 2014.

FSC
www.fsc.org
MIX
Papier | Fördert gute Waldnutzung
FSC® C083411

Kolibri 360 GmbH
Ferdinand-Jühlke-Straße 7
99095 Erfurt, Deutschland
produktsicherheit@kolibri360.de